Joh
and His People

John Henry and His People

The Historical Origin and Lore of America's Great Folk Ballad

JOHN GARST

Foreword by ART ROSENBAUM

McFarland & Company, Inc., Publishers
Jefferson, North Carolina

Lyrics to Rich Amerson's "John Henry" (recorded in 1950) are from *Negro Folk Songs, U.S.A.* by Harold Courlander. Copyright © 1963 Columbia University Press. Reprinted with permission of Columbia University Press.

LIBRARY OF CONGRESS CATALOGUING-IN-PUBLICATION DATA

Names: Garst, John F. author.
Title: John Henry and his people : the historical origin and lore of America's great folk ballad / John Garst.
Description: Jefferson : McFarland & Company, 2022. | Includes bibliographical references and index.
Identifiers: LCCN 2021054454 | ISBN 9781476686110 (paperback : acid free paper) ∞
ISBN 9781476645803 (ebook)
Subjects: LCSH: Henry, John (Legendary character)—Songs and music—History and criticism. | Folk songs, English—United States—History and criticism. | Ballads, English—United States—History and criticism. | Folklore—United States. | BISAC: SOCIAL SCIENCE / Folklore & Mythology | SOCIAL SCIENCE / Ethnic Studies / American / African American & Black Studies
Classification: LCC ML3561.H36 G37 2022 | DDC 781.62/13—dc23
LC record available at https://lccn.loc.gov/2021054454

BRITISH LIBRARY CATALOGUING DATA ARE AVAILABLE

ISBN (print) 978-1-4766-8611-0
ISBN (ebook) 978-1-4766-4580-3

Front cover artwork: illustration depicting those at the race between John Henry and a steam drill, as well as others who later figured in the ballad and lore: scholars, traditional singers, and more. *Left to right*: Unidentified people in crowd; man holding water bucket is C.C. Spencer, foreground in profile, Rich Amerson, Alabama African American singer, men in hats unidentified; woman, John Henry's wife; John Henry Dabney, driving steel in his contest with a steam drill; African American man with suspenders, unidentified. *Background*: the West Portal of the Oak Tunnel, Dunnavant, Alabama; man in hat with paper is chief engineer Fredrick Yeamans Dabney, John Henry's "captain"; young man, name not known, John Henry's shaker; Fiddlin' John Carson. *Lower right*: Uncle Dave Macon, man on hillside, Alabama blind singer W.T. Blankenship, two figures at right, Dr. Carl Marbury of Leeds, Alabama, and Dr. John Garst (artwork by Art Rosenbaum)

Printed in the United States of America

McFarland & Company, Inc., Publishers
 Box 611, Jefferson, North Carolina 28640
 www.mcfarlandpub.com

Contents

I'm gonna ring this old hammer.
I'm gonna ring this old hammer,
And then go home, oh partner,
And then go home.
—Henry Grady Terrell

Foreword
by Art Rosenbaum

John Henry, the African American hero of what Alan Lomax has called America's greatest folk ballad, worked as a steel driver—driving steel drills with a hammer into rock to blast through mountains for railroad tunnels. In 1887 John Henry Dabney, working for Fredrick Yeamans Dabney, for whom he had been a slave as a boy in Mississippi, raced a steam drill. John Henry won but died from the effort. The location was Dunnavant, on a spur of the Columbus and Western / Central of Georgia Railroad, near Leeds, Alabama, east of Birmingham. John Garst's years of research into the ballad which celebrated this event has convinced me that all this is so.

Not everyone has agreed: the first two book-length studies of John Henry, by Guy Johnson (1929) and Louis W. Chappell (1933), place the event at the Big Bend Tunnel in West Virginia, as does a line from many twentieth-century versions of the ballad: "The Big Bend Tunnel on the C & O Road / Gonna be the death of me." In 1960 Alan Lomax wrote: "[John Henry] probably did not die from the effects of his victory as the song says, but later on from one of the frequent cave-ins that made the Big Bend the grave of many workers. The work went on, but a grim note now sounded in the lines:

> This old hammer—WHAM!
> Killed John Henry—WHAM!
> Can't kill me—WHAM!
> Can't kill me—WHAM!"

There are some problems here. Lomax is guessing—"probably"—about a death by cave-in. The source of Lomax's surmise was Neal Miller, one of Guy Johnson's West Virginia informants, whose account Garst will refute. A worker's contest with a steam drill not coupled with a dramatic death "with his hammer in his hand" would have been an

1

unlikely inspiration for a narrative as powerful as the core John Henry ballad. Moreover, as John Garst will show in these pages, places in folk ballads are frequently relocated in oral transmission. The Big Bend Tunnel is named most frequently, but not to the exclusion of other locations. Significantly, an article in the *Central of Georgia Magazine* of October 1930, "Old Negro Folk Song Commemorates Spike Driver on Our Line," asserts that "'Jawn Henry' is no mere fiction hero, for in the mountain side near Leeds, at the east end of our Oak Mountain tunnel, there stands a monument to him—the last steel he drove before he fell dead...." The article includes a photograph of the steel (or "drill") in the rock face as well as a text of the ballad, "sent to the magazine by Mr Peter A. Brannon of the Alabama Anthropological Society of Montgomery." The article prints a text of the ballad, very similar to one Carl Carmer writes of hearing from an Alabama convict laborer—giving the railroad as the Central of Georgia, not the C & O—in an account given below. Carmer's text and the magazine's suggest either that Brannon and/ or Carmer had the same informant, or that Carmer, for convenience, referred to the magazine's text; in any event, the ballad gives Alabama as its source and location.

There are two categories of John Henry songs: the work songs and the narrative ballad. Some African American work songs include references to John Henry; in addition to Lomax's example I can think of one I recorded from the singing of Henry Grady Terrell in Athens, Georgia:

> Ol' John Henry—WHAM!
> Died on the mountain—WHAM!
> He was a-whuppin' steel—WHAM!
> He was a-whuppin' steel—WHAM!

The work song and the ballad occasionally overlap, but the ballad only rarely has been used as a work song—Lomax did record at least one such performance. In the third book on John Henry, Scott Nelson (2008) placed the contest at the Lewis Tunnel in Virginia. John Garst's is the fourth book, and in it he convincingly refutes the West Virginia and the Virginia locations. Nelson argued that the ballad emerged out of work songs that were used by steel drivers. In a way this harks back to the discredited "communal" theory of ballad creation. I believe that the ballad was composed by an individual ballad-maker at some time after the event and that from the beginning it was stanzaic and narrative. Many scholars, including Garst, Phillips Barry, Lomax and Nelson, have acknowledged its relationship to British balladry. Whatever its origin, the John Henry ballad "John Henry" did not appear in collections or print until the twentieth century—Garst presents extensive research into W.T. Blankenship, a blind Alabama singer who printed the first broadside of the ballad in the early 1900s—as it was becoming increasingly widespread in the repertoires of black and white singers, with myriad versions. It sings well, works well with unaccompanied voice or sung with banjo, guitar, fiddle. It is a great song with a great story, to reuse Alan Lomax's adjective. Most versions retain the memorable line "A man ain't nothing but a man." This stands alongside Robert Burns' "A man's a man for a' that."

John Henry and His People is an apt title for John Garst's book. After years of research into a song in fluid oral tradition, as well as in recordings, popular narratives, and political and social culture, Garst has interwoven, analyzed, and interpreted much of what we can know about John Henry and his people: his life and death, his wife, the life and ancestry of Frederick Dabney, new information about C.C. Spencer, the most detailed and credible eye-witness to John Henry's race with the steam-drill, the story of singer and broadside printer Blankenship, the research, the findings and the controversies of scholars who have examined John Henry—Johnson, Chappell, Nelson, Norm Cohen, and others.

Importantly, John Henry's *people* are also the singers, mostly from the South. Among the white singers were Georgia's Fiddlin' John Carson, who waxed the first commercial recording "John Henry Blues" (1924), and Tennessee's Uncle Dave Macon, whose recording "Death of John Henry" (1927) seems to hark back to an early form of the ballad— Garst points out the "people out West" in Macon's version who heard of John Henry's death and took an eastbound train may well have been his Mississippi folks. Another signal performance is that of the black Alabama singer Rich Amerson, whose emotional rendering is discussed by Garst at length. In my own experience recording traditional music in the field, "John Henry," the story, the meanings, the musical drive, all seem to fuel performances with remarkable inner passion and expressive energy. One example: Mose Parker, a black guitar player from the deep South whom I recorded in Indianapolis in 1961, virtually transported himself and his listeners into John Henry's work struggle, grunting as he sang, his bottleneck guitar slide ringing like a hammer on the steel:

> Heard a mighty rumblin', well, well, hittin' on steel.
> John Henry told his captain, that's my hammer catchin' air!

Recently Professor Sam Pezzillo brought to our attention a reference, mentioned above, to John Henry in Carl Carmer's book based on his experiences in Alabama in the late 1920s, "Stars Fell on Alabama" (1934). Although he changed some names in view of highly charged issues and occurrences, the author assures us that "all the events related in this book happened substantially as I have recorded them." Carmer visited the home of a man in south Alabama whose life and livelihood were almost totally supported by black convict laborers leased from the state; this practice has been convincingly called "slavery by another name." The host's house servants were leased convicts, as were the workers in his sawmill, who wore black and white striped uniforms and were guarded by men in khaki with shotguns. Only one of the workers was permitted out of the barracks in the evening, "Philip," who sang and played guitar for the white folks on the porch. Philip was asked to "sing us about John Henry, about the time he killed himself beatin' the steam drill." The convict prefaced his singing of a fine and lengthy version of the ballad with the explanation: "That was over to Leeds, in Jefferson County, my daddy seen 'im do it…. My daddy say his shaker could hardly get the drill turned halfway roun' fo' John Henry'd whop it agin. Nobody ever tetched that drill sense John Henry drapped dead. It's still stickin' in the hole at the mouth o' the tunnel 'twixt Donovan [sic] and Leeds." All of this rings as true as the ring of John Henry's hammer. We have a specific Alabama location for the event, an Alabama singer who claims his father was an eyewitness; a steel was indeed visible in the rock. (A steel was visible for many years in the rock face near the Oak Mountain tunnel near—yes Leeds and Dunnavant, Alabama, widely believed to be the steel driven by John Henry. Further confirmation: Philip's first verse includes "The Central of Georgia railroad gonna be the death of me." That line tunneled through the Oak and Coosa mountains at Dunnavant, near Leeds. This narrative is a capstone to eye-witness accounts of the Alabama contest with the steam drill, notably that of C.C. Spencer, whose letters to Guy Johnson as well as corroborating material are evaluated by Garst. John Garst has pointed out that "eye-witness" accounts may be unreliable, but when several, from diverse sources, begin to accumulate, they can make for a convincing case).

Local traditions also, as Garst will acknowledge, are not probative; but they can certainly bolster the case for a noteworthy event giving rise to a ballad. He will show that local reports have been weak in West Virginia, absent in Virginia, and very strong, and ongoing, in Alabama. I will give two recent examples. The *Birmingham News* reported that "a Birmingham native Jo Ann Powers said she grew up hearing about 'John Henry's tunnel over in Dunnavant. My grandfather, John William Powers, used to take me over to the tunnel and tell about John Henry. 'I remember sitting on his knee and listening to him sing the song about John Henry when I was about 6 years old.'" In 2019 Dr. Carl Marbury, former president of Alabama A & M University, an African American who grew up and now lives in Leeds, Alabama, told me that in 1942, when his older sister Cleo was "in the 8th grade, and when I was in the 2nd grade, she came home, said they were going on a field trip down to Oak Mountain, in a science class, because they wanted to see the metal stave [staff, steel] that was driven into the rock that goes back to the time of John Henry. And they did ... and she came talking about it. The stave that was driven into the rock was still there." (In another conversation Marbury said that the steel was removed in the 1940s by the railroad company, concerned that the site near the Oak Mountain Tunnel portal was dangerous to the many people coming to view "John Henry's steel." And although there has been some skepticism, John Garst has found no evidence that the steel was not the original, dating to John Henry's race with the steam drill.) Marbury went on to tell me that "when I came back, much later, from college, the whites [in Leeds] wanted to do something to memorialize John Henry; and I was kind of surprised ... because I didn't know that the John Henry story was that well known—I was surprised that white people found it interesting."

John Garst's book is discursive, moving adroitly through historical evidence, insights into transmission and transformation in folksong, interpretation of meaning, and scholarly disputes. He would be the first to say that there is more to be learned about John Henry. But as of now, his book is the definitive work on the ballad and the man—and his people.

Art Rosenbaum is a painter and taught studio art at the universities of Iowa and Georgia. He has collected, written about, and performed American folk music for over sixty years. He has written instruction books on traditional banjo styles and authored three books based on his field recordings in Georgia; among released issues of his field recordings is the Grammy-winning Art of Field Recording, Vol. I: Fifty Years of Traditional American Music Documented by Art Rosenbaum.

Preface

Since its inception, the philosophy of this book has changed. As a career scientist, I was inclined to approach John Henry with something like the scientific method: find and interpret facts. Along the way, I kept bumping into John Henry's people, interesting persons with connections to John Henry. I could not leave them out, so the title became *John Henry and His People.*

My perspective changed in another way. A number of previous scholars concerned themselves with the origin of John Henry. I think they all reached the wrong conclusion. In my effort to set the record straight, I focused originally on the origin and tended to neglect the lore itself.

How folklore gets started is important to a comprehensive understanding. Origins must be studied, and folklorists have done so assiduously. Leaving origins out of studies of folklore would be like leaving legs out of descriptions of animals. On the other hand, leaving out everything except origins would be like leaving out everything except legs.

People caused me to broaden my interest in John Henry. I interviewed several who were passionate on the subject. Despite being feeble and knowing that he would die within days, Archie Green, a 91-year-old shipwright and scholar of laborlore, was eager to spend forty minutes talking about "that powerful, powerful legend." Commenting on the absence of newspaper reports of John Henry's mighty feat, Bill Dillon, retired postmaster of Talcott, West Virginia, was sure that whites would have suppressed the news because it would have given a tremendous boost to black morale. Ed Cabbell, a native of Eckman, West Virginia, who is himself black, saw John Henry and his wife, Polly Ann, as symbols for the black people of Appalachia, black laborers everywhere, labor in general, and more—"just *so* many things John Henry stood for." John Henry's impact on these and other people matches the might of his legendary feat.

My perspective had to change. Everything about John Henry is important, works of scholarship, fiction, and art as well as the lore itself and its origin. Even unfounded effusions and outrageous claims must be appreciated for their enrichment of the John Henry fabric.

Bearers of a tradition often have deep feelings for their material, which can seem as important as life itself. I learned this from a host of singers from *The Sacred Harp* and from a number of traditional instrumentalists and singers of ballads and other folksongs. I don't know how to convey this adequately, but I think it important for readers to try to understand. It is best, I think, to have a personal stake in the material, rather than to take something like a detached anthropologist's view.

John Henry scholars have believed that he was a real person. John Henry has always been real to bearers of the tradition, who have claimed him for many states in the South and for several railroads.

Here we consider new data and reconsider old, trying to judge on the basis of the whole body of available evidence. I conclude that one John Henry candidate, John Henry Dabney, a Mississippian who died in Alabama, probably in 1887, stands out from the others. The least that can be said is that he is favored by a "preponderance of the evidence." I consider it to be "beyond a reasonable doubt."

I have three purposes, to investigate the origin of John Henry lore, to describe some of John Henry's people, and to review more than a century of John Henry. The review cannot be comprehensive—the subject is too large. Even so, I address most facets of the subject.

Some day I hope a definitive recording project could assemble the most important recorded performances of "John Henry." In the meantime, an internet search will provide many of these recordings.

I am a folksong enthusiast, hobbyist, and amateur scholar. My credentials for this work are a natural curiosity, an education and academic career in chemistry, and a sixty-five-year interest in American folksong.

I try to be simple, direct, and clear.

As a step toward readability, I use the first person where it seems appropriate and where I judge that it does not compromise integrity. For the errors that are bound to appear, I am responsible.

When I started working on this book in 2007, I intended to take five years to complete it. I would continue research as I wrote. An illness that year convinced me that I ought to stop research and write what I could while I could.

Fortunately, my subsequent health has been good. As a mixed blessing, important new findings have kept me from keeping my resolution. I have felt forced to balance writing with additional research. Like biscuits and molasses, they never come out together, but there comes a point where you must stop.

More could be done. Perhaps most significant would be locating and examining construction records of the Columbus & Western Railway Company for the years 1886–88. Also, there still could be, somewhere, a contemporary account of John Henry and his contest, and there are bound to be documents telling more about some of John Henry's people. I hope that someone will pursue these and other opportunities for further research.

This project has not been a one-person effort. Many fellow knowledge seekers, mostly interested individually in one relevant area or another, have provided important information. I am grateful to all.

In remembrance and appreciation of my wife, Edna Swindoll Garst, for her support over the years.

Special thanks to my daughter, Dr. Jennifer Garst, for her encouragement and support.

I would also especially like to thank the following:

Marie Cromer, the late
Carl Marbury
Lonnie Marbury
James Lowery
Ed Cabbell
Bill Dillon
Katherine Biedleman Thompson
Gregg Kimball, director of education and outreach,
    Library of Virginia, and other librarians there
Bill Oursler
Jonathan Lighter
Peter Turner, who started the "Origins: John Henry" thread
    at the Mudcat Café, http://mudcat.org/thread.cfm?threadid=
    4018#21244, and all of the other contributors to that thread
Norm Cohen
Ed Cray
Art Thieme
Art and Margo Rosenbaum
Neil Rosenbaum
John Cuthbert, director and curator, the West Virginia &
    Regional History Center, and other librarians there
Laurie Matheson, editor-in-chief, University of Illinois Press
David Cowart and Donna Maddock-Cowart
Roger C. Vogel, who notated all musical examples (except figure 7)

Introduction:
Leeds, Alabama,
July 10–12, 2011

For ten years Art Rosenbaum, my friend and fellow resident of Athens, Georgia, had heard me argue that John Henry, the legendary steel-driving man, had raced a steam drill and died at a railroad tunnel at Dunnavant, Alabama, just south of Leeds and about fifteen miles east of Birmingham. He was convinced, but he wondered if more local lore could be found, so he urged that we take a field trip. Maybe we could find an interesting version of the "John Henry" ballad. Failing that, we still might be able to broaden our knowledge of the local John Henry legend, so off we went.

We arrived in Leeds in mid-afternoon, Sunday, July 10, 2011, and decided to drive around looking for people. We came across a young African American man whose wife knew about the John Henry celebrations in Leeds. The first one was on September 15, 2007. I was a speaker, and Art sang "John Henry" to his own banjo accompaniment.

I had thought that Dr. Carl Marbury would be a good source of leads in the black community around Leeds, but my efforts to contact him by telephone had failed. He didn't answer his phone that Sunday evening either.

Recalling that Carl has a brother, Lonnie, I found him in the telephone directory. When someone answered my call, it sounded like party time. Carl's high-school class was having a reunion, and Lonnie was hosting them.

Carl came to the phone, and I told him our mission. He would think about it. We should call him Monday afternoon, and he would tell us what he had come up with.

On Monday morning we decided to scout along AL State Route 25 south of Leeds. It goes over Oak and Coosa mountains to points south and east, following the tracks of the old Columbus and Western (C & W). Testimony given in 1927 associated John Henry with these mountains. He was said to have worked at Coosa Mountain Tunnel and to have raced a steam drill and died at Oak Mountain Tunnel. These tunnels are two miles apart. The community of Dunnavant lies between, south of Oak Mountain and north of Coosa Mountain.

As we crossed over Oak Mountain, we spotted a man in his yard, stopped, and asked about John Henry. Gary Brasher pulled out some folding chairs, got us cold drinks, and fetched a stack of issues of the *Central of Georgia Magazine*. He had no information on John Henry, but as a retired engineer, he loved to talk about the railroad.

An hour later we reached Vandiver, south of Coosa Mountain. The postmaster gave us a lead, but we found no one at home. On the way south toward Sterrett, we stopped and chatted with Roy Hartsfield, who suggested that we go on to Calcis and visit Frances Warren. She knew all about local history. We found her receiving a delivery at her back door.

Her knowledge of John Henry went back at least 75 years, to about 1936. Her mother told her that he raced a steam drill and died at Dunnavant.

Back in Leeds that afternoon, we spoke with Carl. He had arranged for us to interview Alex Parker on Tuesday morning and Lonnie that afternoon (Figure 1). Alex lives in Detroit, but he grew up in Leeds and was there for the reunion. We would interview Alex and Carl together.

Born in 1935, they were five or six years old when they first heard of John Henry. For about ten years, 1940–1950, they rode a mule-drawn wagon to the blacksmith's shop nearly every Saturday.

The blacksmith shop was the most integrated place in town. From the men standing around and talking, Alex and Carl heard about John Henry, mostly from black men.

To these men, John Henry was fact. There was no doubt that he had raced a steam drill and died at "little tunnel mountain." Local people don't use formal names for the mountains or tunnels. They speak instead of the "little" or "short" tunnel and the "big" or "long" tunnel. The tunnel through Oak Mountain is half as long as that through Coosa Mountain.

At home, Alex's father told stories similar to those heard at the blacksmith shop, but with a difference. John Henry was possible but not indisputable.

For most of his life, Carl was under the impression that only blacks knew about John Henry. He was stunned to discover in 1997 that Revis Brasher, Marie Cromer, Glenn Spruiell, Jerry Voyles, and other local

Figure 1. Left to right: Art Rosenbaum, Lonnie Marbury, Alex Parker, Carl Marbury, July 12, 2011 (photograph by the author).

whites were publicizing Leeds as "John Henry country." He joined in and became a leader in spreading the word.

I first visited Leeds in mid–November 2001. Jerry showed me the place "where John Henry fell dead."

Marie had organized the Leeds Historical Society in 1998, and she invited me to speak at their meeting on January 6, 2002. It was there that I met Carl.

He holds a Ph.D. in religious studies from Harvard, other graduate degrees from Oberlin and Vanderbilt, and a bachelor's degree from Alabama A & M, which he served as president from 1987 to 1991. Now retired, he is active in Leeds civic affairs, especially those involving history, education, culture, and African Americans.

Carl's and Lonnie's Cherokee grandfather, Cisero Davis (1850–1929), worked on the C & W when it was being put through Shelby County. His crew started at Goodwater, Coosa County, and built the line northwest. Along the way, he met his wife-to-be, Melissa Hood, a daughter of "Free Bob" Hood. They became the first African Americans to live in Leeds, which was incorporated on April 27, 1887.

Carl tells a story handed down from Cisero. There were frequent

Figure 2. Professors Carl Marbury (left) and John Garst standing beside the John Henry historical marker at the depot in Leeds, Alabama (courtesy Art Rosenbaum).

steel-driving contests, and a man named "John" always won. As the story survives, John Henry is not mentioned, but "John" must have been John Henry.

After lunch we met Lonnie at his home. He was born in 1938, served in the army, and had a twenty-nine-year teaching career. Mementos from his travels to distant lands fill his house. Like Carl, he is active in civic affairs.

He is the family genealogist and historian, and the results of his research fill a number of binders. In addition, he keeps an African American museum in a house that Cisero built in downtown Leeds.

When he was young, Lonnie heard old people tell about John Henry. A new machine was going to put men out of work. "John Henry said there ain't no machine outdo him." At the little tunnel, John Henry raced a steam drill, beat it, and died from his effort.

Lonnie believes that John Henry lies buried along the track somewhere near where he died. He is certain that Cisero and John Henry knew one another.

When asked to sing an old song, he burst into snatches of railroad work songs he had heard as a child. "John Henry was a mighty man! Huh! A mighty man was he. Huh!" ... "Yeaaa, we cain't a-lift these rails. Huuunh."

This is as close as we came to a version of "John Henry," but we *did* document the living tradition. Four informants, one white and three black, had heard some seventy or seventy-five years ago that John Henry raced a steam drill and died at Dunnavant.

It was a good trip.

1

The Gist of Things

Folklorists at the Library of Congress call it the most
researched folk song in the United States, and perhaps
the world.
                        —Scott Reynolds Nelson

The "most researched folk song" is the widely known and highly
esteemed ballad "John Henry, the Steel Driving Man," or, simply, "John
Henry" (Nelson 2006, Cohen 2000, Williams 1983). In folklore, a ballad is a story told in song. John Henry's story has fascinated Americans
since the early twentieth century.

"John Henry" is widely known and admired among both blacks and
whites. This is unusual for an American ballad.

John Henry was a steel driver, a skilled laborer who drilled holes in
rock by pounding on a steel drill with a sledgehammer. His crew was boring a railroad tunnel through a mountain somewhere in the American
South at some time in the nineteenth century after the Civil War. A recent
invention, the steam-powered rock drill, was under active development.

John Henry worked for the Captain. Believing that John Henry
could outdo a steam drill, the Captain arranged for a contest. John
Henry vowed, "Before I'll let that steam drill beat me down / I'll die with
my hammer in my hand." He beat the steam drill, then collapsed and
died, his hammer in his hand.

John Henry made his first appearance in print in 1909. Over the following decades, scholars collected and published considerable material
including transcriptions of commercial sound recordings, which aug-
mented the oral tradition.

Six scholars have concluded that John Henry was a real man, but
they reached five different conclusions. John Harrington Cox identified
him as the outlaw John Hardy and placed him at Big Bend Tunnel, Summers County, West Virginia, in 1870–72, working for the Chesapeake &

Ohio (C & O) Railroad (Cox 1925). Guy Benton Johnson and Louis Watson Chappell correctly separated him from John Hardy but agreed that he had been at Big Bend Tunnel (Johnson 1925, Chappell 1933).

C.S. "Neal" Miller convinced Johnson that Big Bend Tunnel was the John Henry site. Chappell also relied on Miller. His testimony is mistaken.

MacEdward Leach suggested that John Henry died in the Blue Mountains of Jamaica, ca. 1894–96. The ballad was sung in America before 1890 (Leach 1966, Chappell 1933).

Scott Reynolds Nelson put John Henry at Lewis Tunnel, Virginia, ca. 1870. The evidence for that place and time is not definitive (Nelson 2005, 2006).

Johnson obtained testimony about John Henry in Alabama (1929). Additional evidence makes a compelling case (Garst 2002).

The story of John Henry is that of actors in the legend, bearers of the tradition, and scholars. The better we know these people, the better we know John Henry.

The central figures are John Henry, the Captain, John Henry's wife, and the steam-drill salesman. We know a great deal about the Captain. He was Frederick Yeamans "Fred" Dabney, who moved at age six months from tidewater Virginia to Raymond, Hinds County, Mississippi, where his father Augustine ("Gus") was a lawyer and probate judge. Fred became a civil engineer, Confederate artillery hero, and railroad builder. At the end of the war, he was a captain in the Corps of Engineers.

The steel-driving man was John Henry Dabney, probably the Henry Dabney of the 1870 census of Copiah County. He was born a slave in Hinds County in 1849–50 on Burleigh Plantation, owned by Captain Dabney's uncle Colonel Thomas Dabney.

In about 1875, Captain Dabney moved to Crystal Springs, Copiah County, Mississippi. Henry Dabney lived in Hazlehurst, Copiah County, in 1870, and at nearby Hall's Hill in 1880.

Raymond, Crystal Springs, Hazlehurst, and Hall's Hill are all within twenty miles of Burleigh Plantation. Captain Dabney and Henry Dabney were probably in frequent contact throughout Henry's lifetime.

Charles C. Spencer, the only known eyewitness to John Henry's contest, is our closest link to the steel-driving man. He was an excellent witness. In 1887, at age sixteen, he carried water and steel for John Henry at Coosa Mountain Tunnel, Alabama. Outside the east portal of Oak Mountain Tunnel, two miles north of Coosa Mountain Tunnel, he watched John Henry race a steam drill.

These tunnels were bored for the extension of the Columbus & Western (C & W) Railway from Goodwater, Alabama, to Birmingham, in 1887–88. As chief engineer of the C & W, Captain Dabney was in charge of construction.

According to Spencer, John Henry "lived for honor." This is not surprising for someone raised with the Dabney family, which was noted for excellence of character.

Around 1910, W.T. Blankenship published his famous broadside, "John Henry, the Steel Driving Man." After losing his sight and nearly his life in a dynamite explosion, Blankenship became a street musician and sundries seller in Athens and Huntsville, Alabama. He is an exemplar of the poor, white, mountain musician who embraced the song "John Henry."

Margaret Riddlesperger, an ex-slave from South Carolina, preserved the only known copy of the Blankenship broadside. After the Civil War, she lived in Rome, Georgia. Her granddaughter inherited the broadside and sold it to folklorist Guy Johnson, who published and preserved it.

Leon R. Harris was born in Ohio in 1886 to a white mother and a black itinerant musician father. He was an amateur John Henry scholar whose long version of "John Henry" won a 1927 contest sponsored by Johnson through the *Chicago Defender*.

Rich Amerson was an illiterate genius from western Alabama. He sang a powerfully emotional and highly irregular "John Henry," perhaps the best ever recorded.

Riddlesperger, Harris, and Amerson are exemplars of the black person who embraced John Henry as a great hero.

Blankenship's, Harris's, Amerson's, and other versions of "John Henry" contain lines that point to Alabama.

For every proposed John Henry site other than Alabama, the evidence is weak. That for Alabama is overwhelming. It consists of the testimony of a credible eyewitness to John Henry's contest with a steam drill, the concurring testimonies of two others with direct or second-hand knowledge, testimonies of some with less direct links to John Henry, a body of facts about the C & W and Captain Dabney, and relevant lines of "John Henry," all of which are remarkably self-consistent.

꒓꒓ ꒓꒓ ꒓꒓

Much of the John Henry tradition is folklore, but there is oral history and literature as well.

2

Hammer Like John Henry

'Twas the biggest race th' worl' had ever seen.
—Leon R. Harris, "John Henry"

John Henry lore is found in the ballad "John Henry" and in work songs, narratives, tall tales, and works of fiction. Many texts of "John Henry" appear in books by Johnson and Chappell, and Johnson's book includes thirteen tunes as well (Johnson 1929, Chappell 1933).

"John Henry"

Figure 3 gives a typical "John Henry" tune.

The stanzas below are selected to tell the story, albeit sparsely. Frequently, in performance, the fourth line of each stanza is repeated, often after an interjection such as "Lawd, Lawd" (very common), "O dad," "this

Figure 3. A typical John Henry tune (transcribed by the author).

day," "on the job," "O boss," "O boy," "so sad," "must go," "po' boy," etc. Repetitions and interjections are omitted here.

John Henry was a little boy
Sittin' on his mama's knee.
Said, "The Big Bend Tunnel on the C. & O. Road
Gonna cause the death of me."
—Robert Mason, Durham, North Carolina, ca. 1927 [Johnson 1929, 126]

Cap'n said to Jawn Henry,
"Gonna bring me a steam drill 'round;
Take that steam drill out on the job,
Gonna whop that steel on down."
—Collected by Peter A. Brannon, Alabama [Crawford 1930, 8]

John Henry said to his captain,
"A man, he ain't nothin' but a man,
Before I'd let that steam drill beat me down,
I'd die with the hammer in my hand."
—Edward Douglas, Ohio State Penitentiary, ca. 1927 [Johnson 1929, 102]

John Henry had a little girl,
Her name was Polly Ann.
John was on his bed so low,
She drove with his hammer like a man.
—Odell Walker, Chapel Hill, North Carolina, 1925 [ibid., 100]

John Henry said to his shaker,
"Shaker, you had better pray.
If I was to miss this six-foot steel
Tomorrow will be your burying day."
—Jesse Sparks, Ethel, West Virginia, ca. 1930 [Chappell 1933, 111]

"Oh, if I die a steel-driving man
Go bury me under the tie,
So I can hear old number four
As she goes rolling by."
—W.S. Barnett, Holstead, West Virginia, ca. 1930 [ibid., 115]

The man that owned that old steam drill
Thought it was mighty fine,
But John Henry drove fourteen long feet
While the steam drill only made nine.
—N.A. Brown, U.S.S. *Pittsburgh*, ca. 1930 [ibid., 105]

John Henry was hammering on the right side,
The big steam drill on the left,
Before that steam drill could beat him down,
He hammered his fool self to death.
—W.T. Blankenship, [N.d., n.p. and Johnson 1929, frontispiece and 89]

John Henry made a steel-driving man;
They took him to the tunnel to drive;
He drove so hard that he broke his heart;
He laid down his hammer and he died.
—W.S. Barnett, Holstead, West Virginia, ca. 1930 [Chappell 1933, 114]

John Henry hammered in the mountain
Till his hammer caught on fire.
Very last word I heard him say,
"Cool drink of water before I die."
—Mrs. Tennessee Spears, Lorado, West Virginia, ca. 1930 [Ibid., 122]

Who gonna shoe yoh pretty liddle feet,
Who gonna glove yoh han',
Who gonna kiss yoh rosy cheeks,
An' who gonna be yoh man?

Papa gonna shoe my pretty liddle feet,
Mama gonna glove my han',
Sistah gonna kiss my rosy cheeks,
An' I ain't gonna have no man....

They took John Henry to the White House,
And buried him in the san',
And every locomotive come roarin' by,
Says there lays that steel drivin' man.
—Onah L. Spencer, Cincinnati, Ohio, ca. 1927 [Johnson 1929, 98–99]

These stanzas are taken from various sources and assembled so that they tell the story. No original or "official" version of "John Henry" is known. All known longer texts show evidence of having been cobbled together.

Hypertext

Professor David K. Farkas, of the Department of Human-Centered Design & Engineering at the University of Washington, gives his Information Design students a "John Henry Hypertext Exercise" (Farkas 2009b, Syllabus). For convenient reference, he gives each stanza a title.

John Henry Hypertext Exercise

The Prophecy	Epilogue

When John Henry was a little baby
Sitting on his mama's knee,
He picked up a hammer and a little piece
   of steel
And he said "Steel's gonna be the death
   of me, Lord, Lord.
Steel's gonna be the death of me."
	Well they took John Henry's body
	And they buried it in the sand.
	But every locomotive that comes roarin'
	   through that tunnel
	Is cryin' "There lies a steel driving man,
	   Lord, Lord.
	There lies a steel driving man."

No More Work	**Polly Ann Fills In**

The Captain said to John Henry,
"Gonna bring a steam drill 'round,
Gonna take that steam drill out on the job,
Gonna whop that steel on down,
   Lord, Lord.
Gonna whop that steel on down."
	John Henry had a little woman
	Her name was Polly Ann.
	When her John got sick and had to go
	   to bed,
	Polly drove steel like a man, Lord, Lord.
	Polly drove steel like a man.

The Challenge	**Shaker, Why Don't You Sing?**

John Henry said to the Captain,
"A man ain't nothin' but a man.
But before I let this steel drill beat me down,
I'll die with that hammer in my hand,
   Lord, Lord,
Die with that hammer in my hand."
	John Henry said to his shaker,
	"Shaker, why don't you sing?
	I'm throwin' twenty pounds from my hips
	   on down,
	Just listen to the cold steel ring, Lord, Lord,
	Just listen to the cold steel ring."

The Triumph	**Polly Carries On**

The man that invented the steam drill,
Thought he was mighty fine.
But John Henry drove his fifteen feet,
And the steam drill only made nine,
   Lord, Lord.
The steam drill only made nine.
	John Henry had a little woman
	Her name was Polly Ann.
	She picked up his hammer went down
	   to the tunnel.
	And she drove steel like a man, Lord, Lord.
	She drove steel like a man.

Death	**The Boast**

John Henry hammered on the mountain,
With the blood runnin' down his side.
He drove so hard he broke his poor heart,
And he laid down his hammer and he died,
   Lord, Lord,
He laid down his hammer and he died.
	John Henry said to the Captain,
	"Look yonder what I see—
	Your drill's done broke and your hole's
	   done choked,
	An' you can't drive steel like me, Lord, Lord.
	You can't drive steel like me."

The Captain Is Afraid	Shaker, Why Don't You Pray?
The Captain said to John Henry, "I fear the mountain's cavin' in." John Henry laughed and he said to the Captain, "It's only my hammer suckin' wind, Lord, Lord. It's only my hammer suckin' wind."	John Henry said to his shaker "Shaker why don't you pray? Cause if I miss that little piece of steel, Tomorrow be your burying day, Lord, Lord, Tomorrow be your burying day."
John Henry Was the Best	**John Henry's Birthplace**
Some say John Henry's from Georgia, Some say he's from Alabam, But never I say in the whole USA. Was ever such a steel-driving man, Lord, Lord Was ever such a steel-driving man.	Some say John Henry's from Georgia, Some say he's from Alabam, But it's wrote on the rock at the Big Bend Tunnel, That he was a West Virginia man, Lord, Lord, That he was a West Virginia man

A reader proceeds through linear text in a fixed order, a succession of elements such as the words in a sentence, the sentences in a paragraph, the paragraphs in a chapter, and the chapters in a book. Hypertext is nonlinear. At certain points, a reader must choose from among two or more options, as Farkas explained in an email (2009a).

> Basically, I introduce the John Henry legend (which most of the students have never heard of) and I even sing it. Then I ask the students to imagine that they have a friend who is a folk singer. The folk singer would like their advice on the possible sequences of stanzas that would be effective. In other words, some of the stanzas are "core nodes," which pretty much have to be included or the song won't make sense. Other nodes are optional—a singer would have freedom in how to sequence them. But, some choices are better than others. For example, I think that "Shaker why don't you sing" is better if it comes just before "Shaker why don't you pray." I don't especially care what sequences the students prefer. I'm just showing them that you can have multiple pathways through any network of nodes (the stanzas) and that there are various constraints (John Henry should not die before he's born) and other options. Also, I'm connecting this to other forms of hypertext.
>
> By the way, many bluegrass musicians, I've found, sing the verses in a totally illogical order, but that's because they assume their listeners already know the story.

Hammer Like John Henry

In double-jack rock drilling, the steel driver and shaker must be highly coordinated to execute their individual tasks efficiently and effectively. It is a kind of ballet. To time and coordinate their actions, the shaker and driver may sing a "hammer song." The hammer falls during the pause after each line.

> If I could hammer
> Like John Henry,
> If I could hammer
> Like John Henry,
> Lord, I'd be a man,
> Lord, I'd be a man.
> —Negro laborers, Columbia, South Carolina [Johnson 1929, 2]

These lines emphasize John Henry's ability. Indeed, steel driving is highly technical. Excellence requires great skill.

When hammer songs are sung separately from the labor for which they are meant, the singer often marks where the hammer would fall by a grunt or other ejaculation, as Lead Belly explains in his commercial recording of "Take This Hammer."

> Back down south when the boys is workin', every time you hear 'em say "Hah," that's when the hammer falls, and the hammer rings. The boys gives the hammer a swing, and then they gonna sing. They got rhythm, and they got swing, as they sing.

> > Take this hammer, (Whah!)
> > And carry it to the captain, (Whah!)
> > Take this hammer (Whah!)
> > And carry it to the captain, (Whah!)
> > Take this hammer (Whah!)
> > And carry it to the captain, (Whah!)
> > You tell him I'm gone, (Whah!)
> > You tell him I'm gone. (Whah!)
> > —Lead Belly (Huddie Ledbetter) [October 1944]

John Hardy

This story is from West Virginia governor (1893–1897) William Alexander MacCorkle (1857–1930, often misspelled "McCorkle"). In about 1900 he learned a ballad in which John Hardy was a steel driver at Big Bend Tunnel, Summers County, West Virginia. Part of his letter to Henry S. Green, state historian, follows (Ramella 1992, 49).

> John Hardy was not a railroad man or operator, but he was a steel-driver and was famous in the beginning of the building of the C. & O. Railroad. He was also a steel-driver in the beginning of the extension of the N. & W. Railroad. It was about 1872 that he was in this section. This was before the

day of steam drills and the drill work was done by two powerful men who were special steel drillers. They struck the steel from each side and as they struck the steel they sung a song which they improvised as they worked. John Hardy was the most famous steel driller ever in southern West Virginia. He was a magnificent specimen of the genus *Homo*—was reported to be six feet two and weighed two hundred and twenty-five or thirty pounds, was straight as an arrow and was one of the most handsome men in the country, and, as one informant told me, was as "black as a kittle in hell."

Whenever there was any spectacular performance along the lines of drilling work, John Hardy was put on the job, and it is said that he could drill more steel than any two men of his day. He was a great gambler and was notorious all through the country for his luck in gambling. To the dusky sex all through the country, he was the "greatest ever" and he was admired and beloved by all the Negro women from the southwest Virginia line to the C. & O. In addition to this, he could drink more whisky, sit up all night and drive steel all day to a greater extent than any man ever known in the country.

The killing in which he made his final exit was a "mixtery" between women, cards and liquor, and it was understood that it was more of a fight than a murder. I have been unable to find out where he was hung, but have an idea that it was down in the southwest part near Virginia, but I am not positive about this. In other words, his story is a story of one of the composite characters that arise so often in the land. A man of kind heart, very strong, pleasant in his address, yet a gambler, a roué, a drunkard and a fierce fighter.

The song is quite famous in the construction camps and when they are driving steel by hand in a large camp, the prowess of John Hardy is always sung.... Of course, you understand that all this about John Hardy is merely among the Negroes. I cannot say that the John Hardy you mention was hung is the same John Hardy of the song, but it may be so, for he was supposed to be in that vicinity when he last exploited himself. He was never an employee of the C. & O. He was an employee of the Virginia contractors, C.R. Mason & Co., and the Langhorn Company.

When Henry Spencer and John Bell, two of my colored friends each of whom is a gambler and keeper of a dive, come around, I think I can get some information, but my friends are not always in a condition to be seen by policemen and so I don't know just when I can get this information....

—W.A. MacCorkle to H.S. Green, February 16, 1916

"Tall, Gaunt, Alabama Negro"

Elbert McDonald described a Kentucky and Alabama John Henry (1934, 2).

THE SAGA OF JOHN HENRY
The Story of How an Alabama Negro Steel Driver Pitted
His Strength Against Air Compressor Drills
by ELBERT McDONALD

"John Henry Was a Steel Driving Man" is the title of one of the most popular of the mountain ballads sung nowadays wherever groups of men gather with guitar banjo, and old home-made mountain "fiddles." Section crew workers, highway workers, and general construction workers sway to the rhythmic beat of the John Henry song as they perform their labors. In many construction crews where negroes are employed a singer is employed who sits nearby and in rhythmic, barbaric monotone chants mountain ballads and spirituals to the workers. Construction foremen insist that in many instances it would be impossible for the workers to pursue their tasks unless a singer or a "chanter" kept the men gaily about their duties by his renditions.

The story of John Henry is well-known by every old-timer in the Cumberland Valley. Legend has it that John Henry's famous death occurred near Varilla, Kentucky, a short distance from Pineville while working on the construction of the railroad from Pineville to Harlan. The crew was engaged in carving but of the solid rock a roadbed for the railroad which was to open up the richest coal field in the world according to area, the rich Harlan county field. They were laboring at the now famous "Seven Sisters," one of the most beautiful and awe-inspiring sights in the Cumberland Valley. John Henry, a tall, gaunt, Alabama negro, was the most powerful steel driver of the crew. Wherever he had worked, all over the Southland, he had been the champion. He had never tasted defeat. His duty was to drive steel drills into the solid rock with mighty blows from a sixteen-pound sledge hammer.

The foreman on the job was introducing the new pneumatic compressed air drills for drilling the holes for the charges of dynamite. A foreign crew was using these new drills. John Henry and his men formed another crew, but they used the old-time method. Rivalry was keen. There was much bandying back and forth between the crews. One day the foreman of the crew using the new-fangled machines issued a challenge to John Henry and his Alabama huskies. To John Henry it was more than a challenge; it was an insult to think that "them machinery contraptions" could beat him as a steel driver. With scorn and ridicule he accepted the offer. The element of time was that they would begin the next day as the sun peeped its first ray over the top of Pine mountain and the contest was to end as the sun cast its last glimmering ray in the west.

The battle began at the appointed time the next day. From miles up and down the right-of-way of construction, the laborers had gathered to watch the mighty battle between man and the machine. It was a partisan crowd, as they took sides, some with John Henry and some with the machine. No gladiators ever had such ardent supporters as these two factions on that day as they perched on the hillsides and cheered their favorites. Blow after blow rained upon the drills from machine and muscle as the steel chewed its way through the sandstone blocks. Minutes became hours, and hours became ages as the weary crews fought ceaselessly. Sweat poured from the men as they fought desperately to gain an advantage—a margin of victory which could only be determined when the day was done and the holes were measured.

Late in the afternoon, men began to drop here and there from shear exhaustion. This served only to redouble the efforts of John Henry and his valiant warriors. The sun was slowly sinking in the west. Would the end ever come? One hour more—maybe two hours, ages, ages and ages. Finally the last glimmering ray of the sun dropped gently behind the mountains to the west as John Henry, tightly gripping his sledge slipped gently to the earth, covered with dust from his labors. A mighty cheer echoed throughout the surrounding hills as the spectators rushed up to begin the job of measuring the holes that the victor might be determined. They did not notice the near-lifeless body of John Henry lying convulsively near the last steel wedge he had driven. Did we say all of them? Nay, not all of the onlookers. One man who throughout the entire contest had watched with reverential awe the smooth, rhythmic muscular movements of his idol in almost parental devotion, stooped to gather into his arms the fallen John Henry. That man was John Henry's foreman, his name long since lost to the ages. As he gathered John Henry close to his bosom tears were streaming down his face. He realized that John Henry had given his all in a last supreme effort for his sake.

Through tear-dimmed eyes he saw John Henry's lips move in a barely audible whisper—"Boss, I sho' hopes we've won." With these last words, John Henry sagged gently in the foreman's arms as he passed into the realm from which no steel driver returns. He did not hear the exultant shout of triumph his friends sent up as the last hole was measured.

But John Henry won. He won two victories—the champion steel driver of all time and—Death.

That is the story of "John Henry, the Steel Driving Man." It is, however, mistakenly attributed to the "Seven Sisters." John Henry worked on the crew at the "Seven Sisters" but it was the next construction job wherein his battle to death for supremacy of the machine drivers occurred in just such a manner as has been told. The battle was staged at Ewing, Virginia, near what is now known as Sand Cave. But John Henry's body rests immortal in the eyes of his heroes somewhere in the mud flats of Alabama, near Birmingham.

Middlesboro, Kentucky

McDonald puts John Henry in three states: Alabama, Kentucky, and Virginia. Similar claims have been made for every southern state.

Tall Tale

The following story is from an African American in Chapel Hill, North Carolina, but probably came originally from Stone Mountain, Georgia.

One day John Henry lef' rock quarry on way to camp an' had to go through woods an' fiel'. Well, he met big black bear an' didn't do nothin' but shoot 'im wid his bow an' arrer, an' arrer went clean through bear an' stuck in big tree on other side. So John Henry pulls arrer out of tree an' pull so hard he falls back 'gainst 'nother tree which is full o' flitterjacks, an' first tree is full o' honey, an' in pullin' arrer out o' one he shaken down honey, an' in fallin' 'gainst other he shaken down flitterjacks. Well, John Henry set there an' et honey an' flitterjacks an' set there an' et honey an' flitterjacks, an' after while when he went to git up to go, button pop off'n his pants an' kill a rabbit mo' 'n' hundred ya'ds on other side o' de tree. An' so up jumped brown baked pig wid sack o' biscuits on his back, an' John Henry et him too.

So John Henry gits up to go on through woods to camp for supper, 'cause he 'bout to be late an' he mighty hungry for his supper. John Henry sees lake down hill and thinks he'll git him a drink o' water, cause he's thirsty, too, after eatin' honey an' flitterjacks an' brown roast pig an' biscuits, still he's hongry yet. An' so he goes down to git drink water and finds lake ain't nothin' but lake o' honey, an' out in middle dat lake ain't nothin but tree full o' biscuits. An' so John Henry don't do nothin' but drink dat lake o' honey dry. An' he et the tree full o' biscuits, too.

An' so 'bout that time it begin' to git dark, an' John Henry sees light on hill an' he think maybe he can git sumpin to eat, cause he's mighty hongry after big day drillin'. So he look 'roun' an' see light on hill an' runs up to house where light is an' ast people livin' dere, why'n hell dey don't give him sumpin' to eat, 'cause he ain't had much. An' so he et dat, too.

Gee-hee, hee, dat nigger could eat! But dat ain't all, cap'n. Dat nigger could wuk mo' 'n' he could eat. He's greates' steel driller ever live, regular giaunt, he wus; could drill wid his hammer mo' 'n' two steam drills, an' some say mo' 'n' ten. Always beggin' boss to git 'im bigger hammer, always beggin' boss git 'im bigger hammer. John Henry wus cut out fer big giaunt driller. One day when he wus jes' few weeks ol' settin' on his mammy's knee he commence cryin' an' his mommer say, "John Henry, whut's matter, little son?" An' he up an' say right den an' dere dat nine-poun' hammer be death o' him. An' so sho' 'nough he grow up right 'way into bigges' steel driller worl' ever see. Why dis I's tellin' you now wus jes' when he's young fellow; waits til' I tells you 'bout his drillin' in mountains an' in Pennsylvania. An' so one day he drill all way from Rome, Georgia, to D'catur, mo' 'n' a hundred miles drillin' in one day, an' I ain't sure dat wus his bes' day. No, I ain't sure dat wus his bes' day.

But, boss, John Henry wus a regular boy, not lak some o' dese giaunts you read 'bout not likin' wimmin an' nothin'. John Henry love to come to town same as any other nigger, only mo' so. Co'se he's mo' important an' all dat, an' co'se he had mo' wimmin 'an anybody else, some say mo' 'n' ten, but as to dat I don't know. I means, boss, mo' wimmen 'an ten men, 'cause, Lawd, I specs he had mo' 'n' thousand wimmin.' An' John Henry wus a great co'tin' man, too, cap'n. Always wus dat way. Why, one day when he settin' by his pa' in san' out in front o' de house, jes' few weeks old, women come along and claim him fer deir man. An' dat's funny, too, but it sho' wus dat way all his

life. An' so when he come to die John Henry had mo' wimmin, all dressed in red an' blue an' all dem fine colors come to see him dead, if it las' thing they do, an' wus mighty sad sight, people all standin' 'roun', both cullud an' white.
                    —Construction-camp laborer, ca. 1925 [Odum 1926, 238–40,
                                                        Johnson 1929, 144–46].

Literature

Roark Bradford's 1931 novel *John Henry* tells a different story (1931a).

When John Henry is born in the Black River country, the Mississippi River runs upstream for a thousand miles. He weighs forty-four pounds, has a cotton hook in his hand, and tells everybody that he is a "natchul man." When he finds out that everybody else has had supper, he gets really mad and declares, "Don't let me git mad on de day I'm bawn, 'cause I'm skeered of my ownse'f when I gits mad." Then he tells them what he needs to eat, enough for any hundred or so ordinary people, and he walks away and leaves the Black River country.

When he gets to be a man, John Henry becomes a "rousterbout" and starts loading cotton onto a riverboat, the *Big Jim White*, walking a bouncy plank between the levee and the boat. He carries a 500-lb bale on his shoulders and walks with a weaving step that he invents and others imitate. It comes to be called the "coonjine."

When hogs get to be in short supply, they go to the Black River country, where the woods are full of wild, tall, razor-backed hogs that are mighty tough to handle. After dogs run some into a pen, they have to get them onto the *Big Jim White*, but none of the roustabouts can handle them, except John Henry. John Henry talks hog talk, makes friends with the hogs, and then flips them and hoists them out onto the shoulders of other roustabouts. They load ten thousand hogs that way.

One year there was a big cotton crop and at the Bends they are having such trouble picking it that the boss man gives up. He decides to just let it go. John Henry objects. He shows the hands how niggers are such natural cotton pickers that the cotton will jump off the plants to stick on their hands. It takes some educating, but he shows them all how to do it, backs bent, hands cupped, and pretty soon they have all the cotton picked and at the gin, where it stands in a pile as high as the treetops.

John Henry comes to the Yellow Dog Railroad camp when they are trying to start construction but can't get it going. With a special pair of mules the boss gets for him, he starts the grading and gets things underway. Then he tells the boss, Billie Bob Russell, that he needs to get his mules out of the shade and to stop driving his niggers: "Shade is made fo' white fo'ks and hosses. Sun is made for mules and niggers." Following John Henry's directions, they build the Yellow Dog Railroad, a thousand miles long, before the sun goes down that day.

John Henry gets off the *Big Jim White* at New Orleans bent on play. His big muscles cow John Hardy and everybody else in a gambling house into donating money to get John Henry dressed up like a fine sport.

In New Orleans John Henry meets Julie Anne, six feet tall and, like John Henry, from the Black River country, "whar de sun don't never shine." "You's my man, John Henry," she tells him, because there is a *gris gris* on her and him. John Henry tries several other women, but they are all too coy or too forward, or something, so he goes to Julie Anne's house. Julie Anne tells him he can come and go as he pleases but he will always come back to her.

When John Henry gets tired of New Orleans and goes out to travel, he jumps on the Red Ball freight train. The fireman, the best there is, is having trouble keeping enough coal under the boiler for the rate at which the engineer is using steam, so John Henry takes over and they are in Memphis before sunset.

In Argenta, John Henry goes to see Poor Selma, a "low-down devil" whose business is men. She tells John Henry that no man can quit her, but John Henry does.

Dressed up fancy, John Henry meets Stacker Lee, "de baddest man in dis town," in front of Poor Selma's house. As they talk, Stacker Lee shoots off John Henry's shoestrings, coat buttons, hatband, necktie, and belt. While Selma and Ruby have a big fight, Stacker Lee claims to have lost interest in John Henry and puts all the shot-off clothes back on John Henry. John Henry knows better—he knows Stacker Lee is scared. He takes Stacker Lee's gun and watch and chain, and he knocks him in the river—twice.

After a conjure woman in the Black River country says she had cured John Henry of Poor Selma, he lays around for awhile, but the conjure woman tells him he has to stop that and bear his burden, he could work or he could play but he couldn't lay around, so he goes to New Orleans to see his Julie Anne.

He finds Ruby there, and she makes a play for him, but he insists that his woman is Julie Ann. According to Ruby, Julie Ann has gone off with Sam. John Henry quickly disposes of Sam. He gets a job as a roust-about on the *Big Jim White*, and he signs on to do the work of three men so he can earn Julie Ann's way on board.

When John Henry gets to Billie Bob Russell's Yellow Dog railroad camp in the Mississippi Delta, he finds Sam driving spikes and bragging that since the best was dead now, he is the new best. John Henry steps up and challenges Sam, and they have a spike-driving contest. Sam quits part-way through, but John Henry keeps going till sunset and finishes driving the spikes for the Yellow Dog line. When he gets back to camp, he calls for Julie for his supper, but she doesn't answer. An old woman tells John Henry that she has run off with Sam, so John Henry takes up with Ruby.

When John Henry gets tired of Ruby and his job, he walks off to the river, finds the *Big Jim White* just landing, rolls cotton bales on board, and gets on. The *Big Jim White* is bound for New Orleans. The other roustabouts tease John Henry about Julie Ann and how he had worked for three men to bring her along. John Henry vows to get her back when he gets to New Orleans.

He finds her there being abused by Sam and missing her John Henry, so he chases Sam off and takes over, but he can't stop himself from slapping her down three times, then he walks out on the streets. After he passes Sam and knocks him down, he comes upon Blind Lemon, singing a sad song about women, and Old Aunt Dinah, who talks him into going back to Julie Ann. Julie Ann welcomes him, but he sees Sam's fresh, muddy track going out the back door. She promises not to let Sam come again, and John Henry decides to stay.

John Henry goes to the dock and gets a job rolling cotton for the *Big Jim White*. When he gets home, he finds the front door locked. Julie Ann opens it, but John Henry sees fresh tracks going out the back door again. After Julie Ann fixes his supper, he declares he isn't hungry, goes out, and finds Blind Lemon singing a sad song about women, the one about gin and cocaine.

John Henry goes to Mink Eye's place, where Ruby talks him into a few shots of gin and cocaine. He says he doesn't like it, beats up Mink Eye, tears the place up, and leaves to find Julie Ann back home. She has fed his supper to Sam.

One day John Henry goes out, passes Blind Lemon, and goes into the Old Ship of Zion Church, where Old Aunt Dinah is in the congregation and Hell-buster is preaching. After Dinah and Hell-buster get John Henry to ask the Lawd to bear his burden away, he is hit with the Spirit. He is knocked dead, and he moans and groans and froths at the mouth. For forty days and nights he is "struck dead on the floor." Finally, he gets up, says he is saved, says his farewells to Hell-buster and his congregation, and leaves. He goes home, gets his stuff, and says good-bye to Julie Ann and tells her not to grieve after him.

At the *Big Jim White*, the mate tells him they don't need any roustabouts because they have a new machine, a donkey engine that pulls cotton bales up the plank and onto the ship. "That winch rolls cotton like ten good men, and it only takes one nigger."

John Henry challenges the winch to a contest, so they put down another stage for him. Julie Ann tries to bet on John Henry, but there are no takers. The contest goes on till sundown, and about that time John Henry goes down. He dies with his cotton hook in his hand.

Hell-buster preaches his funeral. Old Aunt Dinah and Poor Selma are there, but Julie Ann isn't. Finally, Sam comes in carrying something wrapped in a blanket. He lays it beside John Henry. It is Julie Ann. When she saw John Henry die, she followed.

Hell-buster's funeral sermon ends as follows.

> So come on, you liars, and come on, you gamblers, and come on, you low-down women; git down on yo' knees, and git yo' heart right, and give yo' soul to Jesus, 'cause dat's how John Henry and Julie Ann done when de burden got too heavy [Bradford 1931a, 225].

ᗒᗕ ᗒᗕ ᗒᗕ

"John Henry" tunes have British antecedents. African American performers often simplify them.

3

Great Folk Tune Patterns

In the "Birmingham Boys" pattern the British
folk muse produced something closely akin to the
descending strains of Africa. It is no wonder that black
musicians seized on it so avidly.
—Peter van der Merwe

Ballads are sung. Therefore tunes matter, but ballads are more than
texts and tunes. Style and milieu contribute much of what makes a ballad performance interesting. Here we are limited to texts and tunes.
Transcriptions capture only the skeletons of ballad tunes, but that is
enough for recognizing tune kinships.

Francis James Child (1825–1896), Professor of English at Harvard,
gathered texts for 305 English-language ballads that he thought traditional (1882–98). They are often cited in the form "Child 278," meaning ballad number 278 ("The Farmer's Curst Wife") in Child's collection.

"John Henry" tunes have British ancestors. Phillips Barry has identified a "John Henry" tune with the Appalachian tune for a much earlier
British ballad, "Earl Brand" (Child 7). Peter van der Merwe found that a
tune for another British ballad, "The Birmingham Boys," is widely used
in America for "John Henry" (1989, 196).

"Earl Brand"

The "John Henry" tune to which Barry refers came from Leon Har-
ris, Moline, Illinois, in 1927 (Johnson 1929, 90–95). In Figure 4 the "Earl
Brand" tune from Mrs. Moore, Rabun Gap, Georgia, 1909 (Campbell and
Sharp 1917, 14), is compared, phrase-by-phrase, with Harris' "John Henry."

For the first two phrases, the resemblance of the "John Henry" and
"Earl Brand" tunes is striking. For the last two phrases, the two tunes have
similar ranges and contours. Barry spotted two sets of the "same" tune.

Earl Brand / John Henry

Figure 4. Comparison of the tune of "Earl Brand" from Mrs. Moore (Campbell and Sharp, 1917, 14) with that of "John Henry" from Leon Harris (Guy B. Johnson, *John Henry: Tracking Down a Negro Legend*, p. 91. Copyright © 1929 by the University of North Carolina Press. Used by permission of the publisher). For ease of comparison, both tunes have been transposed to the key of C by the author.

The Harris "John Henry" tune is not typical, but a typical one also resembles the Appalachian "Earl Brand." In Figure 5 the "Earl Brand" tune from Mrs. Mary Sands, Allanstand, North Carolina, 1916 (Campbell and Sharp 1917, 11), is compared with "John Henry Blues," by Earl Johnson and his Dixie Entertainers, Okeh 45101, Atlanta, Georgia (Johnson 1929, 113–14).

Sharp et al. found twelve variants of this "Earl Brand" tune in North Carolina, Georgia, Virginia, and Kentucky, suggesting that it has long been in the Appalachian Mountains (Sharp 1932, 1: 14–25). It surely predates "John Henry," and it almost certainly originates in Britain, even though it does not closely resemble British "Earl Brand" tunes, several of which are found at the "abc notation" website (Walshaw 1995).

"The Birmingham Boys"

Under various titles, Roud's index contains over thirty entries for "The Birmingham Boys" (1985, No. 665). The tune sung by Harry Cox (1885–1971) is a close match for "John Henry."

Earl Brand / John Henry

Figure 5. Comparison of the "Earl Brand" tune from Mrs. Mary Sands (Campbell and Sharp, 1917, 11) with that of "John Henry Blues" from Earl Johnson and His Dixie Entertainers (Guy B. Johnson, *John Henry: Tracking Down a Negro Legend*, p.113. Copyright © 1929 by the University of North Carolina Press. Used by permission of the publisher). Both tunes have been transposed down one whole tone to the key of C by the author.

Harry Cox (Figure 6) was one of the most revered English traditional singers of modern times (Kennedy 1958 and 1971). His repertoire and singing artistry were both remarkable. It included at least one song that he could trace back 200 years in his own family. Using the same tune that he recorded for Peter Kennedy in 1953, he sang "The Birmingham Boys," as "In Burnham Town," for E.J. Moeran in January 1922 (Kennedy 1975).

Figure 7 is van der Merwe's Example 84 (1989, 194–95). Figure 7(a) is Cox's "The Birmingham Boys." Figure 7(b)-(d) are collected versions of "John Henry." Figure 7(b) is from Sandburg, (c) is from the Lomaxes, and (d) is from a recording by Etta Baker (Sandberg 1927, 24, Lomax 1934, 5, Baker 1956, Guida 2009). Etta Baker was a noted instrumentalist, an African American born in Caldwell County, North Carolina, at the base of the Blue Ridge Mountains (Lucas 2011).

The first three melodic phrases Figure 7(a) and Figure 7(b) are nearly identical, and their fourth phrases share some contours. For three phrases, "The Birmingham Boys" and "John Henry" (I) track one another almost note-for-note with the feeling that the key is C major

Figure 6. Harry Cox with homemade toy at his home in Sutton, England, 1953 (photograph by Alan Lomax, from the Alan Lomax Collection of the American Folklife Center, Library of Congress, courtesy Association for Cultural Equity).

(Ionian). "Boys," however, ends on D, rather than the C of "John Henry." For this reason, it could be classified as Dorian, but it can also be seen as an Ionian tune with a surprise ending. There would be a tendency to "correct" "The Birmingham Boys" by changing the ending note to C, as in "John Henry."

Figure 7. "The Birmingham Boys" and "John Henry" tune comparisons (*Origins of the Popular Style*, Peter van der Merwe, copyright © 1989 Oxford University Press. Reproduced with permission of the Licensor through PLSclear).

Africanization of "The Birmingham Boys" in America

Van der Merwe assigns an important role in the development of American popular music to the "John Henry" tune.

> The "Birmingham Boys" pattern … was thoroughly African. Sensing its kinship to their ancestral music, the blacks seized on its African features and exaggerated them. The whole process can be seen in Ex. 84 [Figure 7]. It is the Africanization of British folk music in a nutshell [van der Merwe 1989, 194–97].

Almost no one challenges the idea that American popular music grew out of its varied musical cultures, with British and African strains dominant. In *Origins of the Popular Style* and *Roots of the Classical* van der Merwe analyzes this process (2004).

The "descending strains of Africa" are "so typical." As ancient Near-Eastern music spread across Africa and Europe, it left in its wake slow musical styles featuring high degrees of ornamentation and high-pitched, nasal voices. Polyrhythms (superimposed rhythms of different kinds, giving rise to syncopation), call-and-response (short statements alternating with short responses), and improvisation are also typical of African music (van der Merwe 1989, 9–14, 35–36).

All of these features occur in the blues, where descending phrases, high voices, ornamentation, syncopation, and improvisation are found frequently. Call-and-response is found in the common blues form, AAB, where the repetition of the first line of text is a response.

The repetition of the fourth phrase of "The Birmingham Boys" is a response that carries over into "John Henry." Further, as van der Merwe notes, a large part of the tune consists of repetitions of short musical phrases with variation, a thoroughly African trait (1989, 196).

The tunes of Figures 7(b) and 7(c) are tetratonic, using only four degrees of the scale. Tune (b) "feels" like it is in C major (Ionian). Tune (c) is treated as A minor (Aeolian) by van der Merwe, but for comparisons with the other tunes of Figure 7, it seems better cast as C Dorian (Figure 8).

Africans have tetratonic, pentatonic, hextonic, and heptatonic tunes (van der Merwe 1989, 30). Examples noted by van der Merwe suggest that African Americans tend to reduce tunes to bare essentials.

In the Africanization of music in America, nothing stands out more that style. African American voices resemble African voices, and white Americans have not been very successful in their attempts to imitate them.

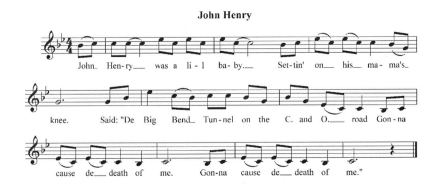

Figure 8. Tune of Figure 7(c) ["John Henry (II)"] recast in the key of C (recast by the author).

When two or more people are singing together, whites tend to try to synchronize their voices, whereas blacks tend toward a kind of "raggedness," with bits of syncopation resulting from anticipated and delayed attacks. In general, African Americans tend toward "looser" styles with more improvisation.

Rich Amerson, an African American from western Alabama, provided what may be the ultimate structural distortion and improvisation in a rendition of "John Henry" recorded in 1950 (1956).

Rich Amerson's "John Henry"

According to the census of 1900 for the Sumterville Precinct, Sumter County, Alabama, Richard Amerson was born in May 1893. Thus, he was 56 when he was recorded in early 1950. His full name was Richard Manuel Amerson. His sister, Eartha ("Earthy") Anne Coleman, called him "Bud." To other relatives he was "Manuel," and to Courlander he was "Rich" (Courlander 1956).

Although his father, Spencer Amerson, could read and write, Rich did not admit these abilities.

> By occupation, Rich Amerson has been farmer, lumberjack, track-liner, storm pit builder, and lay preacher. "Anything at all that man has to do to keep on living, I can do it," he says. "I can preach the Gospel, I can moan and groan, I can counteract conjur stuff, and I can play my mouth harp. And I can look and I can see, that's the biggest part of it all. Livingston County is full of people looking back and forth, but what do they see, I ask you? And do they understand what they see? What good is it to be born if you don't

Figure 9. Richard Manuel Amerson (left) and John Lomax, 1940 (Library of Congress).

see, and if you don't understand what you see? In the ordinary sense I can't neither read *nor* write. But the sense God gave you don't depend altogether on schooling. I was schooled in hard work, and I can read with a hoe and write with a plow." Though illiterate, Rich knows the Testament backwards and forwards, and he is able and ready to preach or sing on almost any Biblical allusion or theme....

He is always on the move, looking for "values." He disappears on foot, reappears months later on a bicycle. He goes down to the general store for groceries and is next heard of two years later living in another county.

Rich has been among the poorest of the poor most of his life. "I ain't proud to be poor," he says, "but I ain't too poor to be proud. And I'm not too poor to be rich in values. Music is in everything you see and hear. Railroad, now that's music, isn't it? And church, that's music too, isn't it? And if you come right down to it, music is church too. Some folks, now, they won't sing

no sinful songs. The way I see it, if a song is in you you got to sing it, and it's just another aspect of the Holy Spirit. When life is big, music is big."
   ... His sister Earthy Anne says: "Bud ain't much but breath and britches, but he sure can sing" [Courlander 1956].

Amerson spoke of "Livingston County." There is no such county in Alabama. The town of Livingston lies in Sumter County.

Through Ruby Pickens Tartt, of Livingston, John Lomax met Amerson in 1937. Lomax's impression of him was a bit different from Amerson's self-representation.

He needed a "French harp" to give imitations of a train, a fox-hunt, and barnyard festival. I bought one and presented it to him. When he failed to appear at the appointed time, after a long stretch I found him. He had loaned the harp to a friend who at that time was fifty miles away. Later I learned that he had converted the harp at half price into a pint of bootleg liquor. But he made me feel that I had done him a great wrong. Richard, as he insisted, was a paragon of virtue, unappreciated by his white friends. Yet, somewhere down in the raw collap of nature, lived a spark of genius. "I'se got a dancin' mind," said Richard. Liar by practice ("I wuz educated on hard work in de field an' graduated in lies"), a drunkard whenever and wherever possible, unkempt, a "no-'count black man," he was, at the same time, a most interesting man [Lomax 1947, 193–94].

Rich had a rule: "I never does lie unless I am by myself or wid somebody." Nevertheless, Lomax recognized his genius, calling him "a running mate for Professor Howard Odum's Left-Wing Gordon" (Ibid.). John Wesley Gordon provided Odum with material for several books.

Figure 10 is a transcription of the second stanza of Amerson's "John Henry," recorded by Courlander in 1950 (Amerson 1956, Courlander 1960, 32–40 and 1963, 112–15 and 1976, 385–90). Irregularity and improvisation are apparent. Whereas a conventional stanza consists of five phrases, including the repeat of the fourth, this stanza has fifteen.

In a typical version of "John Henry," the dress worn by his "little woman" is the only thing that is red. Amerson extends redness to her shoes, hat, and eyes. The additional red items add phrases 3–5 to the stanza. Extra phrases 6–8 elaborate the story. Amerson pays little attention to rhyme in this part of the stanza, but when he finally gets to the end, at phrase 10, "dead" rhymes with the "red" of phrases 2–5, the same rhyme that occurs with phrases 2 and 4 of a typical stanza.

At phrase 9, Amerson's tune prepares for ending by dropping to the lower tonic ("troublin' your mind"). Phrase 10 ("man fell dead") is like phrase 4 of a typical version. Amerson repeats it in phrase 11, the typical practice for a phrase 4, but then he repeats it twice more in phrases 12–13. Finally, he introduces another textual phrase ("He done

John Henry

Figure 10. The second stanza of Rich Amerson's "John Henry," recorded in 1950 (*Negro Folk Songs, U.S.A.* by Harold Courlander. Copyright © 1963 Columbia University Press. Reprinted with permission of Columbia University Press).

hammered his fool self to death"), musically similar to the preceding ones, and repeats it, phrases 14–15.

Amerson uses a typical "John Henry" tune. He simply repeats musical phrases as needed. Let a typical tune (Figure 3) be represented by I–II–III–IV–V, where the Roman numerals index the phrases. In these terms, Amerson's tune is I–I–I–II–I–II–II–I–III–IV–V–IV–V–IV–V.

Such extraordinary elaboration by distorting the text and tune are not found in white tradition in America. It is not uncommon for traditional white singers to drop beats or insert extra ones as needed to fit the text, or to drop or add lines and adjust the tune accordingly, but I am not aware of any example of a white singer making modifications to the extent to which Amerson does in his second stanza of "John Henry." This is not the only stanza that Amerson gives this kind of treatment. Here are the numbers of lines in his stanzas, taken in order: 5 15 20 15 11 17 11 13 26.

In his second stanza, Amerson heightens the emotional impact by introducing "blood." The woman's dress is "red like blood," and her eyes "turned red with blood." Further, she came "a-screamin' and a-cryin' that day" as she was walking down that railroad track, going where her man fell dead, where he had hammered his fool self to death. In similar ways, Amerson dramatizes the story in subsequent stanzas. Thus, as John Henry is dying he tells his wife, "my knee bones begin to grow cold," "the grip of my hands givin' out," and "my eyes begin to leak water." The eight-minute performance is focused on human drama and tragedy.

John Henry

John Henry said to the Captain
That a man is not but a man.
Said before I let this steam drill beat me down
I'll hammer my fool self to death
I'll hammer my fool self to death.

John Henry had a little woman
Well the dress she wore it's a red like blood
And the shoes she wore it's a red
Well the hat she had on it's a red
That woman eyes is turned red with blood
Well she come a-screamin' and a-cryin' that day
Come a-walkin' down-a that railroad track
The Captain supplied to the woman
Said tell me woman what's troublin' your mind
Says I'm goin' where my man fell dead
Says I'm goin' where my man fell dead
Says I'm goin' where my man fell dead
Says I'm goin' where my man fell dead

He done hammered his fool self to death
He done hammered his fool self to death.

John Henry had another woman
Well her name was Pearly Anne
Well Pearly Anne she heard about this man's death
Well what you reckon she said
Said before I stand to see my man go down
Says give me a ten pound hammer
Gonna to hook it on to the right of my arm
Gonna bring me a nine pound hammer
Gonna hitch it on to the left of my arm
Before I stand to see my man go down
Say I'll go down 'tween-a them mountains,
And before I stand to see [my] man go down
Say I'll hammer just like a man
I'm go' hammer just like a man
I'm go' hammer just like a man
I'm go' hammer just like a man.
I'm go' whup-a this mountain down
I'm go' whup-a this mountain down
He say I'll hammer my fool self to death
I'll hammer my fool self to death.

John Henry had a little baby boy
You could tote it in the palm of your hand
Well every time-a that baby cried
He looked in his mother face
Well his mother down-a in her baby's face
Tell tell me son what you worryin' about
The last lovin' words she would hear the boy say
Mamma I want to make a railroad man
Mamma I want to make a railroad man
I wanna die like papa died
I wanna die like papa died
Son papa was a steel drivin' man
Son papa was a steel drivin' man
But he hammered his fool self to death
Yes he hammered his fool self to death.

John Henry had another little baby boy
He was layin' in the cradle kickin' and cryin'
Every time mamma rocked the baby bumpa-bumpa-bump
I want to make a railroad man
Say I want to make a railroad man
Wanna to die like papa died
I want to die like papa died
Son your daddy was a steel drivin' man
Your daddy was a steel drivin' man

But he hammered his fool self to death
But he hammered his fool self to death.

When Henry was 'tween them mountains
The Captain saw him gwine down
He supplied to Henry one day
Tried to pacify-a his mind
Says Henry you know you's a natural man
Well what you reckon that he said
Says the steam drill drive one hammer by steam
Well the steam drill drive one by air
How in the world you 'spect to beat steam down
He says how in the world you 'spect to beat air down
Henry supplied to the Captain that day
Steam is steam I know air is air
'Fo' I'll let the steam drill beat me down
Say I'll die with these hammers in my hand
I'm'o' die with these hammers in my hand
I'm'o' hammer my fool self to death
I'm'o' hammer my fool self to death.

When-a Henry was 'tween them mountains
His wife could hear him a-cryin'
When she went out 'tween them mountains
Tried to get 'im lay the irons down
He supplied to his wife that day
Said my knee bones begin to grow cold
Said my grip of my hands givin' out
My eyes begin to leak water
Before I lay-a these hammers down
I'll die with these hammers in my hand
I'm'o' die with these hammers in my hand.

Take John Henry to the cemetery
Laid him in his lonesome grave
Wife she walked up at the foot of the grave
Cast her eyes in her husband's face
Comin' a-screamin' and a-cryin' that day
Preacher looked 'round an' read the woman's face
Tell me woman what you screamin' about
Last lovin' words that supplied to him
'Tain't but the one thing trouble my mind
That certainly was a true man to me
That certainly was a true man to me
But he hammered his fool self to death
Hammered his fool self to death.

John Henry wife sittin' down one day
Just about hour of sun,

Come a-screamin' and a-cryin'
Papa said daughter what's troublin' your mind
I got three little children here
Who goin' to help-a me carry 'em along
Who goin' to shoe my children's feet
Who goin' to glove my children's hands
Who goin' to shoe my lovin' feet
Who goin' to glove my lovin' hands
Papa looked 'round in his daughter's face
Tried to pacify his daughter's mind
Daughter I'll shoe your lovin' feet
Daughter I'll shoe your children's feet
Daughter I'll glove your lovin' hand
Daughter I'll glove your children's feet
Brother he looked-a in his sister's face
Tried to pacify his sister's mind
Sister I'll kiss-a your rosy cheeks
But you can't be my lovin' man
Brother can't be my lovin' man
Papa can't be my lovin' man
Papa can't be my lovin' man
'Cause you can't file the whole deal down
Brother can't file the whole deal down
Papa can't file the whole deal down
Papa can't file the whole deal down.

That's old "John Henry" from the mountains directly.
—Rich Amerson, 1950 [Amerson 1956]

Arthur Bell's "John Henry"

On his 1939 field trip of the Southern states, John Lomax visited Cummins State Farm, a state prison near Varner, Arkansas. There he recorded Arthur Bell, whose "John Henry" tune begins distinctively (Figure 11) (Lomax 1941, 260–61). Despite the beginning, it fits comfortably among typical "John Henry" tunes.

Bell's performance can be heard online at the *American Memory* site of the Library of Congress (Bell 1939). As he sings he keeps time by striking something, as if hammering or chopping.

Richard Sheadrack's "John Henry"

In about 1927, on St. Helena Island, South Carolina, Guy Johnson found two black men who could sing "John Henry." They could not agree

John Henry

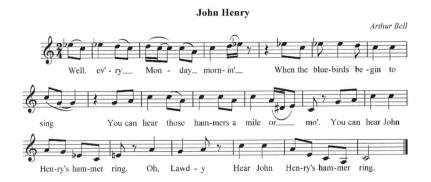

Figure 11. Arthur Bell's "John Henry," 1939 (the Lomax Collection at the American Folklife Center, Library of Congress. Reprinted courtesy of the Association for Cultural Equity). Bell's tune has been transposed up one whole tone from the original key of B-flat by the author.

on how to sing it, so they sang it separately. Thomas Watkins used a typical tune, but Richard Sheadrack's is slightly deviant (Figure 12) (Johnson 1929, 123).

Sheadrack's tune is heptatonic if grace notes are included, hexatonic otherwise. It is a typical "John Henry" tune except for the pitch of the last part. The third phrase does not include the usual drop to the lower tonic, and the third and fourth phrases are an octave higher than usual. In a sense, it can be seen as intermediate between a typical "John Henry" tune and the following one.

John Henry

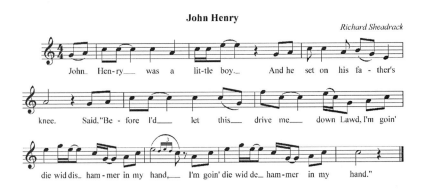

Figure 12. Richard Sheadrack's "John Henry" (Guy B. Johnson, *John Henry: Tracking Down a Negro Legend*, p. 123. Copyright © 1929 by the University of North Carolina Press. Used by permission of the publisher). Transposed up one whole tone from the original key of B-flat by the author.

Uncle Dave Macon's "John Henry"

Uncle Dave Macon (1870–1952) was a beloved performer on the Grand Old Opry (Figure 13). He was born at Smart Station, near McMinnville, Tennessee, about thirty-five miles east and slightly south of Murfreesboro and a little over sixty miles southeast of Nashville. At thirteen, he moved to Nashville. A meeting with a circus banjo player, Joel Davidson, when Dave was fifteen led to his interest in the banjo and in the many old songs he learned from every possible source. After his father was murdered, he moved to Readyville, ten miles south of Murfreesboro. As an adult, his businesses always included music and farming. On November 6, 1925, he played with fiddler Side Harkreader on Nashville radio station WSM. This led to the WSM Barn Dance, which became the Grand Ole Opry in December 1927, after master of ceremonies George D. Hay, the "Solemn Old Judge," remarked, "For the past hour, we have been listening to music taken largely from Grand Opera. From now on we will present the 'Grand Ole Opry.'" Hay also gave Uncle Dave his nickname, the "Dixie Dewdrop" (Matteson 2005).

For the rest of his life, Uncle Dave appeared on the Opry whenever his schedule permitted. His artistry, joviality, and showmanship made him a favorite.

He cut over 350 records. For folk music scholars, his recorded repertoire is a treasure. His "Death of John Henry (Steel Driving Man)" was recorded on April 14, 1926, and issued as Vocalion 15320 (Figure 14) (Russell 2004, 574, Johnson 1929, 117).

Uncle Dave's tune is pentatonic. It can be accompanied by just one chord.

Figure 13. Uncle Dave Macon with his banjo (JblattnerNYC, Wikimedia Commons).

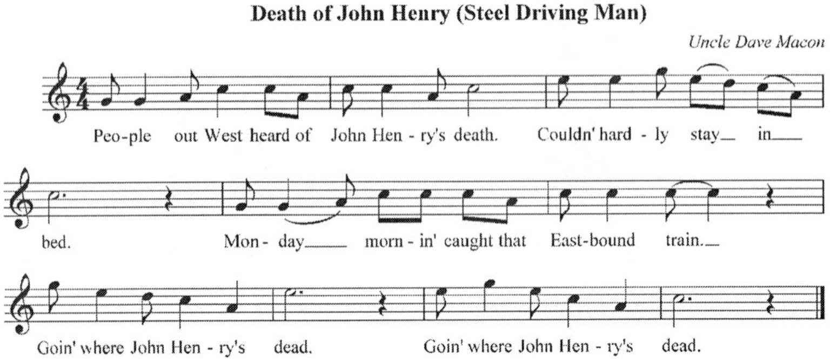

Death of John Henry (Steel Driving Man)

Uncle Dave Macon

Peo-ple out West heard of John Hen - ry's death. Couldn' hard - ly stay__ in__ bed. Mon - day__ morn - in' caught that East-bound train.__ Goin' where John Hen - ry's dead. Goin' where John Hen - ry's dead.

Figure 14. Uncle Dave Macon's "Death of John Henry" (1926). (Guy B. Johnson, *John Henry: Tracking Down a Negro Legend*, p. 117. Copyright © 1929 by the University of North Carolina Press. Used by permission of the publisher). Transposed up one whole tone from the original key of B-flat by the author.

Uncle "Eck" Dunford's "John Henry"

Alexander W. "Eck" Dunford was born May 30, 1875 (Dunford 1918). In the census of 1880, he lived with his mother, Sally Dunford, in the Sulphur Springs Magisterial District of Carroll County, Virginia. In 1900 they lived in the Old Town District of Grayson County, Virginia.

In 1910 Eck was listed as an artist, a photographer who lived with his wife, Callie (Frost), in the Pipers Gap Magisterial District of Carroll County. In 1920 he lived with Callie in the Old Town District of Grayson County and was a cobbler with his own shop. Callie died in 1921 (Tribe 1993, 57).

Figure 15. Alexander W. "Uncle Eck" Dunford (1875–1953), photographic self-portrait (Library of Congress).

Eck was a wonderful musician, a fiddler, guitarist, and singer, a founding member of the Ballard's Branch Bogtrotters, a great old-time string band (Blue Ridge Music Makers 2008, 13). "Bog-trotter" is a derogatory term for "Irishman"—Dunford is an Irish surname (Woolfe 1923, 505). Uncle Eck died in 1953 (Stern 2009).

In 1937 Uncle Eck sang "the original 'John Henry'" for John Lomax's recording machine (Figure 16) (Library of Congress, AFS 1363A3).

This pentatonic tune would fit comfortably among typical "John Henry" tunes if parts were moved up an octave. Typically, the second phrase ends on the sixth degree. Atypically, that note is the highest in the tune.

John Lennon's "John Henry"

John Lennon's "John Henry" was recorded at home and can be heard on the bootleg CD, *The Complete Lost Lennon Tapes*, Volume 1, Track 4 (Walrus Records, 1996). The tune is pentatonic.

Snakefarm's "John Henry"

Snakefarm consists of Anna Domino and Michel Delory, vocals by Domino. Their first release was *Songs from My Funeral* (CD, Kneeling

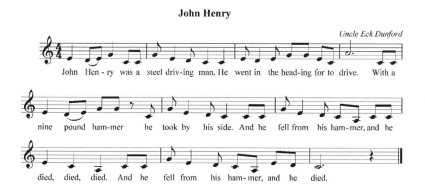

Figure 16. Uncle Eck Dunford's "John Henry," recorded in 1937 by John Lomax. Transcribed by the author and transposed to the key of C (Library of Congress, https://lccn.loc.gov/2009655428; track data: https://memory. loc.gov/diglib/ihas/loc.afc.afc9999005.4620/default.html).

Elephant Records, 1999), a compilation of traditional American songs involving death. Their "John Henry" tune is tritonic.

Cultural Amalgamation

"John Henry" tunes derive from British antecedents. Texts may contain irregularities, but they are metrically similar to the British ballads that were selected by Harvard scholar Francis James Child, numbered from 1 to 305, and published in a series of books.

Harry Smith's *Anthology of American Folk Music* opens with five Child ballads from commercial 78-rpm records—"Henry Lee" (Child 68, "Young Hunting"), "Fatal Flower Garden" (Child 155, "Sir Hugh"), "The House Carpenter" (Child 243, "James Harris"), "Drunkard's Special" (Child 274, "Our Goodman"), and "Old Lady and the Devil" (Child 278, "The Farmer's Curst Wife") (Smith 1997, originally 1952). All have instrumental accompaniments, but many traditional ballad singers perform without instruments.

van der Merwe's idea that the flexibility of the "The Birmingham Boys" tune, and by extension the "Earl Brand" tune, was especially attractive to African Americans is supported by the variations of Leon Harris, Etta Baker, Rich Amerson, Arthur Bell, Richard Sheadrack, and the unnamed sources of Sandburg [Figure 7(b)] and the Lomaxes [Figure 7(c)], African Americans all. The tune that seems most deviant is that of Uncle Dave Macon, a white man who got much of his repertoire from blacks.

The British aspects of "John Henry" do not imply a white author. In America, both whites and blacks were fond of Child ballads. We do not know who applied the "Earl Brand" tune to the "John Henry" text.

≥⊂ ≥⊂ ≥⊂

American ballads tend to be based on fact.

4

Based on Fact

All that is necessary is the sovereignty of the folk, the
denial of an author's individual rights to the song.
—John Meier

"John Henry" is "probably America's greatest single piece of folklore" (Lomax 1941, 258). It has been sung for at least a hundred twenty-
five years. "It ain't good because it's old—it's old because it's good."

Fine art maintains its original form. Museums are full of painted
and sculpted masterworks, and orchestras faithfully play the notes written by great composers, albeit with interpretation.

"Time winnows art." As time passes, the great is distinguished from
the lesser.

For folklore, time also brings recognition of value, but folklore has
a great advantage over fixed art. Folklore is winnowed in another sense.
It is changed.

American Ballads

In the mid-twentieth century, G. Malcom Laws selected a canon of
256 ballads native to America and labeled them with a letter representing a category and a number designating the item within that category
(1964). "John Henry" is "Laws I 1," ballad "1" in Laws's category "I," "Ballads of the Negro."

Historical Stories

Most of the ballads in Laws' American canon are based on historical events. "As a working rule, the investigator assumes that the

51

American ballad is based on fact. In most cases this assumption has proved correct; documentary evidence which corroborates information given in one ballad or another is constantly being discovered" (Laws 1964, 56). On this basis, it can be presumed that John Henry was a historical person.

Folklore and Folksong—Old View

The prevailing view of folklore in the early twentieth century is illustrated in the following quotations from two folklorists:

> The word was invented by W.J. Thoms (1846), from folk + lore, after analogy with German compounds. In all civilizations there is a considerable part of the population whose habits of thought are relatively unaffected by the advances of culture, and who retain, by tradition and the conservatism of custom, something of the mental and material life of bygone periods of development. The collection of the customs, superstitions, myths, and lore of this "unlearned and least advanced portion of the community," and the systematic exposition and interpretation of these in the light of historical civilizations, of analogous primitive conditions among savages, and as an aid to the ethnology of races, is the object of the study of folk-lore [Jastrow, 1901].
>
> ... It is now well established that the most civilised races have all fought their way slowly upwards from a condition of savagery. Now, savages can neither read nor write; yet they manage to collect and store up a considerable amount of knowledge of a certain kind, and to hand on from one generation to another a definite social organisation and certain invariable rules of procedure in all the events of life. The knowledge, organisation, and rules thus gathered and formulated are preserved in the memory, and communicated by word of mouth and by actions of various kinds. To this mode of preservation and communication, as well as to the things thus preserved and communicated, the name of Tradition is given; and Folklore is the science of Tradition [Hartland 1904, 6–7].

In this view of folklore, illiteracy, low social status, and oral tradition are paramount. The whole body of information passed on in oral tradition is "folklore," and the body of song is "folksong."

Folklore and Folksong—Present View

Problems arose with these concepts. Class distinctions became blurred, and new methods of transmission of information, accessible to everyone, became available. As soon as some became literate, handwritten texts of songs were passed around. With the invention of printing, broadsides were sold on the streets.

Handwritten and printed copies of texts, called "(song) ballots" (also "ballits" / "ballets") are commonly found among bearers of folk-song traditions. These texts are "often on sheets of paper pinned or sewed (or glued) together into a long ballot-like strip and kept in a box or tied in a roll and kept in a trunk or drawer" (Chase 1971).

With the advent of broadcasting (radio and television) and recording (sound and video), everyone could hear songs in the physical absence of the singer. Literacy started the demise of the oral tradition, and inventions of mass communication finished it off. It must have been a very long time since there was a pure oral tradition in an English-speaking country.

Information is now transmitted by every possible means. It would be counterproductive to insist that something is not folklore because its transmission was not purely oral.

For example, jokes have been seen as folklore. Today, e-mail is a common mechanism of joke transmission. Under the requirement of a pure oral tradition, there might not be any current jokes that could be considered folklore.

Further, because anyone can bear and transmit folklore, all of us have roles in which we are folk and roles in which we are not. An interest in great literature does not preclude passing on jokes, nor does a job as a violinist in a symphony orchestra preclude passing on old fiddle tunes.

Here is a modern definition.

> The present authors see folklore as something voluntarily and informally communicated, created or done by members of a group (which can be of any size, age, or social and educational level); it can circulate through whatever media (oral, written or visual) are available to this group; it has roots in the past, but also present relevance; it usually recurs in many places, in similar but not quite identical form; it has both stable and variable features, and evolves through dynamic adaptation to new circumstances. The essential criterion is the presence of a group whose joint sense of what is right and appropriate shapes the story, performance, or custom—not the rules and teachings of any official body (State or civic authority, Church, school, scientific or scholarly orthodoxy) [Simpson and Roud 2000].

Folklore is informal, shaped by groups that know "what is right and appropriate" and dissociated from external authority. There is no insistence on oral tradition.

Norm Cohen defined "folk music as the music that survives without complete dependence on commercial media" (Cray 1992). Commercial media *can* have a role.

Ed Cray required of a folk song that "the singers must remain unconcerned with changes in the song. Change is not mandatory, only permissible" (1992).

The eminent German folksong scholar, John Meier, stated his view of "folk poetry," which includes folk ballads, as early as 1897 (1906).

> [Elsewhere] I have strongly emphasized the "folk's sovereign ownership of the material" as a necessary prerequisite to folk poetry and have characterized this [sovereignty] as the uniquely ascertainable and constant force which is operative at all times and places and in all genres of folk poetry, and which accordingly characterizes folk poetry as such.... All that is necessary is the sovereignty of the folk, the denial of an author's individual rights to the song [Translated by Engle 2008].

Those who possess folk poetry control its form. As the owners of their songs, traditional singers feel free to change them.

Engle suggested that if Meier's 1906 book, *Kunstlieder im Volksmund* (*Folk Songs from Art Songs*), "had been translated into English at the time, the 'Ballad Wars' (as DK called them) would have been over half a century sooner" (2008). "DK" is Wilgus, who took 120 pages to describe "The Ballad War" (1959, 3–122). The question was that of "communal composition," the hypothesis that ballads are created by groups of people instead of individuals. By tracing a number of German folk songs to art songs with known authors, Meier settled the issue in favor of individuals (1906).

Communal Re-Creation

An individual wrote "John Henry." Variations in what has been recovered result from communal "re-creation," that is, editing by successive singers (Wilgus 1959, 31).

A "chain of transmission" is a sequence of agents that propagate a tradition. Agents can be people, but they can also be written, printed, or recorded documents. If a document is very popular, it can be highly influential. "John Henry" probably owes its current forms almost entirely to documents.

For such a young ballad as "John Henry," the possibility of finding the original is not so remote as for ballads that are centuries old. Nevertheless, no known version of "John Henry" is recognized as the original.

Variety

As "John Henry" was passed around, there was a great flowering of variations. Johnson gives twenty-nine versions of the ballad, the first three of which contain twelve, twenty-two, and twenty-three stanzas, respectively (1929, 88–99). These fifty-seven stanzas are almost distinct. It would not surprise me if over a hundred stanzas were extant. Variation may be most pronounced in ballads that excite wonder, grip the imagination, and become widespread.

Value of Variety

The large number of distinct phrases, lines, and stanzas suggests that there has been a comprehensive recovery of "John Henry," making it likely that *some* fragments survive from the original ballad. Similar considerations apply to informants' testimonies. Ballad versions and testimonies are likely to include truth. The problem is to discern it.

Nodal Ballads

Roark Bradford described a black approach to ballads:

> The whole story [is] in the opening verse, with the remaining thousand or so verses [taking] "pot shots" at the same theme.... When ballad makers get to work on negro songs, arranging verse after verse in the theoretically proper sequences, they sap it of its strength. On the other hand, when the negroes get hold of a long-winded ballad they drive into it with their characteristic directness. Just the other day, my cook paused long enough in her domestic duties to "make a popout" of America's gutter classic, "Frankie and Johnnie":
>
> > Frankie tuck a shot er cocaine.
> > Den she tuck a shot er gin.
> > Den she tuck a shot at her lovin' man,
> > Ah, Lawd, ain't dat's a sin.
> > She shot him down—root-te-toot-toot-toot!
>
> She got over about as much in that one vagrant verse as the usual ballad singer gets over in a hundred [Bradford, 1931b].

This describes "blues ballads," the concept of which was developed extensively by Wilgus and co-workers (1961, 1968, 1985). Because "blues ballad" is easily misunderstood, Oliver preferred "nodal ballad" (1984).

In a nodal ballad, there is a

near-total suppression of narrative sequence in favor of a series of comments upon a story which must in large part be inferred from these comments. In a word, the "ballad idea" in this case boldly departs from the linear narration, gapped or circumstantial, of its congeners: to sing a story not by directly relating that story but by celebrating it; not by following a chronological sequence, but by creating a sequence of concepts and feelings about it. The story is there, but not explicitly delineated; the units by which it is defined (stanzas, commonplace formulae) are ordered, but not in any normative sequence. This way of singing a story [is] elliptical, allusive, organic... [Wilgus and Long 1985].

Singers of nodal ballads may use different selections and sequences of stanzas in different performances. Further, nodal ballads tend to acquire stanzas from other songs. Only a listener who already knows the story can fully appreciate a performance.

Distinguishing Negro from White blues ballads seems to be impossible.

After years of research, D.K. Wilgus and Lynwood Montell could not determine whether "Clure and Joe Williams" was of White or Negro origin... [Ibid.].

Nodal narrative poetry is ancient. Wilgus and Long found it in Celtic Britain of the early Middle Ages (Ibid.).

According to Bradford, "negroes do not make narrative songs" (1931b). This is not justified. "Mystery of the Dunbar's Child" (1927) is a linear ballad by Richard "Rabbit" Brown, an African American "songster" from New Orleans (Oliver 1984, Brown 1927). As early as the eighteenth century, African Americans were writing hymns and poems in the same styles as whites (Robinson 1969).

Bradford's statement that "John Henry" is a "distinctly negro song" is debatable (1931b). Its form and tune come from Britain, and its earliest notices, 1909–1916, are from both whites and blacks (Barry 1934, van der Merwe 1989, White 1928, Bascom 1909, Shearin, Perrow 1913, *Atlanta Constitution* 1913) "John Henry" has been widespread in both black and white traditions.

Cultural sharing between whites and blacks has been too extensive to allow definite conclusions based on ballad characteristics. We cannot insist that form and style are associated unmistakably with race.

"John Henry" as a Nodal Ballad

"John Henry" is commonly found as a nodal ballad. It is performed with as few as one stanza and, rarely, as many as ten. No known version gives all the details of the story. Many are elliptical, allusive, commentarial, and celebratory. The few that might qualify as linear narratives have been put together by ordering stanzas drawn from various sources (Blankenship n.d., Lomax 1915). Accretion is common, accounting for stanzas that begin, "Who's gonna shoe your pretty little feet," from "The Lass of Roch Royal" (Child 76).

Memphis songster Walter "Furry" Lewis varied stanza order and selection in his recordings of "John Henry" (Lewis 1929, 1959, 1961, 1968b, 1969). Many bluegrass musicians "assume their listeners already know the story" and "sing the verses in a totally illogical order" (Farkas 2009a).

Ballad Evolution

As organisms evolve through mutations in genes, ballads evolve through mutations in texts and tunes (van der Merwe 1989). Our focus is on texts because they can contain explicit historical information.

Singers may misunderstand words and pass on mutations. They may forget lines or stanzas, omitting them or supplying reconstructions. Handwritten copies may be misread and miscopied. Printed broadsides may contain copying and typesetting errors.

When a replacement makes some sort of sense, it is a "mondegreen." This word was coined by Sylvia Wright in 1954 and taken into dictionaries recently (Rees 2002). As a child hearing her mother read "The Bonnie Earl of Murray" (Child 181), Wright had understood that they had slain the Earl of Murray "and Lady Mondegreen." She had misunderstood "and laid him on the green."

In "John Henry," "Big Bend Tunnel" occurs frequently. Mondegreens include "big high tower" and "big wheel turning" (Johnson 1929, 86).

"Big Bend Tunnel on the C & O road" could be derived from a phrase such as "big, bad tunnel on the C & W road." The tunnel where John Henry worked, Coosa Mountain Tunnel, is on the C & W. Locally, Coosa Mountain Tunnel is the "long" or "big" tunnel, and it could have been "bad" because accidental explosions there killed more than a dozen men during its construction in 1886–88 (*Atlanta Constitution* 1887c May 5 and 1887d June 8).

Error is not the only force behind ballad mutation and evolution. A singer may change a ballad deliberately. A time restriction could force abbreviation, new elements could be included to tell a better story, a passage could be improved by rewording, an inessential stanza could be left out, or a singer could combine parts of different versions or include pieces of other songs. Sometimes deliberate changes by literary authors are propagated in tradition. Similarly, editors may alter the texts of broadsides.

Localization, changing from an unspecified location to a specific one, and relocalization, moving the scene from one place to another, are common. Relocalization is illustrated abundantly by "The Berkshire Tragedy," which is also known as "The Wittam Miller," "The Wexford Girl," "The Oxford Girl," "The Expert Girl," "The Export Girl," "The Noel Girl," "The Waco Girl," "The Lexington Girl," "The Boston Girl," and "The Shreveport Girl" (Waltz 1996, Keefer 1996, Roud 1985).

Relocalization can also occur in the narrative tradition surrounding a ballad. In this way, "Red River Valley" has gone from Canada to Texas, "Ella Speed" from New Orleans to Dallas, and "Delia" from Savannah, Georgia, to the Bahamas (Fowke 1964, Cowley 2001, Garst 2004). No one should be surprised that "Big Bend Tunnel on the C & O road" is not the historical John Henry site.

Survival of the Fittest

"Survival of the fittest" is a truism. What survives must be the "fittest."

For ballads, "more fit" can only mean "more attractive to singers who bear the tradition." If we knew what made a ballad more attractive, we could predict something about how it would mutate. Coffin warned of the futility of trying to identify what makes a ballad attractive—it would be "an attempt to define human nature" (1950). Even so, we can offer plausible speculations.

Changing the length can improve a ballad. A shorter or longer narrative can be more esthetically pleasing to singers, more fit.

In addition, we can expect tendencies such as these:

> Strong images will drive out weak ones.
> Strong narratives will drive out weak ones.
> The poetic will drive out the prosaic.
> The familiar will drive out the unfamiliar.
> The simple will drive out the complex.
> The clichéd will drive out the novel.
> The emotional will drive out the factual.
> The interesting will drive out the boring.
> The unintelligible will be omitted or rationalized.

Coffin concluded that

there are constants, and there are definite trends. The central or climactic dramatic situation, the outline of the plot, the stanzas with particularly vivid passages, the figure of speech, the imbedded cliché, all tend to hold the story and the text firm. While an inclination to move away from diffuseness toward concentration upon a single part of a single incident and the desire to universalize the material often opposes these factors. Thus, where the trends can operate with aid from personal factors, masses of detail, archaic phraseology, commonly occurring situations, and the excess material sometimes found at the beginning and end of the songs, the constants are frequently overridden. However, it must not be forgotten that such overriding does not invariably, nor even consistently happen [Coffin, 1950].

An element of a ballad based on an historical incident may tend to a stable end point in which the original information is altered. For example, Lead Belly included the following lines in "Ella Speed."

> Bill Martin, he was long and slender,
> Better known by his being a bartender [Ledbetter 1934].

Similar lines are found in other versions, but the historical fact is that Ella Speed's killer, Louis "Bull" Martin, was short and stocky. If Lomax had not recovered the lines below (from a girl in Prairie View, Texas, ca. 1909), we would have been mystified. As it is, we realize that an awkward negative statement, "neither long or slender," gave way to something more fit, "he was long and slender," albeit incorrect.

> Martin was a man, he was neither long or slender,
> Everybody knew he was a barroom tender [Cowley 2000].

In understanding survival, the agents of transmission must be taken into account. Some people can recall only one or a few stanzas of a long ballad, perhaps not even that without error. This can lead to unusual forms.

"Bonny Barbara Allen" (Child 84) has 9–16 stanzas in the versions reproduced by Child. It is reduced to the following in "Boberick Allen."

> When I wus but a girl sixteen,
> I wus in love with Boberick;
> De othah girls did not see
> Why he did always follow me.
>
> He walk to town and den right back,
> To see if I wus on his track,
> But he could neber fin' me dah,
> Becuz I wus away somewhah.
> His name wus Boberick Allen [Bales 1928].

In the usual versions of "Barbara Allen," a young man dies of heartbreak after being spurned by Barbara Allen, who then repents and dies of her own heartbreak. As distant as "Boberick Allen" is from this, it must be seen nonetheless as a product of survival of the fittest.

The fitness of relocalization is obvious. People prefer to sing and hear about familiar, local places instead of unfamiliar, distant ones.

Economics has Gresham's Law: "Bad money drives out good." Historical ballads may be subject to something similar: "Bad facts drive out good." Attractive introduced elements ("bad facts") tend to persist, while non-attractive original elements ("good facts") tend to be lost.

The fittest, original or not, is what survives in quantity. That John Henry died at "Big Bend Tunnel on the C & O road" is highly attractive, making it very fit, and it is found frequently. It is not correct.

Only one early version of "John Henry" specifies the day of the week on which he died: "John Henry died on a Tuesday" (Chappell 1933, 106). This rare statement is a good candidate for historical truth.

"Frozen" Folk Songs

To most Americans, the famous cowboy song "Red River Valley" is as "folk" as "John Henry" and as American as pecan pie. However, Cray challenged the folk status of "Red River Valley" in America. "'Daisy, Daisy' and 'Red River Valley' are not folk songs" (Cray 2005, July 11). "What honor can a fallen woman have? I can accept she was born pure, of sturdy parents, steeped in traditional values, molded and changed by the community around her. But then she fell on hard times, and lost her purity. Thus 'Red River Valley' as currently sung is fixed, frozen by a hundred reprints. One can no longer sing anything BUT the standard, printed version" (Cray 2005, July 17).

As folklore, a static song is dead, but a frozen ballad *was* a folk song while it lived. "It is for the sake of what has been, rather than what is" (Austen 1813).

"Red River Valley" is not entirely frozen. A perusal of recent versions reveals some variation. A north Georgia version, "Bright Brasstown Valley," was sung around 1932 and can still be heard (Smith 2008, Myers 2007). Canadian forms differ from the American cowboy version (Fowke 1964).

"John Henry," as performed nowadays, usually consists of a selection from a few popular stanzas. The period of most active evolution of "John Henry" appears to have been from its origin to about 1940. Since then, previously unknown elements of the ballad have turned up only rarely.

❯❮ ❯❮ ❯❮

Steel driving requires more than brawn and endurance. The best steel drivers were men of enormous skill.

5

Rings Like Silver

This old hammer / Rings like silver (3×)
Shines like gold, boys / Shines like gold.
—Thaddeus Campbell and Herbert Standard,
Big Bend Tunnel, West Virginia, 1927 [Johnson 1929, 71].

As a steel driver, John Henry hammered steel drills into rock to make holes for explosives. It sounds simple, but it isn't. Excellence requires a very high level of skill.

Rapid drilling by hand is not accomplished by use of heavy hammers and forceful blows, but by hammers of proper size handled by men who know how to strike the blow that will cause the drill to cut and keep the bottom of the hole clear so that the drill is working on solid rock and not on a lot of loose fragments. This is an art and is only learned by experience [Gillette 1916, 25].

Henry Sturgis Drinker, John Henry's contemporary, published detailed expositions of rock excavation (Drinker 1878 and 1883). This ancient art is necessary for hard-rock mining, building canals, making road and railroad cuts, boring tunnels, etc.

In antiquity rock was chipped and wedged away using hand tools, or it was shattered by heating it and throwing water on it (Drinker 1883, 1). By John Henry's time, drilling and blasting was the common practice. It appears to have been used first in 1613 at a mine in Freiberg, Germany, under the supervision of Martin Weigel, who claimed to have invented the hand rock drill. The explosive was gunpowder (Ibid., 42).

Tunneling uses the same techniques as mining. It is customary to call tunnel borers "miners," whether or not they had ever worked in a mine (Chappell 1933, 82). John Henry was a miner.

Drill, Load, Blast, and Muck

Drilling is the slow step. Holes drilled by hand are commonly a few feet deep and range in diameter from 0.7 to 1.5 inches, more or less, narrower than those used in the earliest times, which had diameters 2.0 to 2.5 inches (Drinker 1883, 108).

In loading, the explosive must be tamped into position, capped with a plug, and fitted with a fuse or electrical detonator. For 250 years, "black" or "blasting" powders, variations on gunpowder, were used. Nitroglycerine, discovered in 1847, was first used for blasting by Alfred Nobel in 1863. In 1867 Nobel invented dynamite, which was further developed and became the explosive of choice for its relative safety. Dynamite is a solid prepared by infusing an appropriate material, e.g., a porous clay, with nitroglycerine.

Figure 17 illustrates blasting in the railroad tunnel through Hoosac Mountain, Massachusetts (Jacobs 1968, 48).

Hoosac Tunnel was under construction from 1851 until 1875. Its western portal is at the town of North Adams, close to the Vermont and New York borders. At 25,081 feet, it was the longest tunnel in North America from November 27, 1873, to 1916 (Byron 1955, 144). Big Bend is said to have been the longest American tunnel (6450 feet) from May 31, 1872, to November 27, 1873 (Johnson 1929, 30, Lane 2010).

Its early and long period of construction allowed Hoosac Tunnel to serve as a testing ground for methodologies. Here drilling machines were first employed in America with any degree of success, and nitroglycerine was first extensively used for blasting in an American project.

The "American system" of tunneling was in common use (Gillette 1904, 297–99). The upper third or half of the tunnel, a "top heading," is bored some distance in advance of the "bench," the lower part. Drilling in the heading is horizontal. Once the heading has been advanced the desired distance, the bench is removed using holes made by drilling down.

The American system features a pattern of drill holes in the heading that results in an initial "center cut," which is then finished out by drilling and blasting the peripheral rock. It also uses a distinctive pattern of timbering to prevent tunnel collapse. Tunnels are sometimes lined with structurally supportive brick.

Although a top heading was used on the west side of Hoosac Tunnel, on the east side a bottom heading was advanced before the roof was taken out. This method has been criticized severely. "Occasionally some contractor tries an experiment such as driving the 'heading' at the bottom instead of the top. After killing a few men, return is usually made to

Figure 17. **Blasting in the Hoosac Tunnel** (*Frank Leslie's Illustrated Newspaper*, December 20, 1873).

the top heading. It is exceedingly difficult, and in loose rock impossible, to prevent disastrous falls of rock from the roof where the bottom heading method is used. One contractor, an eminent member of the American Society of Civil Engineers, had his life crushed out by a fall of rock in a tunnel that he was driving in New York City by the bottom heading method" (Ibid., 297–98). Even so, bottom headings continued to be used occasionally because they were believed to be more efficient.

Drilling by Hand

After the Civil War, as the development of steam drills continued, they slowly replaced manual drilling. In John Henry's time both were used. Overall, machine drilling would prove to be much cheaper, but for smaller jobs (e.g., a short tunnel) hand drilling was preferred. With hand drilling, a contractor could avoid the time and expense of acquiring the machinery, getting it to the site, and maintaining it.

In double-jacking, the shaker holds a steel in place and the steel driver hits it with a sledgehammer. Double-jack sledgehammers weigh six to fourteen pounds, or more, and are usually fixed on four-foot handles.

In single-jacking, a man holds a steel in place with one hand and hits it with a hammer held in the other. He acts as his own shaker. A typical single-jack hammer weighs four pounds and has a two-foot handle.

Steels are octagonal, hexagonal, or round rods of high-carbon steel with a usual diameter between three-fourths and one-and-a-half inches. The bit is tempered and sharpened. It is also flared, so that it is slightly wider than the shaft. This ensures that t.he hole will have a larger cross section than the steel, helping keep it from "fitchering" (getting stuck) and providing a passageway through which rock dust and fragments can move up (*Rock Drilling* 1907, 2).

Many bit patterns have been used, including straight and curved chisel edges and the star pattern. In the late nineteenth century, the curved chisel bit was standard for hand drilling in hard rock (Drinker 1883, 115, Gillette 1904, 24–25).

The hammered end of a steel is untempered. It develops a "mushroom" cap as a result of deformation caused by repeated hammer blows.

There is more to a hand-drilling crew than drivers and shakers. Blacksmiths are kept busy sharpening and tempering steels. Tool carriers take them back and forth between the drillers and the blacksmiths. Water is essential for sweating laborers as well as drill holes. In the nineteenth century, teenaged water boys and tool carriers were common.

Drilling by Machine

The first steps toward useful mechanical percussion drills, which imitate steel driving by hammering on a drill, were made in America in 1849 (Drinker 1883, 195–96). In some early designs, power was provided by steam delivered to the drill, but this limited the sites at which the drill could be used. Better designs operated with compressed air, which was generated outside the tunnel with a steam-powered compressor and delivered through tubes to the interior. The story of percussive rock drills is as much that of compressors as the drills themselves (Ibid., 135–88).

Couch and Fowle invented the first powered percussion drills in 1849. After improvements by a number of people, Charles Burleigh devised a drill that was used at Hoosac Tunnel from November 1866, until that tunnel was completed (Ibid., 196–203). Burleigh drills were also used at Lewis Tunnel, Virginia, in 1870–71 (Nelson 2006, 81–88).

Simon Ingersoll's rock drill was patented in 1871. J.F. de Navarro and his Ingersoll Rock Drill Company, which became the Ingersoll-Sergeant Drill Company in 1888, secured patents from various companies. In 1905 it merged with the Rand Drill Company to become the Ingersoll-Rand Company, which is still in business (Saunders 1910, Ingersoll Rand 2009).

Early steam drills looked much alike. Here are drawings of Ingersoll drills from 1874 and 1879 (Figures 18 and 19) (Ingersoll Rock Drill 1874 and 1879).

According to William L. Saunders, an engineer and executive who

Figure 18. Ingersoll drill mounted on a tripod (*The Manufacturer and Builder* 6.4 [April 1874]).

Figure 19. Ingersoll drill mounted on a car and steadied by a column (*The Manufacturer and Builder* 11.7 [July 1879]).

worked for Ingersoll, the Burleigh drill had severe faults. By the 1880s the Ingersoll drill had captured the tunneling market.

> It was only because of the support given by the State Treasury of Massachusetts that the "Burleigh" drills were maintained at the Hoosac Tunnel, their weight being so great, and the expense for repairs reaching such a figure, that private enterprise could not afford to drive tunnels with rock-drilling machinery. After the completion of the Hoosac Tunnel, the "Ingersoll" drill reduced the expense of repairs, and has been used in twenty-four of the twenty-eight large tunnels in this country. Among the tunnels driven by "Ingersoll" drills are the "Factoryville," "Snow-Shoe," "Vosburg," "Coosa Mountain," "Wickes," "Cascade," "South Penn," and the "New York Aqueduct" [Saunders 1889, 378].

Coosa Mountain Tunnel, between Dunnavant and Vandiver, Alabama, was bored in 1887–88 during the extension of the Columbus & Western. It is where John Henry worked. The steam drill that he raced was an Ingersoll.

Fred C. Dopp, a champion steel driver, is seen in action in Figure 20. As he swings a sledgehammer, his shaker (bottom center) holds the steel.

Figure 20. Fred C. Dopp, a champion steel driver, in action (Denver Public Library Western History Collection, X-60049).

Dopp's wide hand grip is standard. It provides greater accuracy than a narrow grip. Ty Cobb's baseball batting grip was similar (Cobb 1999).

> The proper use of the hammer requires thought upon the part of the driller. An experienced contractor knowing this usually when hiring a man requires him to give an exhibition of his method of swinging and striking with his hammer. A good hammersman takes advantage of the recoil of the hammer, while the inexperienced man does not, and, consequently, tires sooner. In swinging a stiff-handled hammer, the arms and body do most of the work, while with a limber-handled hammer the arms and shoulders with but slight movement of the body do the work. The breathing should be timed with the blows. The muscles should be relaxed immediately previous to the blow, as the striker is then not seriously affected by the vibration, or force, of the blow, and the hammer is very readily caught on its rebound for the upward swing. Long experience only can render a striker expert in swinging a hammer, or enable him to deliver an efficient blow that will not tire the body [*Rock Drilling* 1907, 10].

Assuming whatever position is necessary and convenient, the shaker holds the steel in place and rotates the steel a quarter of a turn (for a chisel bit) after each blow from the hammer. The rotation presents fresh rock to the bit for each hammer blow and helps keep the hole round. The shaker also keeps the hole clear and swaps out shorter steels for longer ones as needed. In a set of steels, diameters decrease as the steels get longer.

A fitchered steel is wedged against a corner in a crooked or mis-shaped hole. Rock dust and debris can contribute to fitchering. To prevent it, the shaker or steam-drill operator must keep the steel in good alignment and the hole round and clean.

An overhead hole will clear itself, the rock dust falling out as it is formed. For a downward hole, water is poured in, "tending chuck" (Gillette 1904, 17). Water should be used in the holes "whenever possible, as the commotion of the water caused by the drilling process drives the small pieces from the bottom and floats more or less of the fine material, thus keeping the bottom of the hole clean for the drill" (*Rock Drilling* 1907, 12). To prevent the splashing of water or mud in the shaker's face, a collar of hay, grass, leather, or rubber is wrapped around the steel at ground level (Ibid., 13). The shaker can drag mud out of the hole using a specially designed "spoon."

Clang!

It is commonly said that the hammer rings. Thus, Howard B. Thompson commented, "Anyone who has heard the ringing of a hammer when driving steel at spaced intermissions will be quick to get the tune of this song" (Johnson 1929, 77). A few versions of "John Henry" contain lines like "Don't you hear that cold steel ring" and "Listen to that cold steel ring," implying that the steel is what rings, not the hammer (Cohen 2005, 27, Boette 1971, 55).

The hammer *causes* the ringing, but it is the *steel* that rings. Saying that the hammer rings is misleading colloquialism.

According to John Popelish, "any long cylinder of steel is a good resonator for pressure waves that travel back and forth along its length. And, if the rod bounces up off the bottom of the hole for a moment after each hit, it is free to ring for many cycles before it again makes solid contact with rock. Hands on the sides of the rod have little energy absorbing effect" (Garst 2002 Google Groups).

My correspondent and research assistant, Bill Oursler, of Las Cruces, New Mexico, did some experiments.

> The split second that the hammer hits the steel bar drill the holder or shaker releases the bar so the other hand can turn the bar ¼ turn. At that exact moment in a fraction of a second, the drill is free and can ring. It's so fast that the eye can hardly catch it.... The drills are from 2 feet to 15 feet in length. The longer the drill the more and longer the vibrating frequency which is the ring.... The shaker's hand loosening his grip on one hand to turn it with the other (split second timing) lets the whole bar ring [Oursler 2008].

There is abundant witness in song and testimony that ringing was common in steel driving. J.H. Tredwell recounted the following in 1868, reflecting his experiences living in 1866 at high elevations in the Sierra Nevada mountains of California.

> Lounging upon the steps of the rudely-finished but comfortable house known as Polley's Station, at Crystal Lake, we can hear the clear, ringing sound of hammer and drill; now and then a thundering blast rolls away, echoing up and down the great valleys. This is the steady, onward march of civilization, breaking the pathway through forests, and mountains, and solid granite, for the most magnificent enterprise which has prompted mankind for centuries past—the Pacific Railroad [Tredwell 1868].

Ringing may be attractive to spectators, but it wastes energy.

> If too light a hammer is used in a hard rock, it will rebound and a ringing sound will be produced at every blow similar to that produced by striking the face of an anvil with a hammer, showing that more or less energy is being wasted in vibration [*Rock Drilling* 1907, 10–11].

The ringing of silver is thought to be especially beautiful. "This old hammer / Rings like silver" seems to be bragging.

At least one movie, *Tall Tale* (1994), depicts steel driving with audible ringing. It is probably an artificial sound effect.

Many Ways to Die

Tunneling and mining are dangerous.

> In 1892, in a probably unconscious echo of Engels's conclusion that "In the whole British Empire there is no occupation in which a man may meet his end in so many diverse ways as this one," Hall [Henry Hall, Inspector of Coal Mines, North Wales] supported his report of 23 deaths in North Wales alone with the observation that "the character of the accidents have [sic] been very various, and men have met their deaths by burning, drowning, suffocation, and every kind of mangling of body and limbs by falls of roof and entanglement of machinery" [Williamson 1999, 156].

The famous Friedrich Engels statement is from 1845 (Engels 1892, 249). It follows his description of the inhuman working conditions for men, women, and children in the mines, and it precedes a list of types of fatal accidents.

Three years later, he and Karl Marx published *Manifest der Kommunistischen Partei* (*Manifesto of the Communist Party*), arguing that the plights of coal miners and their families were among the evils of capitalism that could be remedied by communism. Over a hundred years

later, in America, Sarah Garland Ogan Gunning sang a similar senti-
ment in "Come All You Coal Miners."

> Coal mining is the most dangerous work in our land today
> With plenty of dirty slaving work, and very little pay.
> Coal miner, won't you wake up, and open your eyes and see
> What the dirty capitalist system is doing to you and me
> —[Romalis 1999, 137] ©1966 Stormking Music, Inc.

Data suggest that hard-rock mining and tunneling are nearly as
dangerous as coal mining. Of 130 fatalities of known cause in coal mines
in the Birmingham area in 1898–1902, 10 percent were from gas (Birmingham Public Library 2009). That leaves 90 percent for hazards that
are also faced in hard-rock mining and tunneling. Rock falls were most
common, 56 percent, followed by accidents involving coal or man cars
(which ran on rails in the mines), 16 percent, and blasting accidents, 13
percent. Accidents with steam accounted for 1.5 percent. Heat stroke
was 0.7 percent.

Blasting accidents include "going back on a shot." If an explosive
charge fails, workers are killed when they go back to check, and the
charge then explodes.

At least fourteen men died in premature explosions at Coosa
Mountain Tunnel, Alabama, in 1887.

> Birmingham, Ala., May 4.—[Special.]—News of a terrible accident at Coosa
> tunnel, twenty miles from here, on the extension of the Columbus & West-
> ern railroad, reached the city late this afternoon. A white foreman and sev-
> enteen negro laborers were at work in the tunnel, getting ready for a large
> blast. While ramming the blast with an iron bar a strata of flint was struck
> with the iron, making a spark, which ignited the powder. Of the eighteen
> men only six came out alive, and all of them were more or less injured....
> [*Atlanta Constitution* 1887b].
> Birmingham, Ala., June 7.—[Special.]—The premature explosion of a
> blast this morning at the Coosa tunnel, on the extension of the Columbus &
> Western railroad, killed two negro laborers and injured five others ... [Ibid.
> 1887e].

Rock falls and cave-ins are very real and ever-present threats. Merle
Travis put it this way in "Dark as a Dungeon."

> The midnight, the morning, or the middle of day,
> Is the same to the miner who labors away.
> Where the demons of death often come by surprise,
> One fall of the slate and you're buried alive [Green 1972, 290].

Mine rats come into mines and tunnels from outside. Sometimes
workers welcome them and feed from dinner pails, thinking that rats

have enhanced senses of danger from rock falls: "as soon as they [rats] began leaving, many workers would cease their tasks immediately and follow them out" (Long 1989, 35). When the rat population gets too large, they gnaw on mules and miners have to fight with them for their lunches.

Water drips constantly from overhead. Sometimes something gives way, and it comes gushing in suddenly. Rainfall causes flash floods.

The air is commonly depleted in oxygen, enriched in carbon dioxide, and full of rock dust. Breathing the dust leads to increasing pulmonary distress. The strangling is not due merely to mechanical obstruction by rock dust. Silica particles cause thickening and scarring of the lung tissue. As far as is known, these effects are irreversible. There is no cure for silicosis.

Further, weakened pulmonary systems are more susceptible to tuberculosis and other lung diseases. "Miners' lung," "miners' asthma," and "miners' consumption," or just "miners' con," are catchall names for this disease complex, which includes silicosis and "black lung," a condition of miners who have inhaled large amounts of coal dust, as well as other conditions. Coal miners have suffered from elevated rates of emphysema, chronic bronchitis, and other lung diseases, as well as coal workers' pneumoconiosis, the specific extreme disease associated with black lung (Derickson 1998, 163).

In Europe, miners' lung has been known for centuries. Coal miners' respiratory disease was recognized in Britain by the early nineteenth century. In 1881, the sputum of a miner with black lung was used as ink to write a sentence that was part of a paper read at the annual meeting of the Colorado State Medical Society. By 1900, there was ample evidence that this was a "debilitating occupational disease" (Ibid., 1–2).

Even so, as late as 1969, President Nixon was prepared to veto the Federal Coal Mine Health and Safety Act because it included the Black Lung Benefits Program, through which the Federal government would "compensate victims of work-induced respiratory disease" (Derickson 1998). As he mulled the matter over, a group of seven widows of coal miners, killed in a recent explosion in a West Virginia mine, appeared at the White House to see President Nixon and demand that he sign the bill. Nixon never saw the widows. He arranged a White House tour for them, signed the bill, and left souvenirs for them lying on his desk, the pens he had used in the signing (Ibid., xi).

Earlier, doctors and scientists sponsored by the coal companies, sometimes assisted by insurance companies, fought a long, hard battle against claims that coal dust hurt miners. Coal dust in the lungs was harmless, they said. Indeed, it could be beneficial! It could protect the lungs against tuberculosis. In the end, such claims were shown to be false and the companies lost, but they succeeded in evading their responsibilities and delaying government action for many years (Derickson 1998).

Silicosis patients fared a little better. Increasingly, they were being compensated through state laws during the 1930s, especially in northeastern states (Ibid., 90).

As the use of steam-powered mechanical drills increased during the second half of the nineteenth century, so did cases of miner's lung and associated deaths. The new machines greatly increased the amount of dust in the air. "Acute miners' consumption, according to a 1904 report, 'has only assumed prominence since the introduction of power drills, which produce a far greater amount of dust than when the work is done by hand'" (Wyman 1979, 92). In 1889 the Montana Inspector of Mines wrote, referring to compressed-air drills, "It seems that death lurks even in the things that are designed as benefits" (Ibid.).

> Death stalks through the dark chambers of the mines in a thousand shapes. Generally his blows are sudden and terrible. More pitiable, however, seems the living death of the doomed man lingering down to the tomb in the never relaxed clutch of miners' consumption [Wyman 1979, 91].

Despite awareness of miner's lung for centuries, an estimated 1500 laborers died of it during and after the boring of Hawk's Nest Tunnel, Gauley Bridge, West Virginia, in the early 1930s (Rosner 1991). Further, "a tightly drawn insurance plan cut off the litigation stemming from" this disaster (Derickson 1998, 105).

The Lure of the Mines

Tunnel work was a route to an early death. Those who survived other hazards died from lung disease. Why would anyone accept a tunneling job?

Part of the attraction for a steel driver was good pay. According to Glendora Cannon Cummings,

> The steel drivers were the highest salaried men. But John Henry's salary was higher than theirs. Nobody ever drove steel as well as him. I mean when I say the steel drivers were the highest paid; that for a negro in those days in South [Johnson 1929, 23].

There are other factors, including "the lure of the mines," which may stem from a "craft outlook" (Long 1989, 59–76). As Merle Travis sang in "Dark as a Dungeon" (1947),

It will form as a habit and seep in your soul,
'Till the stream of your blood runs as black as the coal.

Like a fiend with his dope and a drunkard his wine,
A man will have lust for the lure of the mines [Green 1972, 284].

In the 1870s, the skilled miner resembled a transplanted independent craftsman; certainly he saw the world from that perspective. Like the independent craftsman, he owned his own set of tools and hired his own assistants [Long 1989, 59].

Typically, an assistant was paid at about one-third the rate of the skilled miner.

A miner acquired skills through an apprenticeship that often began, in a mining family, in childhood. The skilled miner worked so independently that he, rather than a foreman, often made important mining decisions.

Because mining is very complex, and because safety and production are both priorities, miners were rightfully proud of their skills. The John Henry of song and legend was proud of his.

Only a Miner

Despite their bravery and skill, miners were not universally admired. Some saw them as common laborers. The fact that they were often black, Irish, Cornish, or members of other minorities, and often recent immigrants, reinforced their low social status.

Reports of mining deaths were so common that members of the general public tended to become desensitized. The reaction to a report of a death might have been something like "Well, he was only a miner."

Although everything that science, skill, and money can devise is done to avert accidents, the average of fatal ones in the Comstock is three a week. "Three men a week" [Crawford 1879].

While in Virginia City, in 1877, a wagon passed up Main Street, with a soiled canvas thrown over it. Some curbstone brokers rushed out to investigate, and when they returned were asked what was the matter. "O," replied one, "It's only a miner killed." Old Commodore Vanderbilt died on the same day and the papers were full of accounts concerning this multi-millionaire. A paragraph in the Virginia City Chronicle, referring to the above incident, suggested the following verses.

Only a miner killed—oh! is that all?
One of the timbers caved, great was the fall,
Crushing another one shaped like his God.

Only a miner lad—under the sod.
(plus four additional stanzas) [Crawford 1904].

Throughout the nineteenth century, in both Britain and America, "only a miner" was a common expression of indifference or contempt. It gave rise to the song "Only a Miner."

> He's only a miner been killed in the ground,
> Only a miner and one more is found,
> Killed by an accident, no one can tell,
> His mining's all over, poor miner farewell
> [Green 1972, 66, Kentucky Thoroughbreds 1928].

Green called it "the American miner's national anthem" (1972, 64). They took the pejorative "only a miner" and made it their own. In the song, it takes a double meaning: "Only a miner" can be seen as sarcastic pride or as simple humility before God.

Miners knew their own value. They knew the dangers they faced, the skills needed to avoid them, and the fact that they had those skills. They knew that "only a miner" was spoken out of ignorant prejudice. They knew their fellow miners and their families, and they bonded with pride in their skill, work, bravery, and humanity.

Pass the Hot Dogs

The skill, intricate movements and timing, singing, ringing, occasional explosion, and ever-present sense of danger give manual drilling and blasting considerable entertainment value. Census records show that Leona Lowery Raymond was about eleven years old in 1887, when she saw John Henry at work at Dunnavant, Alabama. She passed on her recollections.

> She said that people would come from all around just to watch him work. They would bring picnic lunches and spend the day. On Sundays after church, they would come in droves. They would give him gifts of food, clothing, money and drinking liquor.
> The gifts included live chickens, pigs and even a calf. They made a holiday of it [Terry 1999].

William Eleazar Barton, a noted Congregational minister and teacher, left an account of his memories of steel driving from the 1880s in Kentucky and Tennessee.

> To hear these songs ... at their best, one needs to hear them in a rock tunnel. The men are hurried in after an explosion to drill with speed for another double row of blasts. They work two and two, one holding and turning the

drill, the other striking it with a sledge. The sledges descend in unison as the long low chant gives the time. I wonder if the reader can imagine the effect of it all, the powder smoke filling the place, the darkness made barely visible by the little lights on the hats of the men, the echoing sounds of men and mules toward the outlet loading and carting away the rock thrown out by the last blast, and the men at the heading droning their low chant to the *chink! chink!* of the steel. A single musical phrase or a succession of a half dozen notes caught on a visit to such a place sticks in one's mind forever. Even as I write I seem to be in a tunnel of this description and to hear the sharp metallic stroke and the syncopated chant [Barton 1899, 708].

Lay Your Money Down!

Because drilling by hand is really slow, several steel drivers would work on a given project, and if the work site were large or the area contained many work sites, then a considerable number of steel drivers would be there. Their craft outlook and pride must have led to rock drilling contests as soon as drilling and blasting came into use.

In America, in the mining West in the late nineteenth and early twentieth centuries, contests were common enough that there were professional contestants, some of whom made good livings from their winnings (Writers' Program 1943, 223). To this day, rock drilling contests are held in Western mining towns, often on July 4 or a locally designated old-timers' or miners' day (Ninnis 1961, Saxton 1979). Videos of recent single- and double-jack contests can be found online at YouTube.com.

Drilling contests evolved into events with little resemblance to actual work. The time allowed was short, usually fifteen minutes. There were two kinds of double-jack contests, straight away and double hand. In a straight-away contest, the steel driver and shaker maintained their roles throughout (Saxton 1979). In a double-hand contest, the men took turns swinging the hammer and turning the steel, changing places every minute or so.

The change calls for a high degree of cooperation. The top-notchers of the old days could execute this difficult maneuver so expertly that their actions had to be seen to be believed. There are fifteen pieces of steel in a set for a fifteen-minute contest. Double-hand drillers allow three inches difference in length for succeeding steels. This means that if each piece is driven three inches in one minute, a hole forty-five inches deep would be the result at the end of a fifteen-minute period.

A small stream of water was directed into the hole by a helper to make the steel easier to turn and clean out the cuttings. A team of Butte drillers, Page and Reagan, first introduced what is known as the splash method for cleaning the hole. The records disclose that they were also the first to change steel without missing a blow and that they originated the maneuver known as "fostering." This is the striking of two blows by each man as they change. Each has a hammer in his hand and both strike two blows while shifting.

... Ed Chamberlain, Cripple Creek, and Carl Maka, Leadville, drilled what is said to be the deepest hole ever put down in Gunnison granite by two men. Their record is 46⅝ inches, made in Bisbee, Arizona, in 1903 [Writers' Program 1943, 222–23].

The set-up is seen in Figure 21, where one team's turn is about to begin. The steel driver, shaker, and swamper (prone behind the shaker) are all in position. The duty of the swamper is to keep the hole flushed out with water.

As many as 20,000 spectators witnessed a contest in Goldfield, Nevada, probably on September 2, 1906, the day before the Gans-Nelson boxing match (Figure 22).

An idea of the technicalities involved can be gleaned from Frank Crampton's description of how he and Jack Commerford won that double-jack contest.

Figure 21. Contestants in a double-jack rock-drilling contest on the streets of Silverton, Colorado (Denver Public Library Western History Collection, X-60059).

Jack thought that there would be too much celebrating before the fight, and that if we laid off the whiskey straights, we couldn't help but win....

Jack and I took great pains to get our steel just right. We sharpened and tempered twenty steel on two and one-half inch change lengths, with ten extras on five-inch changes just in case an ear broke or a bit chipped. Ordinarily fifteen changes were used, one for each of the fifteen minutes of the contest, and they were for three inch changes. Each of us had selected our double-jack hammers, long, thin, and small faced. The force of each blow would be all on the steel. Handles were of long grained, well seasoned hickory. The hammer and the handle weight combined was limited to nine pounds, by contest regulations.

Before we left for Goldfield, three days before the fight, we had gotten our strokes to sixty and sixty-one a minute; we wanted more but couldn't make it....

We didn't have a walk away in the double-jack contests. Mike Kinsella, and his partner, whose name escapes me, had the same idea that Jack and I did, keep sober, don't celebrate, and win. They were our only competition. It was close but we came in with a short inch to spare; we attributed it to the shorter steel lengths and bits not dulled in that extra half-inch of drilling that the three inch changes had to do.

Figure 22. Twenty thousand spectators at a rock-drilling contest in Gold-field, Nevada, circa 1906 (Protected Art Archive / Alamy).

> Mike made the championship several times and held the drilling record of
> fifty inches, in fifteen minutes, in the hardest rock of the all, Vermont gran-
> ite.... Mike never used three-inch changes again: his experience with us
> taught him a valuable lesson [Crampton 1993, 36–38].

Champion of the World

John Henry "was the champion of [the] world with a hammer"
(Barker 1927). According to Dr. Carl Marbury, of Leeds, Alabama, his
ancestor Ciscero Davis reported that a man named "John" won all the
steel-driving contests when Davis was working on the railroads around
Leeds in the late 1880s (Marbury 2002). The Marbury family's testimony couples with Barker's to make it likely that both spoke of the
steel-driving man.

This explains why John Henry was chosen to race the steam drill.
It also explains his willingness to give an all-out effort—he was used to
winning.

The testimonies of Spencer, Barker, Cummings, and Davis indicate that John Henry participated in straight-away contests, not
double-hand. They were probably the standard fifteen minutes long. His
contest with a steam drill, however, simulated working conditions and
lasted for hours.

Could John Henry Really Have Won?

That the contest was held at all is evidence that John Henry could
have won. On analyzing relevant information, Williams also thought
he could have won (Williams 1983, 11–12). However, there are contrary
opinions.

Freeman Hubbard dismissed the 1887–88 John Henry contest: "the
date 1888 is pretty strong evidence against the authenticity of the legend that a contest between man and machine was staged at Oak Mountain tunnel, for the power drill was widely used in tunneling long before
1888, and there is little likelihood that it would have been challenged
at so late a date" (1945, 62). In fact, the improvements in steam drills
between 1866 and 1888 were in weight, maintenance, and reliability, *not
speed*. Men who thought they could beat steam drills challenged them as
late as 1901, when Bradshaw and Freethy drilled fifty-five inches in fifteen minutes (Armstrong 1901).

> Walter Bradshaw, an old-time Butte double-jack man and co-winner of
> the drilling championship of the world, has often told that the easiest

drilling contest he engaged in was against one of the mechanical drilling machines.

Bradshaw's eyes twinkle as he relates, "It was in Spokane, the day Joe Freethy and I won the world championship by drilling fifty-five inches in fifteen minutes. A salesman bet that his drilling machine could outdrill us for fifteen minutes. We took the bet and then took a look at the machine. The salesman, in turn, took a look at the hard piece of granite and paid off. His was a coal drilling machine." Bradshaw believes that had the salesman's drill been of the hard-rock type, he and his partner could have outdrilled it for the short period of fifteen minutes.

"That's where the machine is better than the man," said Bradshaw. "It can drill twenty-four hours a day, seven days a week, if necessary, without tiring" [Writers' Program 1943, 221].

Bradshaw's confidence was well justified. Over fifteen minutes, competitive double-hand teams drilled at least 3 inches per minute in Gunnison granite (Ibid., 223). Steam drills drilled 1–1.4 inches per minute (Gillette 1916, 547, Drinker 1883, 250, Schaefer 1919).

Under the long hours of working conditions, hand drilling is much slower. The high end of typical hand drilling in hard rock is about 0.5 inch per minute (Hoffman 1999).

All steam drills bored at similar rates. The differences lay in the composition of the rock and the quality of the operator. The best results required great skill.

It is similar for driving steel. F.P. Barker wrote, "I was as far behind John Henry as the moon is behind the sun. The world has not yet produced a man to whip steel like John Henry" (Barker 1927, Johnson 1929, 143).

"John Henry made fourteen feet," according to a common line of the ballad. Charles C. Spencer, self-proclaimed eyewitness to John Henry's contest, gave him more credit, twenty-seven and a half feet (Spencer 1927). For a contest lasting six hours (a plausible guess), fourteen feet corresponds to a rate of 0.47 in/min. If John Henry made twenty-seven and a half feet, the rate was 0.92 in/min. If the steam drill "only made nine" feet, it performed miserably, 0.30 in/min. If it made twenty-one feet, its rate was 0.70 in/min, still less than expected.

A stanza of "John Henry" from J.D. Williams (Eddyville, Kentucky) describes the fitchering and breaking of the steel of the steam drill.

> John Henry said to his Captain,
> "Captain, can't you see,
> Your hole is choked and your steel is broke
> And your hammer can't go down with me?" [Johnson 1929, 105]

This stanza is rare in versions of "John Henry" collected or recorded by the mid–1930s. It could be a residue from an early version, and it could be historical truth.

There is a remarkable record for a single-jack driller.

> We challenge the world to beat the wonderful feat of single-hand drilling accomplished this week by a Cornishman, named James Gooey, in the Golden Chariot mine. In one 8-hour shift he drilled 31 feet in very hard rock... [Wyman 1979, 90].

Fred Dopp once held the single-jack contest record at 17 inches in fifteen minutes (Brown 2007). Continuing the same rate for eight hours would lead to a depth of 45 feet 4 inches. Gooey drilled for eight hours at nearly three-fourths the speed that champion Dopp maintained over fifteen minutes! This is astonishing, but if Gooey had the combination of skill and stamina to do it, John Henry could have been endowed similarly.

A steel driver drilling at just one-fourth the rate of competition double-handers would make 32 feet in eight hours or 24 feet in six hours. Thus, John Henry's reported 27½ feet is plausible.

John Henry, the underdog, gave it all he had. If he was as good as James Gooey, he might have beaten a perfectly functioning steam drill. If the steam drill had problems, then John Henry could have won easily. He really *could* have beaten the steam drill.

⸺

Beginning in 1909 and continuing through 1933, a succession of scholars, collectors, informants, journalists, and recording artists established the core of the documentary record of John Henry.

6

Drilling into John Henry

Johnie Henry was a hard-workin' man,
He died with his hammer in his hand.
—Collected by Louise Rand Bascom
in western North Carolina, ca. 1909

John Henry escaped printed notice until 1909. By 1912 "John Henry" had become an "exceedingly popular" ballad and banjo song in Berea, Kentucky (Bradley 1915).

Early John Henry scholarship focused on Big Bend Tunnel, Summers County, West Virginia. John Harrington Cox, who took John Henry and John Hardy to be the same man, cast the die in that direction in 1919. Guy Benton Johnson and Louis Watson Chappell followed in the 1920s and early '30s with intense efforts to separate John Henry from John Hardy and to establish Big Bend Tunnel as the John Henry site.

Louise Rand Bascom

Louise Rand Bascom (1885–1949) quoted two just lines of "John Henry" in an article on songs and ballads from the southern mountains (1909, 249–50). She wrote with condescension about those from whom she collected. Thus, the contestants in a Fiddler's Convention didn't care who won because "the winner will undoubtedly treat." The sound of a fiddle or banjo is like "one of the strange tom-tidi-tom noises heard on a midway," but "after a few unprejudiced moments of attention, melody, stirring, full of pathos, rich with suggestion, emerges from the monotonous din" (Ibid., 238).

Bascom distinguished John Henry from John Hardy. In her article, she included a four-stanza version of "John Hardy."

Josiah Henry Combs

In 1911 Hubert G. Shearin and Josiah H. Combs included the following in their Kentucky folksong syllabus.

> THE STEEL-DRIVER, ii, 4a3b4c3b, 11: John Henry, proud of his skill with sledge and hand-drill, competes with a modern steam-drill in Tunnel No. Nine, on the Chesapeake & Ohio Railroad. Defeated, he dies, asking to be buried with his tools at his breast [19].

Combs published a full text in France in 1925 and in America in 1967 (Combs 1925 and 1967).

Shearin and Combs clearly distinguished between John Henry and John Hardy.

> JOHN HARDY, iii, 4a3b4c3b, 6: An account of Hardy's shooting a man in a poker game, of his arrest, trial, conviction, conversion and baptism, and of his execution and burial on the Tug River [Shearin 1911, 19].

Eber Carle Perrow

In 1913 Eber Carle Perrow (1880–1968) reported eight stanzas of "John Henry" and two of "This Old Hammer" (163–65). He obtained "John Henry" in 1912 from E.N. Caldwell as a manuscript containing the note "About half of the 'John Henry' here; very long." Perrow noted, "Mr. C.B. House tells me there is a song in Clay County, Kentucky, about John Henry, a steel-driving man."

Bill Hendricks

On September 2, 1913, *The Atlanta Constitution* carried the following article.

Sings "John Henry" In Court to Prove He Was Wronged

But Lover of "Er Steel Driving Man" Gets Fined
on Evidence Given by Neighbors.

"John Henry was er Steel Drivin' Man" proved to be an unlucky song for Bill Hendricks, a granite cutter, of 588 Simpson street, when the latter was arraigned in police court yesterday afternoon on complaint of Mrs. John Meggs.

Mrs. Meggs charged that on both Saturday and Sunday nights her neighbor had come home more or less intoxicated and had shouted and sung bad songs. Bill, who proved to be a stalwart workman with a mustache that Kaiser Bill might well envy, declared that he had only sung one song and that was "John Henry" and that he had sung "John Henry" since his childhood days and no one had ever before taken offense at it.

In order to prove the worth of the song Recorder Pro-Tem Preston let Bill recite it in the courtroom and he delivered the opening verse as follows:

"When John Henry was er little bit o' boy he sat on his father's knee,
"An' he picked up a bit o' steel and says, 'Dad, make er steel drivin' man out o' me.'"

That was all there was to the song, both the defendant and his sister swore, and the granite cutter added that if you wanted to keep on singing it, you just repeated the opening verse as often as you desired.

Neighbors, however, swore that Bill had been disorderly and he was fined $15.75 in one case and $5.75 in the other. The defendant put the court on notice that it was a piece of malice on the part of the neighbors and not their objection to "John Henry" that caused his arrest.

According to the census of 1900, Bill Hendricks was born in March 1873. If he first sang "John Henry" in 1888, the year after John Henry Dabney died, then he was about fifteen, still a child.

W.T. Blankenship

In 1927 Guy Johnson obtained an undated broadside, "John Henry, the Steel Driving Man," published by W.T. Blankenship. Johnson estimated that it dated to "about 1900 or a little earlier" and concluded that the author was "probably a white man." It provides a clue to the John Henry site. John Henry's "woman" got up at midnight to catch "that No. 4 train" to go "where John Henry fell dead" (Johnson 1929, 84–90, Chappell 1933, 82–83).

Blankenship is the subject of Chapter 9.

John Avery Lomax

In 1912 and 1913, John Avery Lomax (1867–1948) was elected President of the American Folk-Lore Society. In December 1913, in New York City, he delivered an address to the Society, "Some Types of American Folk-Song." An eleven-stanza text of "John Henry" is included in the published version as a song "sung along the Chesapeake and Ohio Road in Kentucky and West Virginia" (Lomax 1915, 13–14).

John Harrington Cox

John Harrington Cox (1863–1945) made the first attempt to trace the origin of "John Henry." His 1919 article, "John Hardy," contains the testimony of West Virginia ex-governor W.A. MacCorkle, who believed that John Hardy had been a steel-driver on the C. & O. in about 1872 and an outlaw and murderer in the 1890s (Chapter 2). Cox accepted this story, interpreted other evidence as being consistent with it, and identified John Henry as John Hardy: "The change of name to John Henry ... is not significant...."

John Hardy was hanged for murder in Welch, West Virginia, on January 19, 1894.

Audio Recordings

The first commercial audio recording of "John Henry," made by Fiddlin' John Carson in March 1924, was released six months later (Meade 2002, Russell 2004, Dixon 1997). With that, the floodgates opened. Hundreds of commercial and field recordings of "John Henry" have been made since (Cohen 2000, xxi–xxv, 61–89).

Howard Washington Odum

Sociologist Howard Washington Odum (1884–1954) brought his doctoral student Guy Johnson to John Henry. Odum and Johnson's second book, *Negro Workaday Songs*, contains material collected during 1924–25 in "certain areas in North Carolina, South Carolina, Tennessee and Georgia" (Odum 1926, x).

Chapter XIII, "John Henry: Epic of the Negro Workingman," includes eleven substantial versions of the ballad, four hammer songs, and a long tall tale heard in Chapel Hill. It also separates John Henry from John Hardy.

With this contribution, Odum left John Henry to Johnson.

Guy Benton Johnson

Guy Benton Johnson (1901–1991) (Figure 23) began work on John Henry in 1924–25, when he and Odum were gathering material for *Negro Workaday Songs*. He continued after finishing his Ph.D. dissertation with Odum in 1927. Two 1927 articles are appreciations of the hero (Johnson 1927d, 1927g). His 1929 book, *John Henry: Tracking Down a Negro Legend*, summarizes his findings and conclusions.

Johnson's book contains twenty-nine versions of "John Henry," eleven hammer songs, one version of "John Hardy," and considerable testimony from people who placed John Henry at various sites. The most notable are Big Bend Tunnel, West Virginia; "Cruzee" / "Cursey" Mountain Tunnel, Alabama; and Oak Mountain Tunnel, Alabama.

Johnson distinguished John Henry from John Hardy. Dismissing the Alabama claims, he concluded

Figure 23. Guy Benton Johnson in his office (photograph by Bob Brooks, courtesy Guy Benton Johnson Papers, Southern Historical Collection, Wilson Library, University of North Carolina at Chapel Hill).

that John Henry was probably a real man, a steel driver at Big Bend Tunnel. This conclusion was based largely on the testimony of Cornelius S. "Neal" Miller, who farmed near Talcott, West Virginia (Johnson 1929, 54, 67).

After 1929, Johnson pursued African American sociology only. He never published on folklore again.

Central of Georgia (C of G)

The October 1930 issue of *Central of Georgia Magazine* contains a seventeen-stanza text, "Jawn Henry," submitted by Peter A. Brannon of the Alabama Anthropological Society of Montgomery, Alabama.

> When Jawn Henry was a baby,
> Sat on his granddaddy's knee;
> Said, "The Central o' Georgia Rail Road
> Gonna be the death o' me.
> Gonna be the death o' me" [Crawford 1930].

Figure 24. A steel drill, said to be the last steel driven by John Henry, sticking up from the rock outside of Oak Mountain Tunnel near Dunnavant, Alabama, where it was said in 1930 to have been in place for more than forty years. The drill has long since disappeared (*Central of Georgia Magazine*, October 1930).

The article also summarizes a report from Road Supervisor J. Morgan of Leeds, Alabama, that Jawn Henry had dropped dead with his hammer in his hand by the steel drill "which still sticks in the hole he was driving" outside the east portal of Oak Mountain Tunnel, about two miles south of Leeds.

The C of G owned the Columbus & Western (C & W), whose track was laid through the Leeds area in 1887–88.

This is a rare appearance in "John Henry" of a railroad other than the C & O. It is the first report of a local John Henry tradition in Alabama.

Louis Watson Chappell

Louis Watson Chappell (1890–1981) began work on John Henry in September 1925, when he visited the Big Bend area (Cameron 1988).

He published papers in 1930 ("John Hardy") and 1931 ("Ben Hardin"), reviewed Johnson's *John Henry* in 1930, and published his own book, *John Henry: A Folk-Lore Study*, in 1933 (Chappell 1930a, 1931, 1930b, 1933).

Like Johnson, Chappell separated John Henry from John Hardy. Dissatisfied with Cox's and Johnson's scholarship, he heaped scorn on both men.

Chappell was concerned about Alabama, but he decided that the construction of the C & O had "priority claims" and that the "leaning of the tradition would seem to promise more" in West Virginia (1933, 42). "At all events, it is no longer necessary, or possible, to regard 'John Henry' as made up of whole cloth. The energy and variety of the Big Bend community will not allow it" (Ibid., 60, 92).

≥≡ ≥≡ ≥≡

John Harrington Cox confused John Henry with John Hardy. Louis Chappell, Cox's colleague at West Virginia University, launched attacks on him and Guy Johnson.

7

Feuding Over the Mixtery

The fires of the famous Cox-Chappell feud didn't burn
as long as those of the Hatfield-McCoy feud ... the
only assassins were of character....
—Jim Comstock

The feud between Louis W. Chappell and John Harrington Cox,
his senior colleague in the English department at West Virginia University,
is said to have begun with Cox's confusion of John Hardy with
John Henry (Comstock 1968, Cohen 1981, 61–89, Williams 1983, 59–76,
Cohen 2000, xxi–xxv). In his articles and book, Chappell treated Cox
and Guy B. Johnson with contempt. Johnson, having moved on to
sociology, ignored him.

"John Hardy" and "John Henry" Before 1919

In "John Henry," as reported before 1919, John Henry is a hero (Bascom 1909, Shearin 1911, Perrow 1913, Lomax 1915). In "John Hardy,"
John Hardy is an outlaw and murderer (Bascom 1909, Shearin 1911).

John Hardy

1. John Hardy was a mean an' disperated man,
He carried two guns ever' day,
He shot a man in New Orlean Town,
John Hardy never lied to his gun, poor boy.

2. He's been to the east and he's been to the west,
An' he's been this wide world round,
He's been to the river an' been baptized,
An' he's been on his hangin' grounds, poor boy.

3. John Hardy's father was standin' by,
Sayin', "Johnie, what have you done?"

He murdered a man in the same ole town,
You ought to see John Hardy gittin' away, poor boy.

4. John Hardy's mother come weepin' around
Cryin', "Johnie, what have you done?"
"It's all for the sake of her I love?"
An' they run John Hardy back in jail, poor boy [Bascom 1909, 247].
—Highlands, North Carolina, by 1909

John Hardy

John Hardy had a wife, a child,
A wife and child had he;
But he cared no more for his wife and child
Than he did for the fish in the sea.

He'd play cards with a white man,
He'd play cards with him fair,
He'd play the hat right off his head,
He'd play him for his hair [quoted in Cox 1919, 513–14].
—Berea College, Kentucky, by 1910

John Hardy

JOHN HARDY, iii, 4a3b4c3b, 6: An account of Hardy's shooting a man in a
poker game, of his arrest, trial, conviction, conversion and baptism, and of
his execution and burial on the Tug River [Shearin 1911, 19].
—Kentucky, by 1911

Mrs. Ellie Johnson, Hot Springs, North Carolina, sang "John Hardy"
for Cecil Sharp in 1916. Only stanza 5 contains material not found above.

5. John Hardy's brother was a-standing round.
O John, what have you done?
I've killed my partner for fifty cents,
For the sake of my blue eyed girl, I do know,
For the sake of my blue eyed girl
[Campbell 1917, 257–58, Sharp 1932, 11: 35–36].

In these ballads, steel driving, Big Bend Tunnel, and the C & O are
not mentioned. There is no suggestion that John Henry and John Hardy
are the same.

Cox and the Mixtery

In the 1910s there was growing interest in balladry in America. Cox
got involved. He may have cherished "John Hardy" because it was the
first folk song he collected.

In the early part of 1913, Mr. E.C. Smith, a student at West Virginia University from Weston, Lewis County, procured for me a copy of the popular song, "John Hardy." It was promptly forwarded to Professor Kittredge, and was printed in *The Journal of American Folk-Lore*, April–June 1913, pp. 180–182. That was the beginning of the West Virginia Folk-Lore Collection... [Cox 1925, xv].

It is version *e* in Cox's 1919 article, "John Hardy" (518). Walter Mick, of Ireland, West Virginia, had heard it from people in his community and passed it on to E.C. Smith.

It contains echoes of "John Henry." In the first stanza, John Hardy sits "on his father's knee" and says, "I fear the C. & O. Road / Will be the ruination of me." Stanzas seven and eight, derived from "The Lass of Roch Royal," are often included in "John Henry."

John Hardy

7. "Oh who will shoe your pretty little feet,
And who will glove your hands,
And who will kiss your sweet rosy lips,
When I'm in a foreign land, poor boy!
When I'm in a foreign land?"

8. "My father will shoe my pretty little feet,
My mother will glove my hands;
John Hardy will kiss my sweet rosy lips,
When he comes from a foreign land, poor boy!
When he comes from a foreign land" [Cox 1919, 514–15].

All five versions of "John Hardy" in Cox's 1919 article contain elements of "John Henry." Version *a* came from Governor MacCorkle, who wrote in 1916 that he had known it for about twenty years, that is, from about 1896 (Cox 1919, 505–06). John Hardy, "black as a kittle in hell," was a famous steel driver on the C & O in about 1872. He was hanged for murder at Welch, West Virginia, in 1894. Two of the seven stanzas of MacCorkle's ballad belong to "John Henry," and one uses his name.

John Hardy

2. John Hardy went to the rock quarrie,
He went there for to drive, Lord, Lord!
The rock was so hard and the steel so soft,
That he laid down his hammer and he cried, "O my God!"
He laid down his hammer and he cried.

3. John Henry was standing on my right-hand side
The steel hammers on my left, Lord, Lord!
"Before I'd let the steamer beat me down,

I'd die with my hammer in my hand, by God!
I'd die with my hammer in my hand" [Cox 1919, 514–15].

Cox's version *b*, nine stanzas, opens with a "John Henry" stanza.

John Hardy

1. John Hardy was but three days old,
Sitting on his mamma's knee,
When he looked straight up at her and said,
"The Big Bend Tunnel on the C. & O. Road
Is bound to be the death of me,
The Big Bend Tunnel on the C. &. O. Road
Is bound to be the death of me" [Ibid., 515–16].
—Maude Rucks, Heaters, Braxton County, West Virginia, by 1919

H.S. Walker reported on two John Hardys.

Mr. H.S. Walker, a man of mature years, a student in West Virginia University from Fayette County, through which the C. & O. runs, reports the following as a current belief where he lives:—

John Hardy, a Negro, worked for Langhorn, a railroad-contractor from Richmond, VA., at the time of the building of the C. & O. Road. Langhorn had a contract for work on the east side of the Big Bend Tunnel, which is in the adjoining county of Summers, to the east of Fayette County; and some other contractor had the work on the west side of the tunnel. This was the time when the steam-driller was first used. Langhorn did not have one, but the contractor on the other side of the tunnel did; and Langhorn made a wager with him that Hardy could, by hand, drill a hole in less time than the steam-drill could. In the contest that followed, Hardy won, but dropped dead on the spot. He tells me, also, that there is a current report in this part of the State concerning a John Hardy who was a tough, a saloon frequenter, an outlaw, and a sort of a thug. He *thinks* this John Hardy was a white man, and he is *sure* that he was hanged later on for killing a man in McDowell County or across the line in Virginia [Cox 1919, 510].

Following MacCorkle's lead, Cox equated John Henry with John Hardy.

Probability indicates that these two stories are about the same man. For a white man contemporary with the steel-driver to possess the same name and attributes as he, to operate in the early part of his career in the same region, to drift later to the same locality, to commit the same crime, and to pay the same penalty, is not believable [Ibid.].

In 1924 Cox maintained the same position, but by February 1927, he had had second thoughts. "The final statement as to the exact relationship between the 'John Henry' ballads and the 'John Hardy' ballads must await further investigation" (1925, 175–88, 1927, 226–27). As late as 1929, Cox had not fully accepted that John Henry and John Hardy were distinct. "This obscure matter needs further study."

Scholars who rejected the identification of John Henry with John Hardy include Josiah H. Combs, Howard W. Odum, Guy B. Johnson, Robert W. Gordon, Newman I. White, and Louis W. Chappell (Combs 1925 and 1967, 80, Odum and Johnson 1926, 222n1, Gordon 1927, White 1928, 190, Chappell 1930a).

Chappell vs. Cox

Although the fires of the famous Cox-Chappell feud didn't burn as long as those of the Hatfield-McCoy feud, and although the only assassins were of character, the feud between the two WVU English professors is not forgotten in academic circles in Morgantown.

The fight was almost violent and ended up in the gutter with good old fashioned mud slinging. All of it started, or so I gather ... over John Henry, whether he actually did what he did, whether he was the same as John Hardy, and was he the same as the cotton-picking "Jawn" from down Alabamy way or wherever [Comstock 1968].

I have no details of this "good old fashioned mud slinging," but there is information about the matrix in which it occurred.

On joining the faculty of the English Department of West Virginia University in 1922, Chappell found that his scholarly interests were similar to Cox's. He decided to take up folksong as the topic for his dissertation, emulating Cox, who had obtained his Ph.D. from Harvard with a folksong dissertation in 1923. Chappell hoped to do the same at the University of Chicago.

He accepted a two-year tuition scholarship, effective in the fall of 1925, at the University of Chicago, having by this time discovered that his colleague, John Harrington Cox, had confused John Henry with John Hardy and that the solution to the problem was still unattained. We have just a glimpse of him when about to leave for the "windy city." Having read in the *Bluefield (Va.) News* of Sunday, Aug. 30, 1925, an account of the hanging of Ben Hardin at Tazewell, Virginia, in 1866, he set out for the Big Bend Tunnel of the C&O Railroad to interview L.W. Hill and others in the Hinton area [Cameron 1988, pt. 1, 8].

The "glimpse" to which Cameron refers, in a newspaper article that he attributes to the *Daily Dispatch* (Bluefield, West Virginia), may be this:

Since the publication last Sunday in the Bluefield Virginia News of the hanging at Tazewell in the year 1868 of Ben Harden, notorious criminal, men

of letters have become interested, and during a week a learned professor
was here in pursuit of research work with the probable thought in mind
the crime committed by Harden in the murder of Sanders Burns, the trial
and conviction, may have had some bearing on the so-called "Hardy song,"
the similarity of Hardy and Harden being spoken of ... during the summer
one of the professors engaged in this research work will have to occasion to
address the students of the University of Chicago.... The data concerning
John Henry, the powerful steel driver, it is said, has somewhat become confused with the notorious Negro, John Hardy, who was hanged at Peeryville,
McDowell county.... During the week one of these men of letters visited this
section and called on the Bluefield Virginia News editor, among others...
[*Bluefield Daily Telegraph* 1925, 5].

Chappell was the "learned professor" bound for Chicago. If Cox
read this news item, then he knew in 1925, a few months after *Folk-Songs
of the South* had been published, that Chappell believed that Cox had
confused John Henry and John Hardy.

Chappell's 1928 promotion to associate professor suggests that he
and Cox were then on reasonable terms. Cox had been a full professor
since 1904. He probably could have blocked Chappell's promotion, had
he been so inclined. However, there is a hint that Chappell tended to
avoid Cox after 1925. In West Virginia University's annual, *The Monticola*, Chappell is listed as a member of Cox's club. See Beowulf Gedryht
in one edition only, that of 1926, published in 1925 (Kurtz 1925).

In 1929 Chappell became involved in administration. The new
chairman of the English department, John William Draper, chose Chappell as his assistant (Cameron 1988, pt 1, 4). Draper initiated sweeping
changes to increase the rigor of the graduate program and the value of
its A.M. A faculty revolt led the dean to remove Draper and Chappell
after just one year (Ibid., 5).

During the political brawl in the department, Chappell was prepar-
ing works for publication (Chappell 1930a, 1930b, 1931, 1933).

In July, 1930, with Draper's encouragement, Lou published a remarkable
twelve-page article ("John Hardy") in the *Philological Quarterly* (IX, no. 3, pp.
260–272), pointing out errors in judgement and methodology in the work of
both Guy B. Johnson and John Harrington Cox and thereby indicating that he
was back at work on that literary problem [Cameron 1988, pt 2, 3].

According to Chappell, Cox could characterize the Hardy-Henry
situation as "lacking finality" in 1929, but in 1927 he had "much more
discomfort about his earlier conclusions" (Chappell 1930a, 261). Cox
added "to the confusion of the matter" with "a new series of suggestions
and seemingly incorrect interpretations." Cox misquoted Scarborough,
seemed to misunderstand her, and suggested the strange possibility that

the killing in "the Yew Pine Mountains" ("This old hammer killed John Hardy") might be "one in which the man had his brains knocked out" (Cox 1927, 117). Chappell criticized Cox's dismissal of testimony that a hanged murderer named John Hardy had been white; his dismissal of John Hardy's death after a drilling contest; and his erroneous beliefs about steam drills. Cox accepted testimony that John Hardy drove steel at Big Bend Tunnel as an employee of the Langhorn Construction Company, when, in fact, that company had "no part in building Big Bend Tunnel" (Chappell 1930a, 265).

Chappell had interviewed men who had known John Hardy (Ibid., 266–67). "Mr. Harman says that in the five or six years he knew John Hardy he didn't know of him doing a day's work, and that he had become such a terror to the working people of the camps that hundreds of them went to Welch to testify against him at his trial." A few months later, Harman told Frank T. Walker, "I know John Hardy didn't drive steel in Big Bend Tunnel; he couldn't because he wasn't old enough when it was built, and he didn't work anyway. He got his living gambling and robbing 'round the camps." Lee Holley said, "I remember seeing John Hardy pretty often, and know all about him.... He was with a group of gamblers 'round the camps."

According to those who had known him, John Hardy was neither a steel driver nor any other kind of laborer. He was a loafer, gambler, robber, and killer.

Chappell summarized, "In the light of the foregoing evidence, ex-Governor McCorkle's hearsay tale"—accepted by Cox—"reads like a fairy story" (Chappell 1930a, 271, Cox 1919 and 1925). John Hardy was not the steel-driving hero of "John Henry" (Chappell 1930a, 272).

A feud could account for the treatment Chappell gave Cox in *John Henry: A Folk-Lore Study* (1933). There he devoted five pages of the introduction to Cox's failures as a scholar (1–5). Cox was then retired but still living in Morgantown.

Johnson on the Separation

Johnson addressed Cox's confusion gently.

Now there is much in favor of the conclusion which Cox has reached. When he made his investigation, only one or two John Henry ballads had come to light, and the structure of those was exactly like the structure of the John Hardy ballads. In the absence of data showing the wide diffusion of John Henry lore, it was natural and logical to assume that John Henry and John Hardy were identical.

Within the last few years, however, a great many John Henry songs have been found, and it is now possible to interpret Cox's data in a new light. In fact, Cox himself has indicated recently his belief that his former position is in need of some revision (Johnson 1929, 59).

Johnson considered three "major possibilities."

1. There was no such person as John Henry. The name John Henry was merely an accident, a mispronunciation of John Hardy resulting from oral tradition. This is Cox's solution.
2. There was a man known as John Henry who worked as a driller in railroad construction in southern West Virginia about 1872, but he changed his name to John Hardy and went further south to work in the coal mines, coming to his end on the gallows at Welch in 1894.
3. There was a John Henry, and there was also a John Hardy. The former worked on the Chesapeake and Ohio Railroad and won fame among workmen as a steel driver about 1872. The latter worked as a driver in the coal mines and won notoriety by murdering a man in 1893 and getting hanged in 1894. The two men had no connection.

In the light of what has been said in the preceding chapter, the first of these propositions may be dismissed as untenable (Johnson 1929, 60).

In calling the first possibility "untenable," Johnson treated John Henry as if his existence were settled, even though he admitted that the evidence was frail (Ibid., 53–54, 60). He made other arguments that John Hardy and John Henry were different men: (1) From age estimates, "John Henry in 1872 was about the same age as John Hardy in 1894." (2) In the hammer song it is always, "This old hammer / Killed *John Henry*," not "John Hardy." (3) "John Henry" is an older ballad than "John Hardy" [Ibid., 60–67].

Chappell vs. Johnson

Chappell scorned White's and Johnson's acceptance of Cox's view that John Hardy had been a steel driver. "They are still referring to John Hardy as the steel-driver, and thereby according him the dignity of John Henry's profession" (Chappell 1930a, 261).

In 1933 Chappell detailed his complaints about Johnson's work (Ibid. 1933, 10).

1. Johnson's statement, "When John Hardy came on to the scene, only a few snatches of John Henry remained in general circulation in West Virginia," is not supported by evidence.

Chappell is correct. Johnson's speculation has no foundation.

2. "His statement that the 'author of John Hardy ... must have been familiar with the structure of John Henry, for he cast his product in exactly the same mold,' is made without giving

any evidence that 'John Hardy' had an author. The observed fact of their structural similarity hardly settles the matter of individual or multiple authorship for one or both of the ballads."

Abundant examples of ballad meter were available in 1894, when John Hardy was hanged. If the author of "John Hardy" patterned it after "John Henry," why didn't he use the "John Henry" tune?

"John Henry" and "John Hardy" tend to be performed with the fourth line repeated after an interjection such "Lawd, Lawd," " po' boy," "God knows," etc. This pattern is common in Britain and America. van der Merwe gives two British examples, both with tunes close to a typical "John Henry" tune (1989, 194, 96n22).

3. "The separation of the two ballads is, perhaps, the best thing Dr. Johnson does in his discussion, and that is not altogether satisfactory. His materials and methods are hardly sufficient for his conclusions." In particular, Johnson's sample of tunes is inadequate, as is their analysis (Chappell 1933, 10–12).

Even so, Johnson's position on tunes has stood the test of time. Among the much larger number now available, "John Hardy" and "John Henry" have a strong tendency to remain distinct.

Mixtery and Mischiefry

In 1922–24, Cox, Chappell, and Combs were all teaching English at West Virginia University. Carey Woofter, a student, supplied them with folklore. On examining the Woofter text of "Edward" (Child 13), Wilgus concluded that it is a clever conflation of Child's A and B texts (Wilgus 1967, xix-xx and 1966). This places all of Woofter's contributions under a cloud of suspicion.

In 1924, Woofter and a classmate, Aubrey G. Goff, gave a hammer song, "The Yew Pine Mountains," to Combs, Cox, and Chappell (Combs 1925, Cox 1927, Chappell 1933). It came from Harley Townsend, Dusk, West Virginia, "whose brother heard it years ago in the coal camps near Fairmont" (Combs 1967, 166, 23).

All three printings include a version of this stanza.

> This old hammer killed John Hardy, (3×)
> But it won't kill me, babe, it won't kill me.

Guy Johnson wrote:

I have heard dozens of driving songs and, as far as I know, I have read all that have ever been published by folk-song collectors, but only once have I heard or seen John Hardy's name in one of them. It is always

> This old hammer
> Killed *John Henry* [1929, 61–62].

The exception is "The Yew Pine Mountains."

According to Combs, Woofter was "an eccentric West Virginia mountaineer, as eccentric as his name sounds ... an avid student and collector of folk-songs and Highland dialect; [he] enjoyed getting Cox in deep water" (Wilgus 1967, xviii). Woofter may have tailored "The Yew Pine Mountains" to provide Cox with bogus evidence for the hypothesis that John Henry and John Hardy were the same man.

Cox's failure to acknowledge his error fully left him vulnerable to gentle correction by Johnson and ridicule by Chappell. Johnson built a strong case for the separation of John Henry and John Hardy. Chappell's was even more compelling.

⸻

Chappell accused Johnson of unethical behavior in his John Henry research and its publication.

8

Priority and Slight

> I had written the report to preserve my priority claims
> until I could complete a larger plan of investigation on
> the subject...—Louis Watson Chappell

Scholars have tended to accept Louis Chappell's work on John Henry and John Hardy but have not approved of the way in which he attacked Guy Johnson (Chappell 1933, Pound 1933, 422, Cohen 1981, 66–67, Williams 1983, 60–61).

> Chappell charges that his unpublished report of investigation of John Henry at Big Bend Tunnel, West Virginia, fell into the hands of Guy B. Johnson, who hurriedly made an investigation and published a book ... using some of Chappell's material and making no acknowledgment. Chappell also points out variations in texts printed more than once by Johnson, Cox, and Combs. Chappell's pugnacious tone and carping criticism disfigure his book. But his ugly charges remain unanswered [Wilgus 1959, 398n116].

There is more to this story.

"Carping Criticism"

Here are selected examples of Chappell's "carping criticism."

1. Johnson does not see sufficient vulgarity in some versions of "John Henry" (Chappell 1933, 7–9). This is highly subjective.
2. Johnson's tune for the singing of Odell Walker is not exactly alike in two printings, nor are the texts in several printings (Ibid., 12–13). The variations are minor.
3. Given that others supported John Henry at Big Bend, Johnson need not have relied so heavily on the testimony of Neal Miller: "One man against a mountain of negative evidence!" (Johnson

1929, 53, Chappell 1933, 17). Miller was the only self-proclaimed eyewitness to John Henry's contest with a steam drill at Big Bend Tunnel (Chapter 14).

Priority Claims and Accusations

Chappell made his charges explicit.

In September, 1925, I investigated John Henry at Big Bend Tunnel, and in February, 1927, a 19-page report of my work there fell into the hands of Dr. Johnson. I had written the report to preserve my priority claims until I could complete a larger plan of investigation on the subject, and was trying to get it published at the University of North Carolina. The following is Dr. Johnson's only acknowledgment: "I wonder to what extent collectors have made John Henry famous at Big Bend! I know of at least two others who were trailing John Henry there before I made my visit." John Henry, p. 34 (n). It would be interesting to know the other culprit. (Chappell 1933, 6n33)

Having failed in North Carolina, South Carolina, and Georgia to turn up any biographical material for Henry as a real person, they [Odum and Johnson] concluded that he was "most probably a mythical character."

Their fabulous John Henry apparently did not satisfy Dr. Johnson very long. The following year, after seeing the report of my investigations at Big Bend Tunnel on the Chesapeake and Ohio Railway in West Virginia, he renewed his inquiries, culminating in a change of heart about where to look for the hero and a shift in point of view. "All in all," he writes, on the strength of this new information, "John Henry and Big Bend Tunnel are so intimately connected that ... there, if anywhere ... we must look for the origin of the John Henry tradition"; and prefers "to believe that (1) there was a Negro steel driver named John Henry at Big Bend Tunnel, that (2) he competed with a steam drill in a contest of the practicability of the device, and that (3) he probably died soon after the contest."

In taking this new point of view, however, Dr. Johnson, in 1929, says that he began in February, 1926, "to pursue the idea that the Big Bend Tunnel was the place of origin of the John Henry tradition." What he means by the expression "to pursue the idea" is not altogether clear, but his treatment of John Henry as a myth from investigations elsewhere as already shown, and his statement at the time, several months after February, 1926, are clear enough.

He leaves Big Bend to Hardy and the question of origin of the Henry tradition to the folk-lorist, several months after February, 1926, and these concessions characterize his efforts "to pursue the idea" that the tradition originated in West Virginia until he saw my report on the tunnel.

His marvellous freedom in handling this material would seem to call for an explanation of some sort. But his disregard of my rights is largely personal and need not require the attention of readers who are not interested in trifles, such as an investigator's priority claims may be, where I seem to follow him without reference in this study [Chappell, 1933, 6–7].

Tracking the Situation

Johnson started working on John Henry and John Hardy in 1924–25 (Odum 1926, x, Johnson 1990, folders 1051, 53, 54). Chappell began on about September 1, 1925 (Chappell 1933, 6, *Bluefield Daily Telegraph* 1925). If he didn't know of it before, Chappell became aware of Johnson's interest in John Henry with the publication of *Negro Workaday Songs* in 1926 (copyright June 15). The opinion expressed there is that John Henry was "most probably a mythical character" (Odum 1926, 221).

By January 1927, Johnson was corresponding about John Henry with other scholars, including H.C. Belden (Johnson 1990). Johnson's letter soliciting information was published in *The Chicago Defender* in the issue of February 12, 1927. On February 15, Chappell submitted his "19-page report" to *Studies in Philology* (Chappell 1927). The editor, James F. Royster, passed it on to Howard Odum (Royster 1927a, 1927b). In March Odum accepted Chappell's paper for publication in *Social Forces*, provided that it be shortened (Odum 1927a, Letter 1). At the same time, Odum mentioned that Guy Johnson was "following the same trail." In April Odum informed Chappell that his revised manuscript was received too late for May publication but could be published in September (Odum 1927b, Letter 2). In May Odum returned the manuscript to Chappell, as he had requested (Odum 1927c, Letter 3).

Johnson Explains

As far as I am aware, the only letter Johnson ever wrote to Chappell is that of June 23, 1928.

> Dear Mr. Chappell:
> My interest in John Henry dates back to the time when Dr. Odum and I were writing *Negro Workaday Songs*. I read Cox's article and thought that he was wrong. I wanted to go ahead and get additional data before we published our book but Dr. Odum considered the question of the relation between John Henry and John Hardy of minor importance, and thought that it was best to go ahead and publish what we had. However I went ahead with my plans of getting to the bottom of the John Henry story and even before *Negro Workaday Songs* was off the press I had uncovered some clues which convinced me that there was really something to the story about John

Henry having died at the Big Bend Tunnel. Accordingly I outlined the John Henry story as a project which I should undertake as soon as possible. I was then working towards my doct[o]rate but this was completed in January, 1927. Immediately after that I again took up the story of John Henry with the intention of devoting full time to it until I had obtained sufficient data to make a respectful volume on the subject. In June, 1927, while I was spending my vacation in the Blue Ridge Mountains I made a trip up to Big Bend Tunnel, a trip which I had considered necessary all along for the proper study of John Henry. I make these statements because Dr. Odum intimated that in your letters to him you thought that my interest in John Henry might have been derived from the reading of the article which you sent here in February last year. I did read the article, as an associate editor of SOCIAL FORCES, but rather reluctantly, since I knew that I was soon going to make an investigation at Big Bend myself. I doubt if any of my informants at Big Bend were the same as yours, for in reading the article I purposely avoided concrete data such as names and places in order that my investigation at Big Bend would not be hampered.

When I learned last summer that you were writing a thesis on John Henry and John Hardy I decided to put John Henry aside for a while in order to give you an opportunity to complete your work before I did anything that might spoil your thesis. After nearly a year I supposed that you were within striking distance of the completion of your thesis so I have just in the past month [moved] towards getting my work ready for publication. It will probably be five or six months yet before the book is published, and I hope that in the meantime your dissertation is successfully completed... [Johnson 1928].

Privileged Communication

Chappell treated Odum's and Johnson's statement that John Henry was "most probably a mythical character" as if it signaled the end of Johnson's research on the subject. Actually, it leaves open the possibility that John Henry was real, and it does not imply that Johnson had finished his research.

Johnson's denial of intellectual theft is supported by evidence (Johnson 1990). He initiated a correspondence about tunnels on the C & O with C.W. Johns in January 1926. In January 1927, he corresponded about John Henry with other scholars. His letter asking readers of *The Chicago Defender* about John Henry appeared on February 12. All of this was before February 15, when Chappell sent his manuscript to *Studies in Philology*.

Some thirteen months before he saw Chappell's manuscript, Johnson was investigating tunnels on the C & O. Because it is so frequently mentioned in the ballad, Big Bend Tunnel was everyone's foremost candidate for the John Henry site.

As a reviewer of Chappell's manuscript for *Social Forces*, Johnson cannot be faulted. He recommended that it be published, and Odum offered publication. After missing a deadline, Chappell rejected the offer.

His description of these events is truncated and oblique.

> I had written the report to preserve my priority claims until I could complete a larger plan of investigation on the subject, and was trying to get it published at the University of North Carolina [Chappell 1933, 6n33].

In fact, Chappell changed his mind about "trying to get it published." It was his own choice not to preserve his priority claims in 1927.

Johnson was under no ethical obligation to stop his own ongoing research on John Henry. He should have proceeded as if he had not seen Chappell's manuscript, and this appears to be what he tried to do.

Because both would have been directed to some of the same people, Johnson could not avoid some of Chappell's informants. Consequently, for several informants we have two independent reports of testimony.

Chappell's manuscript came to Johnson as a privileged communication. A reviewer must respect "that the manuscript is a privileged communication, is confidential, and for your eyes only" (Scheife and Cramer 2007). This principle applies universally and is of long standing. Johnson could not have cited Chappell's unpublished work without permission.

By acknowledging that he was not the first to investigate John Henry at Big Bend Tunnel, Johnson took the best action available to him. His statement would corroborate a claim that Chappell might make later. Even so, Chappell used it as a springboard for accusations and sarcasm.

Chappell never acknowledged Johnson's generosity in giving him an extra year to complete his dissertation. It did not help. Lacking a faculty sponsor, Chappell never obtained a Ph.D. (Cameron 1988, pt. 2, 3).

When Johnson received Chappell's letter of June 2, 1928, the publication of Johnson's book was already in progress. Even though he was through with folk songs, he took time to reply to Chappell in a thorough and courteous manner.

Chappell seems not to have accepted that he himself was to blame for his late appearance in print as a John Henry scholar. His life was filled with hard work, bad luck, and poor judgment. By 1933 he had given up on a Ph.D. and had decided to publish *John Henry: A Folk-Lore Study* as an independent book. The economic depression of that time may have been a factor in his seeking a German publisher. His accumulated misfortune must have been frustrating, and it appears that he took his frustration out on Johnson.

Johnson would become a giant in the study of the sociology of African Americans and the promotion of fair treatment. Eventually, Chappell would also be recognized as a giant, the collector of one of America's great archives of sound recordings of American folk music.

⋙ ⋙ ⋙

In Rome, Georgia, ex-slave Margaret Riddlesperger preserved the only known copy of the Blankenship broadside. W.T. Blankenship, its publisher, lived in northern Alabama and adjacent Tennessee.

9

Nothing but a Man

John Henry said to his captain:
"You are nothing but a common man,
Before that steam drill shall beat me down,
I'll die with my hammer in my hand."
—W.T. Blankenship, "John Henry, the Steel Driving Man"

The Blankenship broadside is an important early text of "John Henry, the Steel Driving Man" (Johnson 1929, frontispiece, 84–90). Only one copy is known to exist. It was probably published around 1910, but the story behind it goes back to the days of slavery.

It provides the only known instance in which it is the Captain who is "nothing but a common man." Most often that line is "A man ain't nothing but a man" (Ibid., 104). Occasionally, it is "I ain't nothing but a man" or "You know I'm nothing but a man" (Darling 1983, 233).

When John Henry says, "A man ain't nothing but a man," or "I ain't nothing but a man," he acknowledges his own limits. When he says to the Captain, "You are nothing but a common man," he acknowledges that risking his life for the Captain is not rational. Even so, he will. There is an emotional bond between John Henry and the Captain, and John Henry would do anything for him.

This bond is described several times in tradition. It is balanced by instances of hostility. Because hostility is what is expected between a late nineteenth-century black laborer and his white boss, the more likely direction of mutation is from affection to hostility. Accordingly, affection may reflect early tradition, and it may be historical fact.

As popular as the "nothing but a man" stanza is, it is not found in the earliest known versions (Perrow 1913, 164–65, Lomax 1915, 13–14, Combs 1967, 164–65). The Blankenship broadside could have had a role in disseminating it. If so, it must have mutated quickly from "You are nothing but a common man" to "A man ain't nothing but a man" and "I ain't nothing but a man."

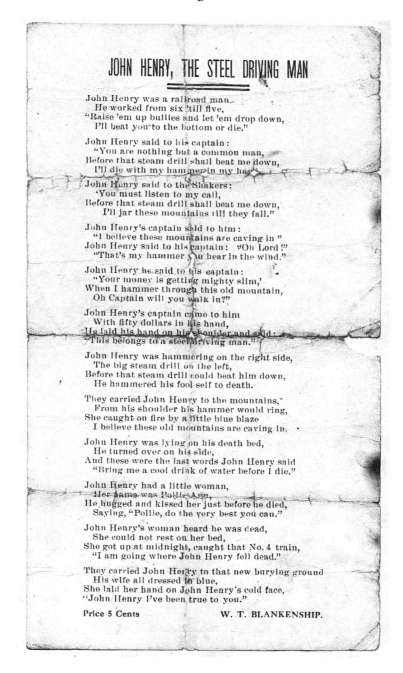

Figure 25. The Blankenship broadside, "John Henry, the Steel Driving Man" (courtesy Guy Benton Johnson Papers, Southern Historical Collection, Wilson Library, University of North Carolina at Chapel Hill).

Guy Johnson's Hunch

> After a short study of *John Henry* ballads I developed the hypothesis that
> there have been one or more printed versions of the ballad circulating. The
> rather formal style and structure of the ballads, standing as they do in con-
> trast to the usual run of Negro songs, led me to this conclusion [Johnson
> 1929, 84].

Johnson ran an advertisement in black newspapers in Virginia,
West Virginia, Georgia, Kentucky, and Ohio, offering $15 for a printed
version of the original ballad. He bought the Blankenship broadside
from Mrs. C.L. Lynn, West Rome, Georgia, for $12.50 (Ibid. 1927f, to
Lynn). She had inherited it from her grandmother (Lynn 1927).

Margaret Riddlesperger

Mrs. Lynn wrote that she had always stayed with her grandmother.
Federal census reports (1880, 1900, 1910, 1920, 1930) show that her
grandmother was Margaret Riddlesperger, born in South Carolina in
August 1829. In the 1880 census, Margaret is a widow. She was already
living west of Rome, Georgia, and she remained in that area until her
death in about 1925.

The 1910 census lists Margaret Riddlesperger as "black" and her
daughter, Mollie, as "mulatto," implying that Mollie's father was white.
Margaret's race, birthplace and birthdate, and surname suggest that she
had been a slave owned by a descendant of Christian Riddlesperger. He
was born ca. 1715 in Europe; emigrated to Pennsylvania in 1733; was
in Lancaster, Pennsylvania, in 1736; had moved to South Carolina by
1742; owned a plantation of more than a thousand acres, adjacent to
the Four Hole Swamp, by 1760; owned slaves; and died in 1790 (Riddlebarger 2010).

According to her granddaughter, Margaret Riddlesperger had
known John Henry. Unfortunately, Johnson did not obtain further
information.

Riddlesperger could have heard of John Henry and gone to see
him in action in Alabama, perhaps witnessing his contest and death. In
1887, when he died at Dunnavant, a rail connection between Rome and
Birmingham was provided by the Georgia Pacific and East Tennessee,
Virginia and Georgia lines (Cline 1997, 132–34). Thus, the trip of something over a hundred miles would have been practical.

Age of the Blankenship Broadside

In 1927, Guy Johnson thought that the Blankenship broadside was probably 25 or 30 years old, that is, that it was printed ca. 1900, possibly a little before (Johnson 1927f, to Lynn). MacEdward Leach challenged this notion: "The ballad here printed is certainly out of a popular literary tradition rather than a folk tradition, and it has little of the structure and style of a Negro folksong.... I feel that it is simply a literary reworking of folk material by a hack writer to capitalize on a growing popularity of John Henry. If that is true, it must be from the twenties" (Leach 1996, 97–98).

Leach's conclusion that the Blankenship broadside does not represent any folk tradition fails to take into account the common and constant musical sharing between whites and blacks. From the beginning "John Henry" belonged to both races. Blankenship's version fits comfortably into white folk tradition.

Leach's date is almost certainly wrong. Lynn provided the broadside in 1927, at which time she thought that Riddlesperger got it around 1895. Surely Lynn would not have entertained this belief if Riddlesperger had obtained it in the twenties, when they were living together.

Johnson could be wrong in dating it as early as 1900. The information given below suggests a date a decade or so later. However, Johnson's early date is supported by one of his colleagues.

> Professor Collier Cobb, University of North Carolina, tells me that he recalls having seen a *John Henry* ballad by Blankenship about 1900. He also says that in collecting folk songs he came across Blankenship productions several times, and he is fairly certain that this author was a white man [Johnson 1929, 86n1].

Two other broadsides published by W.T. Blankenship are self-dating. "The Great Titanic" could not have originated before the tragic sinking, April 15, 1912, and was probably written shortly thereafter (Blankenship 1912). The subject of "Our President" is the pending entry of the United States into World War I, which was in 1917 (Blankenship 1917). This suggests that the period of broadside activity for W.T. Blankenship was the 1910s.

The Blankenship Family

There is evidence of "Blenkinsop" nobility in northern England (Blankenship 2001, Roots Web 2010 and 1997). Thus, Blenkinsop Castle was awarded to Ranulph Blenkinsop ca. 1240 AD (Blankenship 2005). American Blankenships were not so well off early on. Ralph Blankenship (1662–1714) came to Henrico County, Virginia, in 1686, as an indentured servant.

Ralph had five sons in the 1690s. Son John and Elizabeth Hudson had a son, Hudson, a daughter, Amy, and other children. Amy Blankenship (b. ca. 1731) married William Turner. There were several early marriages among Hudsons, Turners, and Blankenships, and in later generations of Blankenships, "Hudson" and "Turner" appear as given names.

In 1880 Blankenships were concentrated in Virginia, West Virginia, Kentucky, Tennessee, and Missouri (Ibid.). Census records for Tennessee and adjacent Alabama suggest that they were "poor dirt farmers," as family members have stated.

Mark Twain's neighbor may have been the most famous Blankenship. "In Huckleberry Finn I have drawn Tom Blankenship exactly as he was. He was ignorant, unwashed, insufficiently fed; but he had as good a heart as ever any boy had" (Twain 1959, 397).

In north Georgia, ca. 1830, Blankenships were strongly allied with Cherokees. In 1836 a group of Blankenships and Cherokees moved to avoid the forced removal of the Cherokees that came in 1838–39. Led by John Buck Blankenship, whose wife was Cherokee, they moved to Coosa County, Alabama, where they married and secured land titles (Clinard 2008).

Coosa County was established in 1832 after the Creek Indians had ceded the land. Over the next few years, the remaining Creeks were forced out.

Forty-four Blankenship men from Alabama fought in the Civil War (Blankenship 2005). Sixty came from Tennessee.

In 1900 there were two areas of high concentrations of Blankenships in Alabama. One consisted of Coosa, Shelby, and Jefferson Counties. This group is partly accounted for by the Cherokee-Blankenship migration of 1836. The other consisted of Lawrence, Morgan, and Madison Counties in north Alabama, spilling over into Giles, Maury and adjacent counties in Tennessee.

The Blankenships have been strikingly musical. English folklorist Cecil Sharp collected ballads and songs from Blankenship women in North Carolina and Tennessee in 1916–1918 (Sharp 1932; I-131, 337, 57; II-129). A BLANKENSHIP-L query resulted in several members telling of family and professional string bands. For ten years, Junior Blankenship (Hillard Blankenship, Jr.) was lead guitarist for Ralph Stanley and the Clinch Mountain Boys (Wright 1993, 225–28). A Google search turned up several Blankenships in opera.

They may have been "poor dirt farmers" at one time, but today Blankenships are represented in every profession, often at high levels. They are frequently on television, in the local and national news, and there are plenty of Blankenship doctors, dentists, and other professionals. On September 21, 2010, a search for "Blankenship" at eBay (http://www.ebay.com/) turned up 162 items involving musicians (popular and classical), artists, authors, baseball stars, racing car drivers, Blankenship brand amplifiers, beauty queens, wedding photographs (such as that of Charles and Rosalind Blankenship, 1960), businesses, photographs of historical places (e.g., Blankenship's Bluff, Pierce City, Missouri), computer programming, Blankenship's Beer and Ale, personal letters (e.g., Mrs. T.B. Blankenship to her cousin, 1940), etc.

The Search for W.T. Blankenship

Jim Blankenship, Tammy Blankenship, Bob Blankenship, Sue Altice, Karen Steele, Pattie Cochran, and many others were generous, patient, and helpful in my search for W.T. Blankenship. Not knowing where the broadside publisher lived meant that all of the many men with that name had to be considered.

In March 2002 Karen Steele was trying to link a blind W.T. Blankenship, born in 1876, with her family. She had a photograph of him with his wife, Josephine. Knowing of the tradition of blind street musicians, this W.T. Blankenship seemed to me to be a promising candidate.

Also in March 2002 Tammy Blankenship notified me that a W.T. Blankenship broadside, "The Great Titanic," was being auctioned on eBay. The seller told me that it had come from an estate in Huntsville, Alabama.

In October 2002 I sent a letter to the editor of *The Huntsville Times*, briefly explaining my quest and requesting help. It was published, and I heard from Cecil Thomas, who had met a blind Blankenship in about 1927. He lived in "either Giles or Maury County," Tennessee. He "was blinded by an accident," and he "played the fiddle.... He was my father's uncle on his mother's side" (Thomas 2002).

Thomas referred me to his cousin, Alma Magowan, for more information, and I had telephone conversations with both (Thomas 2002, Magowan 2002). According to Thomas, "All those Blankenships were fiddlers.... One had one arm, yet played the fiddle." Magowan told me that Willie Blankenship had lived around Athens, Alabama, and that he was a blind singer and fiddler. She had met him in the 1930s. "He was a fine man—mean in his younger days." He had tried to blow up his boss, but the dynamite had exploded prematurely, blinding him. He probably lost his arm in the same accident, which nearly killed him.

If Thomas's recollection is right, his father's uncle had both arms—some other Blankenship was the one-armed fiddler. Magowan, on the other hand, identified Willie Blankenship as blind *and* one-armed. If "all" the Blankenships were fiddlers, confusion would be likely.

There have been one-armed fiddlers. Videos of Leonard Smith (1911–2000) can be found at YouTube 2009. Smith, who had lost his left arm, held the bow firmly upright between his crossed legs while he sawed the fiddle up and down against it, and fingered the strings, with his right hand.

Mrs. Ruby Mooney, Madison, Alabama, also replied to my 2002 query. She sent me a copy of a broadside, "Our President," from her mother's collection. Like "John Henry, the Steel Driving Man" and "The Great Titanic," it has "PRICE 5 CENTS W.T. BLANKENSHIP" printed at the bottom. Unlike the others, it gives a place: Huntsville, Alabama.

In November 2003 Thomas Hutchens, Huntsville Public Library, sent me a packet of information. In the 1920 city directory, Wm Blankenship, wife Tennie, lived at 11 McCullough Avenue. In 1922, Wm Blankenship, wife Tinnie, lived at 424 Washington. According to a 1914 license, W.T. Blankenship, 27, married Mrs. T.M. Morring, 45.

This was the man I had sought, a professional musician and native of Tennessee. He was marrying a native of Alabama. In 2006 Pattie Cochran provided a copy of a draft registration card, dated September 12, 1918, for William Turner "Blakenship," 11 McCullough Avenue, Huntsville.

"Blakenship" was 42 years old, born September 10, 1876. He was a self-employed musician. His wife was "Tinnie." He was of medium height and medium build, and he was blind. In 1914 he was 37 years old, not 27, as stated by the marriage license.

In 1920 William Blankenship, age 42, lived in Huntsville, Alabama, with his wife, Tennie, age 50. William was a "Musician" whose place of business was "Streets." Blindness was not mentioned in the census report, but it was noted that he could not read or write.

A blind street musician was the "perfect" person to have sold broadside ballads. William Turner Blankenship was the W.T. Blankenship of "John Henry, the Steel Driving Man."

In 2008 Pat Blankenship had recently started research on the family of her husband, Rollie Blankenship, Jr.

> W.T. was my husband's "Uncle Willie," his father's oldest brother. He remembers W.T. as being a very talented musician, playing the banjo as well

as any he ever heard. He also remembers very well his singing "John Henry, the Steel Driving Man," but has his doubts that he actually wrote it. He remembers his father singing it also. W.T. was blinded in a dynamite explosion, but he doesn't know at what age, since his (my husband's) memories were always of him being blind, but extremely perceptive.

In October 2010 Pat located Wilma Evans, a ninety-one-year-old daughter of John Wesley Blankenship (1894–1979), W.T.'s next younger brother. Wilma graciously provided information in a telephone interview (Evans 2010).

Uncle Willie, William T. Blankenship (September 10, 1876–March 16, 1960), was the oldest of four sons of Theodore Blankenship (1855–1936) and Delilah Cape Blankenship (1856–1933) (Blankenship 2010). According to the 1880 census, Delilah lived then with her parents, siblings, and young son in Marshall County, Tennessee. In 1900 Theodore and Delilah lived with William and two other sons in Weakley County, Tennessee. In 1910 the family lived in the Wickham Precinct of Limestone County, Alabama, near Athens. It now included "Roley" (Rollie L. Blankenship, age 7; Rollie, Jr.'s father) and Clarence (age 13), Willie's son by his first wife. Willie is "Bl" (blind). He is married and has been for fourteen years, meaning that he married ca. 1896, at about age 20. However, no wife is listed.

Thomas and Magowan think that the blind Blankenship musician they knew was related by marriage to the Attkissons. Indeed, Delilah Cape's mother, Willie's grandmother, was Martha C. Attkisson (Ibid.).

In the 1900 census Willie Blankenship is listed as single, and Clarence does not appear. Willie cannot read or write, but in the margin of the sheet is a handwritten note: "had common education." Clearly, he is blind already, since a "common education" would have emphasized reading and writing. The explosion that blinded him must have occurred before June 9, 1900, when the census was taken. Wilma Evans recalled being told that it happened when Willie was twenty-one years old, in 1897–98. It cost him his wife as well as his eyesight.

Family Recollections

On Wednesday, July 30, 2008, my wife, Edna, and I visited Rollie and Pat Blankenship at their home in a suburb south of Dallas, Texas. We got acquainted over lunch, after which we sat down for an hour and a half of talking for a digital recorder (Blankenship and Blankenship 2008).

At 6'2½" Rollie is an imposing figure (Figure 26). He has a gentle nature; "I am not hard headed." As a habitual reader, he is well informed.

Rollie was surprised to learn of Willie's fame in John Henry circles. As far as he knew, Willie had never been well known.

Willie turned fifty-eight in 1934, the year Rollie Blankenship, Jr., was born. By the time Rollie could form lasting memories, the 1940s had arrived and Willie was in his middle sixties.

Rollie set down his recollections.

MY MEMORIES OF W.T. BLANKENSHIP ("UNCLE WILLIE")

First of all, please bear in mind that my memories of Willie are mostly in the early 1940's at which time he was an old man, with snow white hair and mustache. My earliest memories are of him grabbing me, holding me tightly and tickling me with his mustache. He called it "woolin" me. Obviously, he was blind all of my life.

The account of his blindness was told to me by my father, as well as uncles, and was always the same. That was that he was working on a right-of-way for a railroad. He and another man were trying to remove a tree stump. They dug a hole and tried to place the (wooden) box of dynamite in the hole, but it didn't quite fit. They thought only fire could ignite it and were hammering on the box to force it into the hole when it exploded. The other man was killed and Willie was so badly injured that his internal organs were visible. The doctor said he couldn't possibly live and dismissed

Figure 26. Rollie Blankenship, Jr., at home in DeSoto, Texas, 2008 (photograph by the author).

him from the hospital. Neighborhood women took on the task of helping care for him, making poultices from herbs for his wounds and using whatever home remedies they knew about. Apparently it was spring or summer, because flies were very bad and they also took turns sitting with him fanning him to keep the flies away.

My memories are of him and Josie (Josephine Green, his third wife) living in a little shotgun house in Athens, Alabama. He had an enclosed wagon of sorts, like a gypsy wagon, that he took to the courthouse square on weekends (possibly during the week also—I just don't remember), from which he sold hand-twisted tobacco, soft drinks, candy, gum and such.

He twisted the tobacco himself; and it was in great demand.

I remember that he had very large and strong hands, apparently from twisting the tobacco. He also had a keen sense of hearing and recognition of voices. A story was told that once a man came to his wagon, made a small purchase and gave him a bill, identifying it as $10. Later, when he gave change to another person and gave it as a $10, the man said, "Willie, this is a $1.00 bill." Several days later, the same man came back and tried the same thing again. Willie recognized his voice and grabbed both his hands, almost crushing them. He asked someone nearby to identify the bill, and it was again a $1.00 bill. He held onto the guy, yelling for the police; and they came and arrested the man.

I remember his being a very talented musician, but the singing I remember was at home, or in that wagon. Whether it was just for personal entertainment or for the folks on the streets, I don't know. He played a banjo, juice harp and potato (which you said is called a sweet potato). If he ever played a fiddle, I was not aware of it. I recall him singing "John Henry," "Wildwood Flower," "Wreck on the Highway," "Great Speckled Bird," "Down in the Valley" and others that don't come to mind. I remember his singing a sad and mournful song about the Titanic, but can't recall any words from it. I didn't like it.

I moved from Alabama to Arkansas when I was about 11 and only saw him on very rare occasions after that. The last time I saw him was, I believe, in 1955. I had just gotten out of the Air Force and was visiting family in the area. He and Josie still lived in the same place and I stopped by. Although it had been years since I had seen him, when I walked into the house and spoke, he recognized my voice and called me by name [Blankenship 2010].

Mrs. Tennie Maten Morring was Willie's second wife. She was born in 1868 and had been the second wife of George Ewing B. Morring, whom she had married in October 1893 (Cowles 1999, Smitty 22031 2010). In February 1923 she died of cancer (*Community Builder* 1923).

In October 1924 Willie married Josephine Green (Figure 27) (Blankenship 2010). She was the wife remembered by Rollie Blankenship, Jr.

It is said that Rollie Blankenship, Jr., resembles Willie more than any other family member (see Figure 26). Willie was shorter, about 5'10", whereas Rollie is 6'2½".

Figure 27. William Turner Blankenship and Josephine Blankenship, date unknown. This degraded photograph is the only known image of William T. Blankenship discovered so far. Blankenship published a broadside of "John Henry, the Steel Drivin' Man" circa 1910, among the earliest printings of the song (courtesy Karen Steele).

Willie died in March 1960.

Rollie is the fourth and last child of Rollie L. Blankenship and his second wife, Offie Foster. The family lived in various communities in North Alabama, around Athens. Rollie, Sr., married Etta Viola Hutchinson in 1944. They moved to Arkansas when Rollie was about eleven. At sixteen he came back to Alabama, lived with relatives, and worked in their fields.

Although he loved school, circumstances allowed Rollie to go no further than the tenth grade. In 1951, as soon as he turned seventeen, he enlisted in the Air Force, which sent him to Texas. There he met and married Pat, went to college, and settled down.

All his memories of childhood are bad, and he thinks of Alabama as a "very poor, sorry state." "When I got to Texas, when I was seventeen years old, I thought the Lord had sent me to heaven."

On the farms of North Alabama, they made music, but bad things and hard times were all the people knew, so that's what their songs were about. When they started singing those "old, sad songs," such as "The Great Titanic," Rollie would leave the house.

Rollie, Wilma Evans, and Cecil Thomas agreed that their older male relatives were moonshiners. When Rollie lived in Paint Rock Valley, Alabama, the air was often thick with spirals of smoke from the stills. He said that the moonshiners around Flintville, Tennessee, where some of his relatives live, are now legal whiskey makers who sell their product to a commercial distillery.

Willie Blankenship may have been a leader in the Ku Klux Klan. Rollie recalled being taken to a big Klan rally in Athens, Alabama, one night when he was five or six years old. People were dressed in white sheets, holding burning torches, and there was a lot of shouting and various kinds of "hoopla." Rollie was scared to death by "all those people dressed up like goats."

At the top of the courthouse steps sat a big wicker chair. After the proceedings had gone on for a while, a Klansman dressed in a red robe was led out by two people, one on each arm, and seated in the wicker chair. Rollie supposed that he was the Grand Dragon.

At the end of the rally, the process was repeated. Two people led the Grand Dragon away, one on each arm. Rollie later saw other Klan events, but never again did he see a leader be escorted in that fashion. He thought that the red-robed man must have been blind. Since Uncle Willie was the only blind man in the county, he has always suspected that he was the Grand Dragon.

Rollie recalled that Willie had a lot of common sense. He would not accept charity. He made a living selling candy bars, cold drinks, tobacco, and other sundries from his "little gypsy wagon" with a wooden top and a window in the side. Friends would pull it for him to the courthouse square in Athens, and people would make a point of going by and buying something. A 1923 news account of Tennie's death reads, "Mr. Blankenship is blind, yet he manages to make a comfortable living by making mops and has a small business in this city" (*Community Builder* 1923).

Willie had many ways to earn small amounts. In addition to candy, cold drinks, other sundries, mops, and twisted tobacco, he sang and played on the streets for contributions, and he sold his broadsides. He may be the author of some of the ballads on those broadsides. However, his "John Henry, the Steel Driving Man" does not appear to be the original version.

In November 2010 Edna and I visited Wilma Evans at her home near Somerville, Alabama, and I recorded a lively interview (Figure 28)

(Evans 2010). Wilma told us things about her Uncle Willie that we probably could not have discovered otherwise.

Wilma, who has lived all her life in North Alabama, had good childhood memories and a more favorable opinion of the area than her cousin Rollie. Unlike Rollie's, her family was stable.

Like Rollie, Wilma recalled their Uncle Willie as a kindly man who enjoyed playing with them as children.

> I remember goin' to uncle Willie's house when I was 'bout eight or ten years old. He lived in Athens, Alabama.
>
> He'd been blind since he was twenty-one years old. He used to set me on his knee and pick the banjo and sing "John Henry," and some other songs, too, he would sing to me.
>
> Then he'd decide that we needed fish for supper, and he'd go and buy fish, and bein' blind, he would clean 'em hisself. 'Course Mom and Aunt Josie had to redo it, but, anyway, we'd have fish for supper, and he'd tell us about our grandmothers and granddaddies.
>
> He told us about when he was twenty-one years old, and he was workin' on a road, to build a railroad. He had a bunch of dynamite. He and one of his friends decided to set off a dynamite, and they didn't think that anything but fire would set the explosion. But they got to hammerin' it with a rock, or a hammer of some sort, and it exploded and blinded him completely.

Figure 28. Wilma Evans, outside her home near Somerville, Alabama, November 23, 2010 (photograph by the author).

He was in real bad shape, they said, even his intestines showed some. But some women took him over, and they didn't think he would live, but they took real good care of him, and he survived it. He lived for years after then. Actually, I don't remember how old he was, but he was in his eighties when he died.

So far as I know, my uncle Willie was a real good old feller, and everybody loved him [Evans 2010].

I had packed up my recording equipment after interviewing Wilma, and we were sitting around chatting for a few minutes before Edna and I would leave, when Wilma said something that had me unpacking and setting up again for her to repeat it.

I had heard that my uncle Willie and this black man were friends. Now, I don't know if they were working on the road together or what, but that they got to talkin' and a-singin' together, and I have heard that the black man was involved in writing the songs. Now, whether that's true or not, I have no idea. That was just something I heard when I was a kid. Miss'ippi—that's where they said he was from.... I don't know if his name was the name of the song, "John Henry," or what it was, you know, what his name was [Ibid.].

Perhaps Willie's black friend brought "John Henry" from Copiah County, Mississippi, the home of John Henry Dabney. That could account for the appearance in the Blankenship text of a railroad timetable that is correct for Crystal Springs, Mississippi, ca. 1890: "She got up at midnight, caught that No. 4 train / 'I am going where John Henry fell dead.'"

It was probably around 1910 when Willie was making music with this friend from Mississippi. He was thirty-four years old and living with his parents in Limestone County, Alabama, near Athens. He could have met his Mississippi friend in any North Alabama community where a street musician could make a little money, e.g., Athens, Madison, Huntsville.

Who was the friend? Tommy Johnson was a famous Crystal Springs musician who traveled a lot. He never recorded "John Henry." Still, it is exciting to imagine that Tommy taught it to Willie.

Also in November 2010, Edna and I visited Cecil and Hazel Thomas at their home in Huntsville, Alabama (Thomas 2010).

There are some major discrepancies between the recollections of Rollie Blankenship and Wilma Evans and those of Cecil Thomas and Alma Magowan. Cecil recalled visiting a blind Blankenship who was plowing a field near Columbia, Tennessee, in about 1927. Rollie and Wilma did not recall that their uncle Willie ever lived there or that he ever farmed, though he did keep a garden.

Alma met Willie in the early 1930s, stated correctly that he lived around Athens, Alabama, and remembered him as a blind singer and fiddler. She heard that he was blinded in an accidental dynamite explosion that occurred while he was trying to set a charge to blow up his boss, but Rollie and Wilma were always told that it happened on a construction job. According to Cecil, who got it from Alma, Willie was blinded in the mid–1920s, but both Wilma and the census of 1900 contradict this date. Wilma said that Willie was twenty-one years old when he was blinded, making it 1897–98, consistent with the census indication that he was blind in 1900.

Some of Alma's information about Willie is accurate. However, the story of his trying to kill his boss is hearsay. Rollie and Wilma's account, that Willie's accident occurred on a construction job, is more plausible.

Cecil and Alma are correct in claiming that they are related to Willie by marriage. They are Attkissons, and Willie's grandmother on his mother's side was Martha C. Attkisson Cape (Blankenship 2010). According to Cecil, the Attkisson and Blankenship families of Giles and Maury Counties, Tennessee, and vicinity, are closely allied and have often intermarried.

Misery and Bad Luck and Stuff

For Rollie's people in North Alabama, life there was "misery and bad luck and stuff." Willie's life is an example. His accident blinded him and cost him his wife and baby son. For the next fifteen years or so, he lived with his parents.

He married his second wife, Tennie Morring, in 1914. A year and a half after Tennie's death in 1923, he married Josephine Green, with whom he lived in Athens, Alabama, in a little "railroad shotgun house" until some time around 1955. Then he and Josie moved to Flintville, Lincoln County, Tennessee, where his younger brother, Walter Gray Blankenship (1896–1972), looked after them. Willie died there on March 16, 1960.

His blindness resulted from a careless act of youthful ignorance. He tried to make the best of it, and he succeeded to the extent that he was self-sufficient and gained two devoted wives.

When Guy Johnson printed the Blankenship broadside in 1929, Willie was fifty-three years old. He lived for another thirty years. Ironically, Johnson knew nothing about him, and Willie never learned of his fame.

Leon Harris earned his living as a pipe fitter in the Silvis Shops of the Rock Island Line. He was a writer, social activist, and amateur John Henry scholar.

10

I Had to Eat

I have tried faithfully to get the story of John Henry.
No folk-song fiend has searched more diligently than
have I. But I have failed. Anyone who tries it will fail.
—Leon R. Harris

On February 12, 1927, *The Chicago Defender* published a letter from Guy Johnson to Dewey R. Jones, a prominent African American journalist and later a member of Franklin Roosevelt's Black Cabinet (Johnson 1927b, Hall 2011). Jones' column, "Lights and Shadows: A Little Bit of Everything," published poetry. Members of his club, Lambda Alpha Sigma, were called "Lasers."

> What About This, Lasers?
> Dear Dewey R.: As a constant reader of the Defender and as one who is trying to help the Negro race preserve its great body of folk songs, I am writing to ask if you might not be able to help me out in a certain matter. I am making a study of a song known as John Henry—sometimes as John Hardy ... the most distinctive ballad which the Race has produced.... Would it be at all possible for you to request the Lasers to send you such versions of John Henry or John Hardy as they know? I will go so far as to offer a reward of five dollars to the Laser who sends in the best version, the only conditions being that the version must never have been printed and that the sender shall tell when and where he first heard the song... [Johnson 1927b].

Jones urged the Lasers to comply with Johnson's request, set an eight-week deadline, and added five dollars to the reward (Jones 1927).

Leon R. Harris told of his zeal for John Henry.

> I am sending herewith a version of the song, "John Henry, The Steel-Drivin' Man," as the railroad "Graders" sing it. I agree with Mr. Johnson when he says that it is the most distinctive ballad the Race has produced....
> The ballad, by special right, belongs to the railroad builders. John Henry was a railroad builder. It belongs to the pick-and-Shovel men,—to the scraper and wheeler man,—to the skinners,—to the steel-drivers, to the

men of the railroad construction camps, which they call the "gradin' camp."
It is a song by Negro laborers everywhere, but none can sing it as they can
sing it, because none honor and revere the memory of John Henry as do
they. I have been a "Rambler" all my life,—ever since I ran away from the
"white folks" when twelve years old,—and I have worked with my people in
railroad grading camps from the Great Lakes to Florida and from the Atlan-
tic to the Missouri River, and, wherever I have worked, I have always found
someone who could and would sing of John Henry [1927].

His twenty-two-stanza version won the contest. According to Johnson, it was "by far the best version of 'John Henry' that I have ever seen—
and I have seen a great many. It seems to me to have the real ring of the
hammer in it" (1927 to Harris).

John Henry Scholar

Harris is important in John Henry research. Here are his
conclusions.

I believe ... that the following are facts:
1. John Henry really lived.
2. He beat a steam-drill down and died doing it.
3. Li'l Bill was his "buddie" or helper.
4. He worked for a railroad construction contractor.
5. His wife('s), or his woman's(,) name was "Lucy." [I have never heard any
   other woman's name in a "John Henry" song.]

These are probabilities:
1. He died in the early (')70's.
2. He was a Virginian.
3. He worked on the C. & O. road or on a branch of that system.
4. His "captain's" name was "Tommy Walters,"—probably an assistant
   foreman(,) however [Harris 1927].

It is strange that Harris, with his widespread experience, "never
heard any other woman's name in a 'John Henry' song" than "Lucy." His
contribution to Guy Johnson's book is the only occurrence of "Lucy"
in versions of "John Henry" published from 1909 through 1933. "Polly
Ann" is very frequent, appears in the Blankenship broadside, and was
heard as early as 1915 (Blankenship n.d., White 1928, 191). "Julia Ann"
was recovered ca. 1909 (Combs 1967, 165). Perhaps Harris let his personal preference for "Lucy" guide his recollections.

I accept Harris' facts one, two, and four, and I am neutral toward
three. I reject all of his probabilities. John Henry did not die in the early
1870s, he was not a Virginian, he did not work on the C & O, and his
captain was not Tommy Walters.

Writer

Leon R. Harris describes himself as, first of all, a writer, adding quickly that he also has worked as a farmer, steel mill employee, teacher and railwayman, "because, of course, I had to eat" [1956].

Leon Ray Harris (1886–1960) was "a Poet and a Crusader, for Steel and Railroad Workers ... a Nationally Known Moline Man" (Klann 1952a). The following biography is based on census records (1900, 1920, 1930), World War I and World War II draft cards, and other sources (Mather 1915, Du Bois 1919, Kerlin 1921, 21 and 1923, 180–82, Hope 1940, Klann 1952a and 1952b, Harris 1956 and 1960, Douglas 1997, 716n139, Reid 2010).

He was born on October 18, 1886, in Cambridge, Guernsey County, Ohio. By his own reckoning, he was at least three-fourths white. His mother and paternal grandparents were white. His father was William Harris and his mother Catherine Albright Harris (Mather 1915). Guernsey County, Ohio, is in Appalachia about halfway between Columbus, Ohio, and Pittsburgh, Pennsylvania (ARC 2011).

Leon lived with his mother for his first two years, with his mother's family for the next two, and then in a Cambridge orphanage, which provided his earliest memories (Du Bois 1919). At age six, the orphanage sent him to school. In about 1895 he was placed in a white foster home on a farm near New Columbus, Owen County, Kentucky. For three years or so, Lilly Hudson taught him at home (Mather 1915, Stamper and Stamper 2011).

In the census of 1900, he was a thirteen-year-old lodger in the home of eighty-year-old farmer Silas Hudson. His teacher and foster mother was thirty-two-year-old Delilah "Lilly" Hudson, single.

Leon left the Hudsons to further his education. According to Berea College records, "Lillian Hudson, a teacher," provided his reference for admission in the fall of 1900 (Bradley 2011). In the light of Lilly Hudson's role in securing his admission to Berea College and his later contacts with the Hudson family, it seems clear that Harris did not "run away from the 'white folks.'" He left under cordial circumstances.

It was not a good time to be a black student at Berea. The president, William Goodell Frost, encouraged campus segregation (Baskin 2008). In 1901, after one year, Leon left.

Perhaps he foresaw things to come. In 1904 state legislator Carl Day pushed for legislation to outlaw racially integrated schools in Kentucky (Berea College was the only one). The Day Law was enacted in 1904 (Brinson 2011). In 1908 the U.S. Supreme Court upheld the law over the dissent of Judge John Marshall Harlan, a Kentuckian who had also dissented in *Plessy v. Ferguson* (1896), the case that made "separate but equal" the law of the land.

The February 26, 1903, issue of *The Citizen*, Berea's newspaper, carried this item: "Leon Harris, formerly a student here, is now in Booker T. Washington's school at Tuskegee, Alabama" (Racer 1903). He attended Tuskegee Normal and Industrial Institute in 1901–04, majoring in agriculture (Ferguson 2011). He spent the first year in the Night School, "designed for young men and women who earnestly desire to educate themselves, but who are too poor to pay even the small charge made in the Day School." After that he attended the Day School.

In April 1904, for financial reasons, Leon left Tuskegee without finishing a degree but having made important friends. He went to work for a dairy in Birmingham, where he first heard "John Henry" (Johnson 1929, 91).

He was hired a well-paying job at a dairy in Rock Island, Illinois, intending to earn money for Iowa State College, Ames, where George Washington Carver had studied and worked, but when he showed up for work, he was rejected because he was "colored." In Davenport, Iowa, in 1904–07, he worked first as a yardman and then as a laborer with the McCarthy Improvement Company, which built and paved roads (Mather 1915). At a Baptist church, he met Gertrude May Bell (1885–1955), a well-educated and musically talented woman from Des Moines. They married in early September 1904 and had a daughter, Henrietta, in about 1906.

In about 1909, Leon went first to Danville, Virginia, and then to High Point, Guilford County, North Carolina, where he farmed. He was very successful, and he taught his methods to others. By 1912 he was also teaching school for children and adults living in the vicinity of High Point, Florence, and Jamestown.

Gertrude was not happy living in the South, and as war loomed, steel shortages were rumored. In late 1914, the Harris family left for Portsmouth, Ohio, where Leon worked first for the A. Laughlin Co., Open Hearth Furnaces, and then in the steel mill of the Whittaker-Glessner Company at New Boston, adjacent to Portsmouth (Willard 1916). That year he wrote a poem, "The Steel Makers," and published it in an employees' magazine, "Safety Hints." It was widely reprinted without payment.

THE STEEL MAKERS (stanzas 1 and 8)
Filled with the vigor such jobs demand,
Strong of muscle and steady of hand,
Before the flaming furnaces stand

The men who make the steel.
'Midst the sudden sounds of falling bars,
'Midst the clang and bang of cranes and cars,
Where the earth beneath them jerks and jars,
They work with willing zeal.

For of what they make we are servants all,
They have bound our lives in an iron thrall,
We do their bidding, we heed their call,
As they work with willing zeal.
So tap your heats with a courage bold,
You're worth to your world a thousand fold
More than the men who mine her gold,
You men who make her steel! [Kerlin 1923, 182–84].

From that time, Harris considered himself to be a writer.

In 1918 he left Portsmouth for Richmond, Wayne County, Indiana, where he was a "stationary engineer" in a factory (1920 census). There he founded and edited *The Richmond Blade,* a newspaper for African Americans. The *Blade* disappeared when Harris left under KKK pressure in 1921 (Harris 1956).

He moved his family to Moline, Rock Island County, Illinois, where for the next thirty years he worked as a pipe fitter in the Silvis Shops of the Chicago, Rock Island and Pacific Railroad Company. In 1925 he published his John Henry story, "The Steel Drivin' Man," which was republished with slight alterations in 1957 (Harris 1925 and 1957, Dundes 1973, 561–67).

After Harris retired, he and Gertrude moved to Los Angeles to be near their daughter, Henrietta Whiteside, and her family. Gertrude died five months later, in May 1955. In November 1957, he married Addie Graves, a registered nurse (*California Eagle* 1957).

Leon Harris died on January 22, 1960. At about 8:30 p.m., he suddenly dropped dead in the middle of a telephone conversation (Harris 1960). He was seventy-three years old.

Fact in Fiction

Over the years Leon Harris published many poems, short stories, and articles, as well as four books, the last of which is a novel (Harris 1918, 1946, 1948, 1959). The publisher suggested its title.

Because there is no accepted definition of the Negro who passes as white, I suggest that you title your book *Run, Zebra, Run!* The zebra is black and white. Is he black with white stripes, or white with black stripes? Put him against a white background and he is black; put him against a black background and he is white. When his camouflage fails, he becomes prey to the beasts of the jungle and his only escape is to run [Harris 1959].

Edward Uhlan, President
Exposition Press Inc.

The protagonist of the novel, Leonard Hall, is the son of a white mother and mulatto father. Leonard could pass for white, but as a child he is abused and not allowed to forget that he is a "nigger."

This does not reflect Leon Harris's own life. He could not pass for white.

Even so, the story of Leonard Hall, up to about age thirteen, is partly autobiographical. Harris patterned characters after those from his own life. The fictional names Leonard Hall, Catherine Vanalban, William Hall, and Silas Harker resemble the real names Leon Harris, Catherine Albright, William Harris, and Silas Hudson. Leonard's father, Jaques Halldau, was a musician; so was Leon's father, William Harris. Leonard was born in Bridgeville, Ohio; Leon Harris in Cambridge (about 15 miles east of Bridgeville). Silas Harker was a preacher, farmer, and lawyer in Kentucky; so was Silas Hudson. Leonard and Leon both spent some of their early years in an orphanage.

Run, Zebra, Run! is sprinkled with admirable whites, e.g., George Vanalban, Sr., Catherine Vanalban, Silas Harker, and Bernice Harker. Others are racist bigots.

Harris was coy: "I don't want you or anyone else to say that this is an autobiographical novel, but I can't help what you think" (Klann 1959). Klann inferred that "his early life must have helped him write the book." Harris' real life with the Silas Hudson family in Kentucky was much better than the fictional life of Leonard Hall with the Silas Harker family. He maintained good relations with the Hudson family (Stamper 2011).

At nearly fourteen, Leon Harris left the Hudsons for Berea College. He arrived in time for the fall term, 1900.

Crusader

In 1922 Leon Harris and three fellow Tuskegeeites, James P. Davis, Gilchrist Stewart, and Cornelius R. Richardson, founded the National Federation of Colored Farmers, which was incorporated by Harris and Davis in 1930 and which Harris served as secretary, then president (Hope 1940, Reid 2010). In 1928–39 Harris edited their newspaper, *The Modern Farmer*, the first issue of which is dated March 1, 1929. The organization worked to assist black farmers in every possible way.

National media attention resulted from the personal relationships that NFCF officials had with Claude Barnett, founder of the Associated Negro Press. He likewise attended Tuskegee Institute synchronous with Davis, Harris, and Richardson. The team of urban agrarians, attorneys, political activists, and a publisher proved formidable. Thus the NFCF combined numerous Tuskegee-Institute lessons, agricultural reform and effective business practices with public awareness to gain attention and undermine localized, white opposition to black potential [Reid 2010, 6].

In 1929 Davis set up a black farmers' purchasing cooperative in Howard, Mississippi, a remote community near the eastern edge of the Mississippi Delta, about five miles south-southeast of Tchula (Hope 1940, 49–52). The participating farmers immediately saw the price of their staples cut by more than half. The objections of local white farmers, who operated their own commissaries, were overcome through legal procedures at the state government level. Harris himself had face-to-face dealings with some white farmers.

Leon Harris was very active with the NAACP. For many years he was president of the Tri-City Branch as well as a state director.

He served President Hoover on a housing committee; organized a union at the Silvis Shops; was Worshipful Master of Arsenal Lodge 60, AF & AM; and Superintendent of the Sunday School at St. Paul AME Church (Burroughs 1932, Harris 1960). Among those that he knew and corresponded with were W.E. B. Du Bois; Martin Luther King, Jr.; and Thurgood Marshall.

He did all this while holding a day job and writing prolifically.

Setting an Example

On April 15, 1956, *The Greensboro Daily News*, Greensboro, North Carolina, ran a remarkable piece by Leon R. Harris, who had seen an article "datelined Greensboro, N.C.," in a Los Angeles newspaper about six months earlier (Harris 1956). The report told how a white parent had made two attempts to enroll his children in the local Negro school of the Guilford-Florence community. Thirty-four whites had signed a letter urging that the County Board of Education admit Negroes to the white school.

These were not typical actions of Southern white parents in the wake of *Brown v. Board of Education* (1954). Harris believed that they were a result of his having taught in that community about forty-five years earlier.

Starting in 1909–10, he farmed with great success at High Point,

Guilford County, North Carolina, and he taught his methods to other African American farmers in the area. Further, as he and Gertrude taught Sunday School, they began to have evening sessions, both on Sunday and during the week, emphasizing education.

It didn't take the local people long to figure out that Harris was exceptional. He was intelligent, practical, and well educated, qualities that would make him a fine schoolteacher. When he passed a test in Greensboro and was certified to teach first grade, he became the first certified teacher the colored school at Florence had ever had. He was the principal of the Jamestown Colored School in 1912 (Mather 1915).

Soon he started evening classes, on Mondays and Wednesdays, for adults to learn to read and write. Regular Friday night classes ranged over many subjects, such as the best farming methods, history, hygiene, and current events. White people began coming and listening in at the doors and windows. On one occasion Harris took the class outside for a geography lesson followed by questions and answers. Whites and blacks participated, making a kind of integrated class.

Finally a white tenant farmer from "up in the Blue Ridge" approached him.

> "Prof., I hear you're having pretty good luck teaching those old colored folks to read and write. How about giving me some lessons."
> I seized the opportunity and gave him his first lessons then and there. That winter I taught every adult member of his family [Harris 1956].

Meanwhile, Gertrude was doing needlework and visiting many elderly white women to pick up tips on technique. In exchange, she would teach and brush them up on the three R's.

At the community's big corn shucking, segregated dining was the policy. White men ate in the dining room, black men in the kitchen.

> After washing my hands I entered the kitchen and started to sit down at our table. Our host called from the dining room.
> "Come in here, Prof. You've got to eat in here."
> I walked inside the dining room and took a seat near the center of the table. A white man sat beside me. Our host called again.
> "Here, Pres. Where's Uncle Pres? Come in here, Pres. Sit there at the head of the table. I want you to ask the blessing."
> Uncle Pres Raper asked the longest blessing I have ever heard. He prayed for everybody, sick or well—for our schools and churches [Ibid.].

After Harris showed the county superintendent of schools and other officials how his school was running over with students, they planned a new school for a site adjacent to the church at Florence. Having heard of the Rosenwald Fund, the instrument through which Julius

Rosenwald, President of Sears, Roebuck and Company, had recently begun to fund the construction of schools for black students, Harris applied and received its assistance.

> We should have a school of not less than three rooms. The cost would be evenly divided between the county, the Rosenwald Fund, and the people of the community.
>
> All of us got together, white and Negro. The white people donated all the timber for the rough lumber and some gave money. I took my axe into the woods with the others. We felled the trees, cut the logs and hauled them to the sawmill. But every sill under that schoolhouse was hand-hewn from good old oak—the best of timber from Mr. Fin Hiatt's place [Harris 1956].

Leon Harris knew he would never teach in the new school. "Gertrude's father had passed. Her mother was blind and needed care. The war was going on in Europe. I needed that war work and high wages" (Ibid.).

> I remember the day we went away. We went to Florence and for the last time walked through the completed building. The painters were applying the finishing touches. A seven months' term would soon commence. Three teachers had been employed. Then, too, the county had employed a home economics teacher, Mrs. Faulkner. She would have classes for the girls twice a week. And now we had a Negro farm extension agent. He had to work in three or four counties, but there was no limit to the service he would be able to give Negro farmers.
>
> On our way home Mr. Clay Briggs, his wife and a few of our other white friends stopped us. Mr. Briggs had been one of our best friends. We said our farewells. Only twice during my lifetime have I seen white people shed tears when I was parting from them. Both times they were white people of the rural South [Ibid.].

In the database of Rosenwald schools maintained by Fisk University, there is a Florence school whose construction date is before 1918 (Fisk University 2001). This may be Harris' school.

Its historic name was "Florence School." It was a "two-teacher" type "built under Tuskegee" at a total cost of $1650.00, $395 of which came from "Negroes," $5.00 from "Whites," $950.00 from "Public," and $300.00 from "Rosenwald." The non-monetary contributions from whites described by Harris (timber) could be part of the "Public" amount.

Perhaps Leon Harris paved the way for racial harmony and school integration in the minds of a few dozen rural whites around the community of Florence, North Carolina. However, the first North Carolina public schools to integrate did so in the mid–1960s, and the state first met the requirements of *Brown v. Board of Education* in the school year 1971–72 (Currie 2005).

Harris had deep and complex feelings about the races in America. His resilience under abuse is remarkable. If he harbored resentment or bitterness, he overcame it. Perhaps he really followed the principles that he learned at Tuskegee.

> You must be industrious.
> You must never hate anybody.
> You must help your race [Harris 1956].

The Silas Hudson Family

Leon Harris stayed in touch with the Hudsons. When he attended a Hudson family reunion in Kentucky, he "was treated as a member of the family" (Klann 1959). He "attended a Methodist church and was asked to substitute for the pastor in the pulpit," which he did. He also spoke at the reunion.

It is not clear how many Hudson family reunions Harris attended. Georgia Green Stamper, Silas Hudson's great-great-granddaughter, recalls one in 1952.

When I was a young child, I remember Mr. Harris visiting our home, specifically my grandfather. He was in the area to attend the Hudson Reunion. According to the reunion records, this would have been Labor Day weekend, 1952. My father was the president of the reunion that year and he asked Mr. Harris to offer our prayer of thanksgiving—grace—before we began the meal. I recall my mother commenting afterwards that Mr. Harris recited the same "grace" that my grandfather always did, and she wondered if the prayer had been handed down from Silas Hudson. Later, we came to understand from other older relatives that this indeed was the prayer that Silas—my grandfather's grandfather—recited before meals: "Our Father, accept our thanks for these and our many blessings. Pardon and forgive our sins and save us, in your name we ask it, Amen" ...

According to a newspaper article about the reunion "Leon Harris, of Moline, ILL., ... gave a very interesting talk on the life of S.A. Hudson and Lillian Hudson Cooke who raised him from childhood, and told of the Christian training he received in their home.... He closed with a poem written by himself and dedicated to Mrs. Lillian Cooke, entitled, 'To An Unknown Teacher'" ...

According to my mother's stories, Leon was treated pretty much like a child of the family. Given his intelligence and personality—both of which would have appealed to the Hudsons—and knowing their kindness, albeit not completely devoid of the racial prejudice of their time and place, I suspect this is true [Stamper 2011].

Silas Hudson's daughter Delilah changed her name to "Lillian" (Stamper and Stamper 2011). She turned thirty-three in June 1900, so she was in her late twenties when Leon Harris arrived at her home (census).

Close Relations

A Catharine Albright is enumerated in Cambridge, Ohio, in the census of 1870. She is the one-year-old daughter of Jacob Albright, a day laborer with no real estate and a personal estate valued at $200. She was seventeen years old in 1886, when Leon Harris was born, and she could have been his mother.

Ernie Stamper drew my attention to the Zontini Family Tree at Ancestry.com, according to which Martha Catherine (Emma) Albright was born on October 12, 1869, in Ohio (Ibid.). On February 10, 1890, she married Evan Carl Walters in Cambridge, Ohio. This is probably the year that Leon Harris was put in the orphanage in Cambridge. Martha Catherine Albright could have been his mother.

Charles Jefferson Albright, retired publisher, also lived in Cambridge. His real estate was valued at $15,000 and his personal estate at $12,000. In 1855–57 he served in the U.S. House of Representatives. It is not known how he may have been related to Jacob Albright.

William Harris was a musician who liked circus work and traveled a lot (Klann 1952a). He is said to have taken no interest in his son. Even so, Leon helped his father in his old age.

Leon's father may have been the William Harris who played trumpet with the Silas Green orchestra in 1932, when the show was laying over in Brunswick, Georgia (Abbott 2007, 347). "Silas Green from New Orleans" was a stage character and musical comedy whose name was taken in 1911 for an African American tented minstrel show (Ibid., 314). William Harris is also listed for the Silas Green bands of 1936–38 and 1940 and for the side show band of John Robinson's Circus in 1927 (Ibid., 382, Bradbury 1986).

A reader of Leon's brief biographies could construe that he was estranged from his biological family. For example, W.E. B. Du Bois summarized his early life as follows.

> His father was a roving musician and never took the slightest interest in him. He was separated from his mother at the age of two, and from his mother's family when four years old, being made a ward of an orphan asylum. The asylum placed him in the Cambridge grade schools at the age of six and he was in the fourth grade when they gave him away [1919].

Actually, Leon reconnected with both of his parents. He was able to help his elderly father "considerably, both materially and otherwise" (Klann 1952b). At age ninety, his father lived in Cambridge, Ohio.

When his mother was critically ill, Leon arranged to see her in such a fashion that only she and her pastor would know who he was. She died a few days later, and he attended her funeral, where only her pastor and the undertaker knew his family connection. "They (my half-brothers and other relatives) were pretty prominent people. I didn't want them to know that she was my mother; I didn't want to embarrass them. Maybe, for a minute, my blood did boil a little" (Ibid.).

Run, Zebra, Run! is Leon Harris' statement on race. It is dedicated

TO
MY MOTHER

＝＝ ＝＝ ＝＝

When he was about six months old, in 1835, Captain Dabney's family moved from tidewater Virginia to Hinds County, Mississippi.

11

Mississippi Virginians

John Henry's cap'n Tommy,—
V'ginny gave him birth;
Loved John Henry like his only son,
And Cap' Tommy was the whitest man on earth.
—Leon R. Harris [Johnson 1929, 92]

"The Captain" of the ballad and legend of John Henry was Captain Frederick Yeamans Dabney. He gained his rank in the Civil War and was called "Captain Dabney" thereafter. This may account for the nearly universal appearance of "Captain," instead of other terms for a boss, in "John Henry."

In Leon Harris' version of the ballad (Chapter 10), the boss is "Cap' Tommy." "Tommy" is a plausible mutation of "Dabney." The unfamiliar and awkward "Dabney," though accurate, would not have lasted long in tradition.

Harris' "V'ginny gave him birth" describes Fred Dabney. He was born in Fredericksburg, probably at his mother's home at Snowden. His father was Judge Augustine "Gus" Dabney. Even though Fred's family moved to Hinds County, Mississippi, before he was a year old, his identification as a Virginian was so strong that he went there to enlist in the Civil War.

He was very close to his wealthy uncle, Colonel Thomas Dabney, the leader of the Virginians who established a colony in Hinds County, Mississippi, in 1835. Colonel Dabney was widely known for his humane treatment of slaves (Smedes 1965, 47).

Fred's sister, Mary Dabney Ware "adored" Fred. She wrote, "He was so handsome and big and strong, and his heart and soul and mind were all built on a big scale" (1923). This was the kind of man who could have "loved John Henry like his only son."

John Henry was born and raised on Burleigh Plantation, owned by Colonel Dabney, who was a role model for both Fred Dabney and

John Henry. The character of the Dabneys is consistent with the opinion of Charles C. Spencer, water boy and tool carrier for John Henry, that "good old John Henry" "lived for honor" (Spencer 1927, February). To know the Dabney family is to know John Henry.

Normans

According to Captain Charles William Dabney, "We claim to be of the same origin as the Daubeneys of England, who are descended from Sir William D'Aubigné, Knight, who came over to England with William the Conqueror" (1937). William the Conqueror, Duke of Normandy, led the Norman invasion and conquest of England in 1066. Dabney ancestors are believed to include Vikings who settled in Normandy, and gave it its name (from "Northman" or "Norseman") around 900 AD (Amick 2011a).

From 193 to 197 AD, the province was part of the Roman empire ruled by Clodius Albinus. It is believed that "Dabney" is derived from "Albinus": Albinus—Aubigny—d'Aubigné—Dabney. The English consistently use the spellings "Daubeny" and "Daubeney" and the Americans "Dabney."

England

In England, the Daubeneys were aristocrats.

The d'Aubignes were part of the dominant Norman faction in England, marrying into the English aristocracy, later becoming knights. Thirteen generations of the family lived in Sharrington Hall, a manor house near Melton Constable in Norfolk—by this time they had the surname Daubeney (sometimes just Daubney) [Dabney 2000].

They held various high positions, Knight and Sheriff, Lord, Archdeacon, Baron of Magna Carta. Daubeneys are said to have built King Ina's palace, Barrington Court, and Wayford House, in or near South Petherton. C.W. Dabney cites a "dozen or more" of the family's coats-of-arms listed in Burke's *General Armory* (1937).

Virginia

On September 27, 1664, Cornelius DeBaney was given title to 200 acres in Virginia "on Tottopotomoy's Creek, South Side of York River, a little below the fort of Manaskin" (Dabney 1937). Virginia land grants of 1666 and 1667 name "Cornelius Debney" and "Cornelius Dabony," but a letter of June 29, 1678, is signed "Cornelius Dabney," the standard form the surname took in America by 1700. Cornelius was a British agent who dealt with, and knew the language of, the Pamunkey Indians. Today there is a Pamunkey Indian Reservation and Museum at King William, Virginia.

According to C.W. Dabney, Cornelius Dabney probably came to America following the execution of Charles I, 1649, who had been supported by the Cavaliers (Amick 2011a). "The extent of this sudden influx of Cavalier immigration to the colony was so great that while the population of Virginia was but fifteen thousand in 1650, it had increased to forty thousand by 1870" (Thwaites 1910, 76).

Figure 29 shows part of the Dabney family tree (Amick et al. 2011a, Dabney 1937 and 1888, Smedes 1965, following xlvii). It is believed that the Dabneys descend from Cornelius Dabney, the king's agent.

George Dabney (?–?)
(Dabney's Ferry, near Hanovertown, Pamunkey River)
+ Grace Smith (1)

    Benjamin Dabney (1757–1806)
    (Lawyer, "Bellevue," Pamunkey River, King and Queen County)
    + Sarah Smith (2)
    (Father: Rev. Thomas Smith, pastor to George Washington)
    (Brother: Dr. John Augustine Smith, President of William and Mary's
       College, President of the College of Physicians of New York)

        Thomas Smith Gregory Dabney (1798–1885)
        ("Elmington," Chesapeake Bay and North River, Gloucester County,
           Virginia)
        ("Burleigh," Hinds County, Mississippi)
        ("Southern Planter")
        + Sophia Hill (2)
        (Father: Charles Hill, lawyer, rival of Benjamin Dabney)

            Susan Dabney (1840–1913)
            (Author of *Memorials of a Southern Planter*)
            + Lyell Smedes

    Philip Augustine Lee Dabney (1800 – 1878)
    (Lawyer in Virginia and, from 1835, Mississippi; also Probate Judge)
    + Elizabeth Osborne Smith (2)
    (Father: Yeamans Smith; Mother: Ann Osborne Marye)

        Frederick Yeamans Dabney (1835 – 1900)
        (Civil Engineer, Railroad Construction)
        + Agatha Ann Moncure
        (Father: Dr. John E. Moncure; Mother: Courts Hill)
        (Sophia Hill Dabney and Courts Hill Moncure were sisters)

Mary Smith Dabney (1842 – 1931)
(Author of a memoir)
+ William Lynch Ware

Thomas Gregory Dabney (1844 – 1929)
(Civil Engineer, "Father of Mississippi Levee System")
(Author of a memoir)
+ Frances Bowmar

Anna Letitia Dabney (1852 – 1946)
(Author of a memoir)
+ Thomas Marshall Miller

Martha Burwell Dabney (1802 – 1883)
+ Lewis Webb Chamberlayne
(Father: Edward Pye Chamberlayne; Mother: Mary Bickerton Webb)

John Hampden Chamberlayne (1838 – 1882)
(Subject of collected papers)
+ Mary Walker Gibson

Figure 29. Part of the Dabney family tree. (1), (2) = first, second wife (compiled by the author).

The early Dabneys in Virginia lived in a tidewater area that can be described roughly as extending from Richmond east to Chesapeake Bay and north to the vicinity of Fredericksburg. George Dabney lived on the Pamunkey River at Dabney's Ferry, near Hanovertown. His son Benjamin (1757–1806), a prominent lawyer, made his home at "Bellevue," near West Point, on the Pamunkey near its union with the Mattaponi to form the York River (Moorehead 1951).

In about 1804 Benjamin bought "Elmington," a plantation on the North River and Chesapeake Bay (Mason 1947). It exists today, with attractive gardens and a house that dates to about 1849.

Two of Benjamin's sons, Thomas (1798–1885) and Gus (1800–1878), are important in the John Henry story (Figures 30 and 31). Their childhoods of high privilege were marred by their father's death in 1806.

The next year their mother placed them under the care of her brother, Dr. John Augustine Smith. Thomas remained with Dr. Smith for nine years, but Gus was soon brought home, being deemed too fragile for the climate in Elizabeth, New Jersey, where the boys had been placed in boarding school (Smedes 1965, 7).

Thomas and Gus were very close. Thomas had an "iron constitution," but Gus was "never a strong child." By the time Thomas was nine, his "tender care and admiration ... for his gentle, studious brother, knew no bounds" (Ibid.). Thomas was Gus's protector and, to an extent, provider.

Shortly after Dr. Smith became President and Professor of Moral and Political Philosophy at the College of William and Mary, in 1814, both boys were sent there. They had their own house, and each had a cook and a body-servant (Ibid., 16).

Gus attended William and Mary in 1814–1815 and 1817–1819 (Swem 1941). Thomas did not graduate. When his mother remarried and moved away, Thomas returned home to manage Elmington.

Thomas "always believed that Gus was by nature fitted for a naturalist, and he deplored that his education was not turned in that direction" (Smedes 1965, 7). In fact, Gus became a lawyer and judge.

Thomas continued at Elmington as a planter. He married Mary Adelaide Tyler on June 6, 1820, but she died in 1823, and both their sons died young. On June 26, 1826, Thomas married Sophia Hill (1810–1860), who bore him sixteen children.

Her eighth child became a famous author. In 1887 Susan Dabney Smedes published much of her family's history in

Figure 30. (*top*) **Thomas Smith Gregory Dabney, 1798–1885 (Smedes, 1887, frontispiece).**
Figure 31. (*bottom*) **Philip Augustine Lee "Gus" Dabney, 1800–1878 (courtesy Lucius B. Dabney, Jr.).**

her best-selling book, *Memorials of a Southern Planter*. In the 1965 edition, editor Fletcher M. Green gave a valuable overview of the family.

Thomas Dabney was a very successful and wealthy planter of corn, wheat, rye, and tobacco at Elmington. Comfortable in high social circles, he was a friend of John Tyler, a future President of the United States, and other notables. In 1831 Governor John Floyd made him a colonel in the Virginia militia (Smedes 1965, 26). Thus, he became "Colonel Dabney."

He was a dashing figure and expert horseman. A man who had witnessed the militia's drills later testified, "Colonel Dabney's horse sprang into the air and seemed hardly to touch the ground, and we wondered how he kept his seat" (Ibid., 27).

Gus Dabney's first wife, Ann Robinson, died childless. In 1834 he married Elizabeth Osborne Smith. The eldest of their ten children was Frederick Yeamans Dabney, b. March 22, 1835, in Virginia (Dabney 1922).

The depression of the 1820s and '30s were hard times for Virginia planters (Green 1965, xxxii). Many of them bought cheaper and more fertile lands to the south and west and moved. Colonel Dabney toured Alabama, Mississippi, and Louisiana, looking for suitable property.

Mississippi

He settled in Hinds County, Mississippi, where he purchased 3,953 acres to put together Burleigh Plantation. A number of his relatives and friends caught the Mississippi fever and also moved.

Burleigh was about nine miles southwest of Raymond, where Gus made his home, practiced law, and served as probate judge. Judge Dabney struggled to support his family, while Colonel Dabney prospered. Their families were spoken of as "the Raymond Dabneys and the Burleigh Dabneys" or "the poor Dabneys and the rich Dabneys."

Other Virginians established plantations nearby. Some locations are sketched in Figure 32, where township-range-section examples are referenced to the Choctaw baseline and meridian. Present-day roads are drawn schematically. Burleigh and Locksley Plantations are from maps surveyed and drawn by Fred Y. Dabney (Dabney 1860 and 1873). These maps indicate that H. Campbell Smith owned property that was sandwiched between Burleigh and Locksley Plantations, bordering each. The Campbell Smith property is presumed to have been Midway Plantation, the boundaries of which are not known. Woodburne Plantation is from a map constructed by Charles D. Powell from land records (Powell 1993). The location of Auburn Plantation is approximated from Major Thomas G. Dabney's description.

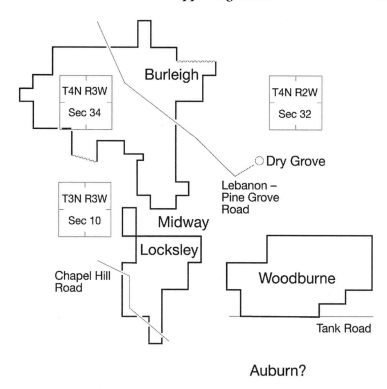

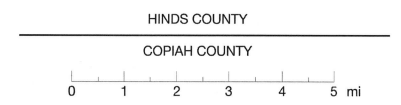

Figure 32. Map of "Virginia" plantations in Hinds County, Mississippi (drawn by the author).

The Hinds County Virginians entertained on a large scale, largely among themselves. Part of the reason for their clannishness was that neither their customs nor their finances were similar to those of their Mississippi neighbors.

Thomas was a scientific farmer, using and advocating crop rotation. In 1839 he helped organize the Hinds County Agricultural Society, chaired the committee that wrote its constitution, and became its first president. Later, he was the president of the Mississippi State Agricultural Society (Drake 1990).

The Dabneys were "Old-Line Whigs" until that party died in 1852 (Green 1965, xxxviii–xlvi). Between 1852 and 1875, Thomas took no active role in national politics.

In 1854–57, Thomas financed Fred's education at the Rensselaer Institute (now the Rensselaer Polytechnic Institute), Troy, New York. On completing his work there, Fred entered on a career of railroad construction.

The Civil War

As war approached, the Dabneys were strong unionists, vigorously opposing secession. Thomas participated in a unionist meeting in Hinds County on February 8, 1860, at which it was held that "the union of the states was the real source of prosperity and that dissolution of the Union would bring strife, anarchy, and destruction" (Ibid., xlii). Less than a year later, Mississippi seceded and joined the Confederate States of America.

The Dabneys had little choice but to join the cause. Thomas briefly considered moving his family to England but decided to stay with his adopted home state (Ibid., xlii–xliii). Thomas's and Gus' older sons, including Fred Dabney, Civil Engineer, went off to fight for the Confederacy.

When Vicksburg fell on July 4, 1863, Thomas Dabney, his family, and about a hundred slaves hid out for a time in the Pearl River Swamp. Gus and his family moved to Burleigh, staying until January 1865. Thomas's group made its way to Mobile. Six months later, they moved to Macon, Georgia. When Macon fell in July 1864, Thomas took his family back to Burleigh and went with his slaves to Montgomery, where they could find work (Green 1965, xliii–xliv, Smedes 1965, 216).

Poverty

During the first year after the war, the situation at Burleigh was marginal, but things went on as best they could. Then came a terrible blow. Before the war, Thomas had signed as security on a friend's loans. In retrospect, he saw it as a trap. The "friend" defaulted and the debt fell on Thomas. In the fall of 1866, the sheriff came to serve Thomas with notices of his debts. Even though Thomas had no means of discharging these obligations, he spurned bankruptcy and resolved to pay every cent he owed (Green 1965, xliv, Smedes1965, 221–82).

During his late sixties and continuing through his seventies,

Thomas worked at hard physical labor for the first time in his life, becoming a gardener and wood-cutter. Even under these circumstances, he continued as a social force in his community.

The Civil War and Reconstruction made Colonel Dabney an ardent Democrat. He was convinced that slavery was right. Only near the end of his life did he change his mind.

In 1878 the community of Dry Grove, near Burleigh, was struck by yellow fever. Thomas's offer of Burleigh as a refuge and medical center was accepted, and the fever was fought there (Smedes 1965, 265–72). He was now 81 years old, and the situation was a terrible strain.

With help from friends and relatives, he managed to discharge his debts by 1882, when he was 84. One of the relatives who helped retire his debts was his nephew Fred Y. Dabney (Ibid., 272).

At some time between 1870 and 1880, Fred settled in Crystal Springs, Copiah County, about twelve miles southeast of Burleigh. He lived there for the rest of his life. At about that time, Gus moved his family to Crystal Springs (Ware 1923).

When not separated by necessity, Thomas and Gus were in contact at least weekly for all their adult lives. Thomas would provide Gus with provisions, and Gus would provide Thomas with advice. When Thomas was faced with any significant decision, he consulted Gus.

Thus it went until January 1878, when Gus and Elizabeth moved to Santa Rosa, California, where some of their children lived (Smedes 1965, 260). He died there on April 25, 1878 (Amick 2011a).

In 1883 Thomas moved to Baltimore. He died there on February 28, 1885 (Green 1965, xv).

Family Traits

A few Dabneys have been wealthy. All have placed a high value on education. They have been planters or have entered professions such as education, medicine, law, ministry, and journalism. For some, high ideals and an unreserved belief in the goodness of humanity may have inhibited their practical success.

> If these Dabneys were not of the nobility, they had all the characteristics of the English aristocracy. They went to work speedily to acquire land and to build up great estates. In three generations they became great landlords and leaders of the people. Captain George Dabney [was] the first sheriff of his county, and his sons and grandsons were magistrates, sheriffs, colonels of militia and burgesses. His grandson Charles Dabney organized the first legion to go into the Revolution from Virginia and became the trusted

officer of George Washington, fighting with him at Monmouth, suffering with him at Valley Forge, and assisting him at the surrender of Cornwallis at Yorktown. Letters in his chest show that Lafayette, Patrick Henry, and John Marshall were his intimate friends [Dabney 1937, 42].

Gus' children's views of their father are consistent with those of his brother Thomas.

My father was visionary; poor, not practical. As a horticulturist he would have been a great success, and he made an excellent probate judge for many years.... My father did a great deal of work in his garden and orchard.... We had fourteen large fig trees, for one item—three varieties. Neighbors sent and got them by the water bucketful. My Father would have been insulted had anyone offered to pay.... My father was really a free thinker, an immediate convert to the Darwinian theory, and an earnest reader of such books of Spencer's as came his way.... My father, on the other hand, was skeptical, philosophical, questioning everything except fiction, for which he did not care. He was very fond of poetry—Pope, Burns, Scott, Hood.... Several times when I was small, a circus came to Raymond. My father considered them low and unfit places for ladies, and would not dream of going himself [Miller 1926].

Thomas provided food for Gus's family. John Davis Dabney, Gus' youngest son, made weekly trips to Burleigh "for meal, corn and an occasional piece of fine beef, or mutton" (Ware 1923).

Gus' trusting nature, in the face of near poverty, is illustrated in another of Letitia's recollections. "Some of my father's slaves had been seized and sold for his debts, and they were the near relatives of those left behind. We hated my Mother's brother for whom this debt had been contracted" (Miller 1926). The brother was Samuel C. Smith.

It is not known whether or not Gus Dabney owned slaves before his marriage to Elizabeth Smith. According to the slave schedule of the 1860 census, he owned eight. Elizabeth's dowry can account for all of them: "My mother brought from Virginia, as her dowry, Uncle Anderson, Aunt Daphne, and their progeny, about seven children" (Ibid.).

Burleigh Today

In late July 2008, Judge Dabney's great-great-granddaughter, Ella Tardy, took Edna and me to O.J. Paige's home on O.J. Paige Lane, off Lebanon–Pine Grove Road, Hinds County, Mississippi. O.J. was not at home, but Ella showed us around. The property was once part of Burleigh Plantation, established by Colonel Dabney in 1835 and owned by him until about 1882. The plantation house once stood in O.J. Paige's yard.

A sketch of Burleigh House, provided to Fletcher M. Green by Mrs. Richard Heath Dabney, is reproduced in Green's edition of *Memorials of a Southern Planter* (1965, opposite p. xiii). Perhaps Fred Y. Dabney drew it.

Edna and I arranged to visit O.J. at his home on July 28, 2008. An articulate man, he welcomed us cordially (Figure 33). He is a police officer and detective in Jackson. As a history buff, he is quite knowledgeable about his family and the local area.

O.J. traces his ancestry to George and Susan Page (Figure 34) (Smedes 1887, facing 246). Among their children was Patsy, b ca. 1863. According to family history, Arthur Paige, Sr., b 1895, was her son. Arthur Paige, Jr., b 1927, was O.J. Paige's father. This makes O.J. the great-great-grandson of George Page, who, as Colonel Dabney's body servant, was arguably his most important slave. George Page was born in Virginia, ca. 1812, according to the 1870 census.

After the Civil War, when Thomas had fallen on very hard times, George Page kept his former master's house supplied with fresh fruits and vegetables. "When George's girl brought over a bucket of strawberries one year, the daughter who received them asked casually if she had

Figure 33. Otis J. Paige, July 28, 2008, outside his home on the site where Burleigh Plantation house once stood (photograph by the author).

Figure 34. George and Susan Page (Smedes, 1887, facing p. 246).

been enjoying the strawberries that spring ... 'No, marm, I ain't tase one,' the child answered. 'Daddy say dat we sharn't tase one 'twell ole marster hab de fust dish, an' dese is de fust" (Ibid. 1965, 235).

O.J. owns several acres that were the heart of Burleigh Plantation. Arthur Paige, Sr., bought a large acreage, once part of Burleigh Plantation, during the 1930s, when the land was a cheap as a dollar an acre. O.J. estimates that about 70 percent of Burleigh Plantation is now owned by descendants of slaves.

This is a remarkable story. George Page's ancestors came from Africa as slaves. They and their descendants remained slaves until the Civil War. Some of George and Susan's children stayed in the area of Burleigh Plantation after the war, living there through the bitter and violent eras of Reconstruction and Jim Crow. Somehow, they persevered and prospered. Now descendants of slaves own most of the plantation land. I suspect that something similar is true of the other "Virginia" plantations in Hinds County. We know, for example, that there are many African American Moncures in the area, some of whom are landowners.

O.J. Paige is rightfully proud of possessing and protecting an important piece of his own history. It is also part of John Henry's history.

⇒⇐ ⇒⇐ ⇒⇐

Fred Y. Dabney, a Confederate engineer, designed the defenses of Port Hudson, Louisiana. He was captured when Port Hudson fell and was incarcerated at Johnson's Island, Ohio, where he became gravely ill.

12

Engineer in the Civil War

I adored this brother. He was so handsome and big
and strong, and his heart and soul and mind were all
built on a big scale.—Mary Dabney Ware

With no preparation "beyond an ordinary country school training, Fred entered the Rensselaer Institute (later the Rensselaer Polytechnic Institute) in 1854 and graduated in civil engi-
neering in the class of 1857" (Figure 35) (Nason 1887, 307). His wealthy uncle, Colonel Thomas Dabney, lent him the money for his education (Dabney 1922). On grad-
uating, he immediately began a career in railroad construction, which was interrupted by the Civil War.

Family

Fred's brother Thomas G. Dabney fol-
lowed in his footsteps as a soldier and civil engineer. Along with Fred, he was captured at Port

Figure 35. Frederick Yeamans Dabney at the Rensselaer Institute, Troy, New York, circa 1857 (AC18, Frederick Y. Dabney, Institute Archives and Special Collections, Rensselaer Polytechnic Institute, Troy, NY).

Hudson, Louisiana, on July 9, 1863. A corporal at the time, he was released along with the others who were not officers, but he later served again in the Confederate army. After the war he lived in Vicksburg, Mississippi; Clarksdale, Mississippi; and Memphis, Tennessee. He would become known as Major T.G. Dabney, and he is now recognized as the father of the levee system in the Yazoo-Mississippi Levee District (Levee Board 2011). He is honored by a marker on U.S. 61 at the levee road, near Walls, Mississippi (Sheer 2011).

Thomas wrote of "a notable episode of my boyhood." In August 1858, about a year after Fred had finished his studies a Rensselaer, Thomas went with him on a preliminary survey for the Gulf and Ship Island railroad. At twenty-three, Fred was in charge of the survey. Thomas, who was a "stake marker" for the survey, would turn fourteen in December. He joined the team about thirty-two miles north of Jackson, Mississippi. The survey route went to the Gulf coast at Mississippi City, which is now part of Gulfport.

They camped along the way, sleeping in tents in the very hot summer weather of South Mississippi. "The life on the survey was hard and rough; that is, we had a great deal of hard walking to do, and suffered much at times from heat and thirst.... Notwithstanding the occasional hardships, this camping experience, and the tramping through the virgin pine forests, with my vigorous appetite and a zest for all adventure, stands in my memory as a bright picture of my boyhood days, with a glamour of romantic interest investing it."

They averaged about four miles a day. "Our line of survey passed four miles east of Jackson, through Rankin and Smith Counties, and when we entered the primeval long-leaf pine region, which was then thinly populated; and the farther we progressed the wilder was the country. There seemed to be an interminable forest of large pine trees, with clean trunks, and no undergrowth; so, through long vistas of big tree bodies, the view was unobstructed. The ground was thickly covered with long pine needles, with red sand beneath, so that there was no dirtying of clothes through wallowing on the ground. The streams were beautifully clear, and schools of trout could be seen in the clear water" (Dabney 1922).

They heard grisly tales of death from rattlesnake bites. Southern Mississippi is home to the extremely venomous eastern diamondback rattlesnake, which can grow to a length of eight feet and a weight of ten pounds or so.

One night they stopped at the farmer's house where Fred's and Thomas' cousin Charles Dabney had died of yellow fever three years earlier. Charles was Colonel Dabney's son.

After they had started back home, Thomas had "a severe attack of bilious fever." They stayed for a few days near the present site of Hattiesburg with a prominent man, Mr. Battson, who lent Thomas a horse. When they reached Summit, they took the train to Terry, not far from Raymond.

Through all of this, we can be sure that Fred looked after his little brother carefully. Surely this experience helped Thomas decide to follow Fred into civil engineering.

Woodburne Plantation, owned by Dr. John E. Moncure, was near Burleigh. Agatha Ann was Dr. Moncure's only daughter, and she was just Mary's age. Consequently, Mary was asked to provide "Aggie" with appropriate company by spending holidays with her.

Fred also noticed Aggie. Before he went off to fight in the Civil War, she accepted his proposal of marriage.

First Maryland Artillery

The Dabneys and their close friends and relatives in Hinds County, Mississippi, were thoroughly Virginian. Fred went to Virginia to enlist in the Confederate forces. Lucius Dabney's grandfather, Moncure Dabney, gave him the names of five young men who were together in Fredericksburg to enlist (Ibid. 2008). All five had Virginia roots, and all were, or would be, related by blood or marriage.

They were Fred Y. Dabney, Charles H. Moncure, Edwin C. Moncure, John E. Glascock, and William Thurmond. Charles, Edwin, and John were first cousins, the children of Dr. John E. Moncure, William A. Moncure, and Agatha Ann Moncure Glascock, respectively. Fred would marry Dr. Moncure's daughter, Agatha Ann, and William would marry Colonel Thomas Dabney's daughter, Sophia (Dabney 1888, 76, 82, 200).

Fred tried to enlist in the Confederate engineering corps, but they would not accept him immediately. They were taking engineers in order from a list on which Fred was not near the top (Dabney 2008).

While his group was in Fredericksburg, some Marylanders there were trying to organize a cavalry unit under Walter H. Jennifer, who was to appear at any time. Jennifer was delayed, and another group of Marylanders arrived. R. Snowden Andrews, a distinguished architect, suggested that they form an artillery unit, and for this purpose they traveled to Richmond.

On July 10, 1861, the First Maryland Artillery, under Captain Andrews, was mustered into service. William F. Dement was elected first lieutenant, Frederick Y. Dabney second lieutenant, and Edwin C.

Moncure corporal. Charles H. Moncure and John E. Glascock, became privates.

Lieutenant Dabney started drilling the troops immediately (Goldsborough 1900, 259). His appointment became official on July 21, 1861, with an effective date of July 14 (Dabney 2008). Virginia's governor, John Letcher, supplied the unit with field artillery, four Napoleons and four Parrotts.

For about three months, the First Maryland Artillery was at Brooks Station, on the Aquia Creek and Fredericksburg Railroad, a Federal military railroad. In October it was sent to Evansport, Virginia, where it helped enforce the Confederate blockade of the Potomac River until March 1862 (Goldsborough 1900, Dabney 1861). By mid–January 1862 Fred had formed a low opinion of Captain Andrews' "petty" regulations, though he appears to have admired him otherwise (Dabney 1862).

Morale was low. "Everything is remarkably quiet in camp & there is nothing to distract our bodily *discomforts* or our *miserable* reflections! The boys have a downcast penitentiary look about them, as if the cup of their bitterness was overflowing, & they obliged to fritter away this highest point of their existence 'cabbined, cribbed, confined' in this dismal hollow" (Ibid.).

From March to very early July 1862, the First Maryland Artillery was part of the force that General Joseph E. Johnston, then General Robert E. Lee, directed against the Peninsula Campaign of General George B. McClellan, whose plan was to take Richmond by advancing up the Virginia Peninsula from Fort Monroe. Despite McClellan's superior forces, the Peninsula Campaign failed.

In the battle of Mechanicsville (Beaver Dam Creek) on June 26, Captain Andrews was wounded, then he was promoted. Dement took over the unit, which gained fame as "Dement's Artillery" (Goldsborough 1900, 260). The First Maryland Artillery was present at Appomattox Court House when General Lee surrendered on April 9 (Ibid., 269).

On December 3, 1861, from "Evansport Batteries," Fred wrote a letter to Dr. Moncure in which he commented, "The roads are becoming worse & worse daily and even now, those in this neighborhood are next to impassable for artillery. In a short time, they will be utterly so" (Dabney 1861). This comment foresaw a later incident.

On the morning of May 5, 1862, the day of the Battle of Williamsburg (Fort Magruder), the Confederate forces were retreating along the Virginia Peninsula toward Richmond. General Joseph E. Johnston had ordered that the road be kept clear, and to that end, anything that got stuck in the mud was to be destroyed. Fred commanded two cannons and their caissons, each of which was pulled by a team of six horses.

After traveling about six miles, the weakest team of horses balked with a 12-pound Napoleon stuck in a mud hole, something Fred had greatly feared from the moment he had heard the orders. The whole line to the rear was halted. As the men were trying unsuccessfully to get the cannon out of the hole, a group of officers rode up from the front, among them General Johnston.

> I gave the military salute and stood like a criminal awaiting sentence. To my surprise he remarked in a very kindly tone: "Well, Lieutenant, you seem to be in trouble." "Yes, sir," I replied; "and I am afraid we shall have to abandon this gun." "Oh, no; I reckon not! Let me see what I can do." Whereupon he leaped from his horse, waded out in the mire, seized one of the wheel-spokes, covered as it was with mud, and called out, "Now, boys, altogether!" The effect was magical, and the next moment the gun jumped clear of the mud-hole. After that our battery used to swear by "Old Joe" [Dabney 1887].

Fred may have been promoted to first lieutenant and assigned to the Confederate engineers as early as February 15, 1862, but he was not detached from the First Maryland Artillery before July. He was sent to Port Hudson, Louisiana, on the Mississippi River about eighteen miles north-northwest of Baton Rouge (U.S. War Department 1891, 40, Goldsborough 1900, 261). Port Hudson came under Confederate control on August 17. Fred probably arrived shortly thereafter.

The Mississippi River in the Civil War

During the Civil War, control of both coastal and major inland waterways was of vital importance to both sides. At various times early in the war, the Confederacy established fortifications on the Mississippi River. Among them were garrisons at Columbus, Kentucky; New Madrid, Missouri; Henning, Tennessee; Memphis, Tennessee; Vicksburg, Mississippi; Port Hudson, Louisiana; New Orleans, Louisiana; and Forts Jackson and St. Philip, below New Orleans.

The Union vigorously pressed offensives from the north and the south. By the spring of 1863, the only Confederate strongholds remaining on the Mississippi River were Vicksburg and Port Hudson.

Each fell to a siege. Historians give the fall of Vicksburg on July 4, 1863, the position of prime importance, but Port Hudson outlasted Vicksburg. The commander at Port Hudson surrendered five days later, only after learning that Vicksburg had fallen. The Union controlled the Mississippi River from July 9, 1863, to the end of the war.

The Red River flows into the Mississippi River between Vicksburg and Port Hudson, near the southern border of Mississippi with Louisiana. Early in the war, the Confederacy used the Red River as a route from the west. It was cut off when the Union gained control of the Mississippi River.

Port Hudson

Léon J. Frémaux was a polymath: civil engineer, Confederate engineering officer, battle map maker, city planner, and artist, known especially for his *New Orleans Characters* (Frémaux 1987, NMD Inc. 2010). In early 1861, he lived with his family in Baton Rouge, but as Captain Frémaux of the Creole Guards, he left Baton Rouge about June 1 for Camp Moore, a Confederate training camp just north of Tangipahoa, Louisiana. On June 15, the Creole Guards became Company A of the 8th Louisiana Infantry. They were sent to northern Virginia, to Camp Pickens, Manassas Junction, where a great battle was fought on July 21. Frémaux included a sketch, "First Mass at Camp Pickens," with his first letter home (Garcia 1987, 66–68). The unit wintered in northern Virginia.

On February 12, 1862, Frémaux was transferred to the Corps of Engineers of the Provisional Army of the Confederate States, commanded by General Pierre Gustave Toutant Beauregard, himself a Creole Louisianan and civil engineer (Kundahl 2000, 143–45). By early April he was in Corinth, Mississippi, where Confederate troops assembled to face a Union army at Shiloh on April 6–7. It was a Union victory with a very high cost, evenly divided between the sides: 3500 men killed; 16,500 wounded; 4700 missing or captured. Frémaux made a sketch of the battlefield (Frémaux 1862).

> The horrors of that battle did my soul with anguish fill,
> The wounded men and dyin' all laid on Shiloh's Hill [Lomax 1960, 349].
> —"The Battle on Shiloh's Hill"

In March 1862, acting on a suggestion from Beauregard, who may have gotten it from Frémaux, Major General Mansfield Lovell began the fortification of Port Hudson (Hewitt 1987, 2, Garcia 1987, 89, 225n18). After New Orleans fell to the Union on May 1, Union forces drove the Confederates out of Port Hudson. By mid–June the only Confederate garrison left on the Mississippi River was at Vicksburg, which had survived Union attacks.

The length of the contested region along the Mississippi River, the distance from New Orleans, and extensive disease among the troops thinned the Union forces at Port Hudson and Baton Rouge. Taking advantage of this, Major General Earl Van Dorn, Confederate commander at Vicksburg, ordered the retaking of Port Hudson and Baton Rouge. An attack on Baton Rouge on August 5 was unsuccessful—the fire of Union gunboats pinned down Confederates. The plan had been to have the CSS *Arkansas* engage the Union navy during the attack, but the engines of the *Arkansas* failed, and her crew burned and scuttled her.

On the day of the attack on Baton Rouge, Mrs. Frémaux and her children had escaped to the home of wealthy plantation owner Valentin Dubroca, across the river from Baton Rouge. When the first sounds of battle were heard, everyone rushed to the garret, the windows of which afforded a good view of some of the streets of Baton Rouge. Twelve-year-old Céline Frémaux (1850–1935) watched the battle through her father's spyglass.

> Kneeling on a trunk near an open ventilator, I saw my first battle, saw guns aim, saw the signal to fire, saw men fall and rise, or try to rise, and fall again, never to move again. In one street the Yankees seemed to be marching twelve or more abreast. The street was packed. All at once a cannon back somewhere shot and shot again, again, and again, I think five shots. Some said it was grape shot, others said round bullets. Be that as it may, it mowed men down at a terrible rate. The street was almost cleared but the sight was terrible. The wounded were carried to the levee to be embarked on gunboats. We could see them plainly. It was awful to see. It was blood, blood everywhere. I felt faint and I was sobbing [Garcia 1987, 83].

Confederate forces led by Brigadier General Daniel Ruggles reoccupied the city on August 17. On August 21 the Union abandoned Baton Rouge and sent its troops to New Orleans (Shea 2003, 31).

Shortly afterwards, perhaps as part of the reassignment on August 29 of Ruggles to Mississippi and of Brigadier General William Beall to Port Hudson, Captain Frémaux and First Lieutenant Dabney came to Port Hudson. Both must have been involved in the redesign and reconstruction of the defenses (Association of Defenders 1886, 306–07). A late 1862 map of a plan of defense, surveyed and drawn by James L. Woodside, Acting First Lieutenant Engineers, as directed by Captain Frémaux, Chief Engineer, can be seen on-line (Woodside 1862). For the rest of 1862, the Confederacy attempted to strengthen their position at Port Hudson while fighting occasional battles with Union gunboats (Hewitt 1987, 16–29, Cunningham 1994, 10–16).

Meanwhile Mrs. Frémaux received word that her husband was at Port Hudson, and she determined that the family would join him there. When they arrived, they found Captain Frémaux and his officers living in the home of James H. Gibbens, thrice widower, south of the town of Port Hudson (Garcia 1987, 91). The Gibbens house still stands (Schulze 2010).

Gibbens was about to acquire his fourth bride, so the family stayed at his home for only about three weeks, after which they moved to a vacant house in Port Hudson. This they shared with some officers, including Fred Dabney, who became Céline's life-long friend (Garcia 1987, 94).

> Capt. Dabney was very friendly to me, particularly. He appeared to have been a wealthy man, all his belongings were fine. Many were silver mounted, and his horse's trapping were very fine. The horse was a most beautiful very dark bay. Mr. Dabney would tell me tales at odd times and always said they were true. I knew better, but if it pleased him, I was willing to appear convinced. He told me all about the girl he was going to marry and showed me her handwriting and picture. I believed it all, then one day he said, "You know my affianced is a Tar Heel." Then I did not believe. I did not know what a Tar Heel was. It sounded derogatory to my ears. Yet the tale was true. She did live in the Miss. Piney Woods, and was very nice, and he married her after the war.
>
> I have in my papers a very graphic account written by himself of his horrible experiences in a Northern prison. He lived to a very old age in Crystal Springs, Mississippi [Ibid., 100].

Fred was not a captain but a first lieutenant when he met Céline, and he died just before his sixty-fifth birthday, not a "very old age," even in 1900. His account of his prison experiences has not been located.

Life in Port Hudson was nearly unbearable. Meat, if it was not already bad on arrival, spoiled quickly, as did corn. The most common rations for the men were "blue beef" and "corn bread" (Hewitt 1987, 24). "The memory of the beef that was served to us for a good while is still nauseating. Poor, gristly blue, gummy, it could be boiled for hours and never an eye of grease on the water. Those old steers, I suppose, were the only animals in existence without a single particle of fat in their composition" (M'Neilly 1919, 337).

There was a shortage of decent cooks. Soldiers coped with homesickness, lice, bad water, and shortages of blankets, shoes, clothing, and cooking utensils. Beds were improvised. "Chills, fever, and mumps plagued the garrison; the death toll mounted daily" (Hewitt 1987, 25). Death was a daily occurrence. In the semitropical climate of South Louisiana, Union forces suffered similarly.

On December 27, 1862, Major General Franklin Gardner, himself a civil engineer, arrived at Port Hudson as the new commander (Cunningham 1994, 19). Captain Frémaux left for Jackson, Louisiana, on January

1, 1863, and Fred Dabney replaced him as chief engineer (Garcia 1987, 103, Hewitt 1987, 42).

Morale at Port Hudson was uplifted by Gardner's command (Hewitt 1987, 43, Association of Defenders 1886, 307). Even so, the hardships of disease, poor food, etc., continued.

Gardner set out to correct the many weaknesses he found in the fortifications and in the discipline of his soldiers. Fred was in charge of redesigning and strengthening the fortifications (Hewitt 1987, 42). Strengthening the garrison was a continuous job until the end and work often proceeded seven days a week. Even though the Confederates would be outnumbered by factors of two to four, and greatly outgunned as well, Fred's defenses would never fail.

General Nathaniel P. Banks was slow to attack Port Hudson, giving the garrison much needed time for preparation. All the while, Farragut's fleet was doing considerable damage to Confederate positions up and down the lower Mississippi.

On February 24, 1863, Fred Dabney wrote to Dr. Moncure from Port Hudson: "We are bound to have peace and that very shortly. Old Abe has played his last trump & might as well give up" (Dabney 1863).

Banks finally moved against Port Hudson in May. By the evening of May 22, 1863, the Confederate garrison at Port Hudson was effectively isolated by surrounding Union forces (Hewitt 1987, 131).

It became evident to Gardner that the Union planned an attack, among others, from the north. "To the north, the ground became suddenly very much broken, densely wooded, and almost impassable, for a few hundred yards, to Sandy Creek, a branch of Thomson's creek.... It had generally been supposed that no attack in force would ever be attempted through the swamp above Port Hudson, nor through the heavy timber back of the town, through which ran Sandy Creek. Fortifications had not been erected there, nor were they considered necessary. But ... the enemy preferred to overcome the natural obstacles of the woods rather than the artificial ones in the shape of fortifications. ... [The] valleys and gorges ... were principally choked ... with fallen timber" (Association of Defenders 1886, 305).

Chief Engineer Dabney, with all available tools and slaves, spent the night of May 25–26 laying out new defenses facing Sandy Creek (Hewitt 1987, 133). Preparation there was not completed until the morning of May 27, the day of the assault (Association of Defenders 1886, 318–19).

It was a bloody day. The First and Third Regiments, Louisiana Native Guard, attacked from the Sandy Creek area (Hewitt 2002). Many among these black troops had been distinguished free men of color in New Orleans.

Reports of the performance of the Native Guard vary widely, reflecting the propaganda needs of the Union and Confederacy, but all agree that the black soldiers followed orders, made several assaults, and were slaughtered. "How many of the poor wretches perished in the fatal trap into which they had been so unwisely driven I cannot say. In conversation with Federal officers and men after the surrender I have heard the number estimated as high as six hundred" (de Gournay). To arrive at a similar figure, Hewitt included the wounded and missing (Hewitt 2002, 96).

Some have raised questions.

Now, why were the colored troops left unsupported? Why were they sent on such hopeless missions? Why were the officers informed by General Dwight that there were clear grounds beyond Sandy Creek? There were white troops who could have been sent to their support; the officers expected to fight the rebels but met the river. Colonel Nelson played General to perfection; during the whole battle he remained on the safe side of Sandy Creek, and had his corps of orderlies to attend him; in plain words he kept his men under fire from quarter before six A.M., till seven P.M. During the day he never saw a rebel's face or back [Wilson 1890, 526].

Whatever the answers may be, the Native Guard at Port Hudson proved its bravery.

Port Hudson held. After bringing in reinforcements, additional cannon, and other arms, Banks attempted a second assault on June 14, 1863. It was as unsuccessful as the first, and perhaps even more costly in Union casualties, which came to 1,805 killed, wounded, or captured on that day alone (Cunningham 1994, 82–93).

By June 29, the last beef in the Port Hudson garrison had been eaten, and the soldiers turned to other meat.

Some horses were also slaughtered, and their flesh was found to be very good eating, but not equal to mule. Rats, of which there were plenty about the deserted camps, were also caught by many officers and men, and were found to be quite a luxury—superior, in the opinion of those who eat them, to spring chicken [Wright 1863].

Skirmishes continued. At several points, Union forces tried to work their way closer to the garrison by sapping, digging trenches ("saps"), usually zigzag, deep enough to shield men from fire from the garrison. They also tried to reach positions under some of the fortifications by digging tunnels ("galleries"). At an appropriate point underground, they could set off explosives so as to cause the fortifications above to collapse.

Union soldiers named one position near the northeastern corner of the Confederate fortifications "the Priest's Cap" (or "Priest Cap"). When the Confederates detected a gallery being dug toward the Priest's Cap, they started digging their own tunnel under the Union miners (Cunningham 1994, 105).

> At one point, where the enemy had undermined a salient in our line of fortifications, Capt. Dabney tunneled beneath them, working in the shaft himself, with the sound of their picks over his head, digging the earth with trowels and sending it back in baskets. He tamped his charge with his own hands, not finding anyone else willing to perform the dangerous service. When the Federal mine was about completed he fired his mine by means of a "friction primer," with a wire attached, passing through sections of cane to avoid the difficulties of angles in his small tunnel, and blew up the enemy before they were ready to spring their mine [Dabney 1900b, 230].

This happened a little after midnight on July 3. No one was injured, but that Union operation was stopped.

On July 4, Vicksburg surrendered. The word reached Port Hudson on July 7. A cease-fire was arranged on July 8 and Gardner's surrender on July 9 (Cunningham 1994, 119). At 48 days, the siege of Port Hudson was the longest in American history.

General Banks paroled the enlisted men and non-commissioned officers, who were on their way home about a week after the surrender, Corporal Thomas G. Dabney among them (Amick et al 2011b). He rejoined his old unit, the First Mississippi Light Artillery. When his unit surrendered at Blakely, Alabama, on April 9, 1865, he was a sergeant.

The commissioned officers were not paroled. On July 16 Fred Dabney was sent to New Orleans on the steamer "General Banks" (Hardy 2011). The captured Confederate officers were treated very well in New Orleans. "Thanks to our friends in the city, [we] were well clad, and dainty food was the order of the day." If such was to be the existence of a prisoner of war, it seemed strange that whole armies did not allow themselves to be captured (Carpenter 1891, 706). This photograph may have been made while Fred was a prisoner there (Figure 36).

First Lieutenant Frederick Y. Dabney is seated at right. "From Anderson's Photographic Gallery, 61 Camp Street, New Orleans" is printed on the back. The seated man at left bears a striking resemblance to Léon J. Frémaux. However, as far as is known, he and Fred Dabney were never in New Orleans together. Frémaux last served the Confederacy in the Department of Alabama, Mississippi, and East Louisiana under Lieutenant General Richard Taylor. He was paroled at Meridian, Mississippi, in May 1865 (Kundahl 2000, 264).

Fred was sent to Fort Columbus, New York Harbor, probably at about the same time as his fellow prisoner from Port Hudson, First Lieutenant Charles Chaney, who arrived at Fort Columbus on September

Figure 36. Group of Confederate officers, with Frederick Y. Dabney seated at the right. The original photograph is of low quality (courtesy LSU Libraries: Item 25720032dr, from the Civil War Photograph Album [Mss. 2572], Louisiana and Lower Mississippi Valley Collections, LSU Libraries, Baton Rouge, Louisiana, USA).

29, 1863 (Conque 2009). On October 15, 1863, from Fort Columbus, Fred arrived at a Union prison for Confederate officers, the Depot for Prisoners of War, Johnson's Island, Sandusky Bay, Lake Erie, north of Sandusky, Ohio (U.S. War Department 1891). Fred's first cousin, John Hamden "Ham" Chamberlayne, son of Martha Burwell Dabney Chamberlayne, was already a prisoner there (Chamberlayne 1932, 203).

Johnson's Island

October 1863 was a bad time to arrive at Johnson's Island as a prisoner. The winter of 1863–64 was unusually severe.

The buildings ("blocks") in which prisoners lived were cheaply constructed and not insulated, in keeping with the "strict economy" ordered by the Union Commissary General of Prisoners, Lieutenant Colonel William C. Hoffman. Also in keeping with strict economy, prisoners were issued minimal clothing and blankets, although Ham Chamberlayne wrote on Christmas day, 1863, that he and Fred had a "full supply of flannels and blankets" (Ibid., 212).

Ham's letters were invariably optimistic. He was fortunate in being sent to Point Lookout, Maryland, at some time between February 4 and March 2, 1864, and released by March 15 (U.S. War Department 1891).

On March 17, 1864, Fred was promoted to captain (Ibid.). On May 7, 1864, he wrote that "nothing worries me now but my captivity, & the last I endeavor to bear with as much fortitude as I can command. I have given up all hope of an early exchange & quietly await the development of future events ... everything is going on pretty much as when [Ham] left—a considerable body of sick men having been shipped lately, being the only interruption to our usual monotony" (Chamberlayne 1932, 218). If Fred himself were not already sick, he soon would be.

Prisoner treatment had become increasingly severe. A cut in prisoner rations and clothing in April 1864 was a step in a Union campaign of retaliation for perceived Confederate atrocities, especially the slaughter of black troops after they had surrendered at Fort Pillow (Sanders 2005, 241). Another cut was implemented on June 1, when the daily ration at Johnson's Island became "a loaf of bread and a small piece of fresh meat," insufficient to sustain good health (Carpenter 1891, 715, Johnson 1901, Shepherd 1917, 13–16). Hoffman gloried in the savings, which went into his beloved "prison funds," the balances of which testified to his "efficiency" (Sanders 2005, 125).

Col. I.G. W. Steedman was Confederate medical doctor who was twice held at Johnson's Island. His 1866 paper for a medical society meeting was subsequently published.

> During the prevailing intense cold of that latitude in winter, the rooms were insufficiently warmed, and there was consequently great suffering; the supply of blankets and clothing being scant for men unaccustomed to cold winters....
>
> The supply of pure water was insufficient, especially for hospital purposes.
>
> There was no drainage from the privies. The substratum being a limestone rock, these sinks necessarily filled up very rapidly, and were constant sources of disease.
>
> The medical supplies were issued to the hospital in accordance with the supply table of the Medical Department, U.S. Army, but were frequently

insufficient, in consequence of the great prevalence of disease among the prisoners.

The supply of food for the sick was generally ample in quantity, but of too coarse a character for sick men. There was a systematic effort on the part of the surgeon of the post, Dr. Eversman [Evertman], to supply the necessary diet suited to the sick, but, from the want of sufficient funds or proper authority, his efforts did not accomplish the good always intended by him. Here I would state that Dr. Eversman [Evertman] and Dr. T. Woodbridge, U.S.A., who were the post surgeons during my connection with the prison, always evinced a desire to do all in their power for the relief of sick prisoners; yet, in consequence of the rigid orders from Washington regulating the treatment of prisoners of war, their good intentions availed but little in relieving the vast amount of suffering, which could at least have been greatly ameliorated by a generous supply of the wants of our sick.

The island having little timber, the prison was constantly exposed to the bleak winter winds blowing from the lake [Steedman 1870, 355–58].

The facilities at Johnson's Island were designed for about 1000 prisoners, but the number confined there was 2000–3000 between November 1863 and April 1865 (Speer 1997, 12, Sanders 2005, 70–71, Steedman 1870, 359). Overcrowding raised the levels of communicable diseases.

According to Colonel B.W. Johnson, "The black hole of Calcutta possibly was worse, but Andersonville could not have been as bad" as Johnson's Island (1901). This is a strange comparison. Of about 45,000 men processed at Andersonville, in southwestern Georgia, nearly 13,000 died. Of about 10,000 at Johnson's Island, fewer than 300 died. Colonel Johnson's claim may be that the intensity of individual suffering was greater at Johnson's Island.

※ ※ ※

Fred Dabney's illness, threatening death, was his ticket home. He recovered, to an extent, and continued his career in railroad building.

13

Railroad Builder

Columbus and Western ... This road is being built in a substantial way. When complete, it will be not only a marvel of engineering skill, but one of the best roads in the south.

—*Railway World,* April 1888

Captain Fred Y. Dabney's stay at Johnson's Island included some of the worst weather and worst treatment of prisoners at that facility. By September, his health had become desperate.

Home

In early September 1864, the Union and Confederacy agreed to "exchange all sick and invalid officers and men who from wounds or sickness shall, in the judgment of the party holding them, be unfit for duty and likely to remain so for sixty days" (Sanders 2005, 260). Fred was "sent to Fortress Monroe, by order of Col. Hoffman Sepr 16th." (U.S. War Department). Fort Monroe, Hampton, Virginia, was at the eastern tip of the Virginia Peninsula, convenient for exchanges and releases of prisoners. By September 27 Ham Chamberlayne had received a letter telling him that "Fred has come" (Chamberlayne 1932, 270). He wrote on December 17, "I hope you have exaggerated Fred's illness" (Ibid.).

Two months after Fred left Johnson's Island the Confederate doctors there stated that "if the inmates of this prison are compelled to subsist for the winter upon this reduced ration of ten ounces less than health demands, and six ounces less than Colonel Hoffman's order allows, *all* must suffer the horrors of continual hunger, and many must die from the most loathesome diseases" (Steedman 1870, 361–65). Similar conditions existed during part of Fred's time there.

Fred "shared the sufferings and privations of that awful prison ... being a physical wreck and a hopeless invalid, he was sent with others, who were completely incapacitated for military service, into the Confederate lines.... He recovered from his prison maladies within some three years" (Dabney 1900b). "The long confinement and the unnecessary hardships he was forced to endure laid the foundation for the ill health that marked the latter years of his life" (Ibid., 1900a).

Family

Frederick Yeamans Dabney and Agatha Ann Moncure were married in Hinds County, Mississippi, in May 1865 (Hinds County MSGHN 2012, Chamberlayne 1932, 330). During the eight months between his release from Johnson's Island and his marriage, Aggie must have nursed him to tolerable health.

In 1870 Fred lived with Aggie and two children, Evelyn, 3, and Susan, 1, in Dry Grove, Hinds County, Mississippi, among the plantations of emigrant Virginians. His real estate was valued at $5000. In 1880 "Montcure" (Moncure), 9, Agatha M., 7, Augustine Lee, 5, Frederick Y., 18 months, and Courts Hill "Montcure" (Aggie's widowed mother) had joined the family, which now lived on Railroad Avenue West in Crystal Springs, Copiah County, Mississippi, about ten miles south of Dry Grove. East and West Railroad Avenues ran north-south, parallel to the tracks of the New Orleans, Jackson and Great Northern Railroad, which eventually became part of the Illinois Central. The house on West Railroad Avenue would be Fred's home for the rest of his life. His and Aggie's ninth and last child, Conway Dabney, was born in 1882 (du Bellet 1907, 125).

Chief Engineer and Superintendent

Fred's career to 1885 is summarized as follows.

Entered railway service 1857 as rodman Southern (now Vicksburg & Meridian) RR; 1858 and 1859, leveler Gulf & Ship Island RR; 1860, transitman Vicksburg, Shreveport & Texas RR; 1866 and 1867, assistant engineer Louisiana levees; 1868, assistant engineer North Missouri RR; 1869 and 1870, in charge surveys New Orleans, Jackson & Great Northern and Natchez & Jackson RRs; 1871 to 1875, road-master and special engineer New Orleans, Jackson & Great Northern RR; 1875 to 1879, locating engineer New Orleans Pacific RR; 1880 to 1881, special engineer Vicksburg, Shreveport & Pacific

Ry; July 1, 1881, to date, chief engineer and superintendent, same road [Talbot and Hobart 1885].

"Rodman," "leveler," "transitman," and "locating engineer" are all positions on railroad surveying teams (Allen 1920). Sixteen years after the Civil War, Fred had risen to the office of Chief Engineer and Superintendent of the Vicksburg, Shreveport and Pacific. On November 1, 1882, he was elected to membership in the American Society of Civil Engineers (American Society of Civil Engineers 1882).

Brief Retirement

His malady from Johnson's Island can account for the following report.

> Capt. F.Y. Dabney, chief engineer and superintendent of the V., S. and P., retired from office on the 1st inst., owing to bad health. He is suffering with a severe cough, and has almost entirely lost his voice. His physicians urge him to try change of climate. The consolidation of the V., S. and P. and V. and M. under one superintendency would relieve him of this part of the work, and he was urged to retain the position of chief engineer, but will be compelled for the reasons stated to retire entirely. His retirement is greatly regretted, as he has been a popular and competent officer. Capt. Dabney will go to San Antonio, Texas, health seeking, and may extend his trip into Mexico [*American Engineer* 1885].

Whether or not he actually went to San Antonio and Mexico, his retirement was brief. On August 27, 1886, *The Meteor* (Crystal Springs) reported, "Capt. Dabney is home again from a trip to Georgia." He had been in Savannah in his capacity as Chief Engineer of the Columbus and Western Railway (*Railroad and Engineering Journal* 1887).

Columbus and Western

In the 1880s, the Central Rail Road and Banking Company of Georgia ("Central of Georgia") saw a great opportunity in a railroad that would connect Birmingham, Alabama, with Columbus, Georgia, and points east and south. According to the 1886 city directory, Birmingham, founded in 1871, had a population of 21,347. It had been only 3,086 in 1880 and would be 26,178 in 1890 and 38,415 in 1890 (Birmingham Public Library 2010). The rapid growth was due to the development and exploitation of mineral resources, which include limestone, coal, and iron ore, raw materials for the iron and steel industry.

In 1886 railroads connected Birmingham with regions in other directions, but not southeast. The C & W would remedy that. The following report is for the year ending June 30, 1887.

> The Columbus & Western Railway, of standard gauge, for the year ending June 30th, 1886, had in Alabama 87.02 miles, of which 19.52 were in steel and sixty-seven in iron rails. The terminal point of this railroad at that time was Goodwater, in Tallapoosa County, and up to June 30th, 1887, this road had not been operated beyond that point. It is now being rapidly extended from Goodwater to Birmingham. This extension will have a length of about seventy miles. It runs as nearly as the nature of topography will permit in an air line toward Birmingham, but from the difficulties of location is forced to bend considerably to the northeast, crossing the Georgia Pacific Railroad at the town of Leeds, and thence parallels that road to Birmingham, a distance of about eighteen miles. Before reaching that point it crosses the Coosa and Oak Mountain ridges by means of tunnels, the first or Coosa Mountain Tunnel being 2,500 feet in length, and the Oak Mountain Tunnel 1,200 feet....
>
> The country through which the line runs, while in many parts rugged, gives promise of excellent traffic as soon as its mineral, agricultural, and timber resources are developed. The connection at Birmingham it is also hoped will give to the road a reasonable amount of through traffic [Shorter 1887].

As Chief Engineer for the C & W, Captain Dabney was in charge of design and construction of the extension. By alternating the "Map" view (which shows railroads) with the "Terrain" view (which shows relief), you can use Google Maps (Google 2010) to get an idea of how the landscape influenced the route of the extension from Goodwater to Birmingham. Captain Dabney found a route through Sylacauga, Childersburg, Vincent, Sterrett, Vandiver, and Leeds (Figure 37).

Oak Tunnel is at Thompson Gap, about two miles south of Leeds. The community of Dunnavant is about one and a half miles south of Thompson Gap, and Coosa Tunnel is about a half mile south of Dunnavant.

Each of these mountains is a southwest-to-northeast lying ridge that rises 500–600 feet above the adjacent land. The tunnel through Oak Mountain is the shorter one, partly because it penetrates at a gap and partly because it penetrates at a higher elevation than Coosa Tunnel.

Work on the C & W started in late 1886.

Contrary to the hope that it would be finished by the end of 1887, twelve miles of track remained to be laid in April 1888. Forty miles had been laid on the east end, twenty on the west, and Oak Tunnel had been completed, but Coosa Tunnel was still being bored (*Railway World* 1888).

The east and west headings of Coosa Tunnel were begun about

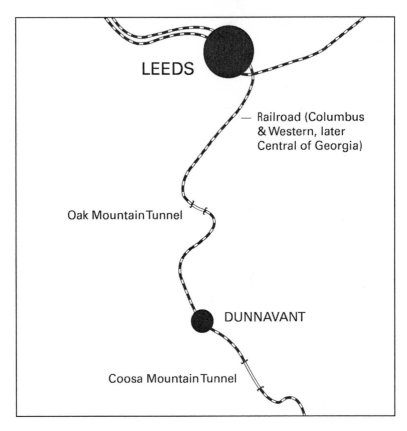

Figure 37. Central of Georgia railroad, formerly called Columbus and Western, between Dunnavant and Leeds, Alabama, as shown on a map redrawn from Coates' 1890 map of the Alabama coal fields. The map also shows the location of the Oak Mountain and Coosa Mountain tunnels.

February 20, 1887, and they met at 11 p.m. on February 23, 1888 (Baker 1888). Removing bench, trimming, and track laying took another four months. The last spike was driven at 9:25 p.m. on June 20, 1888, four hundred feet from the west portal of Coosa Tunnel. The occasion was celebrated, a few hours prematurely, by a dinner party at the site (*Weekly Iron Age* 1888). The line from Columbus to Birmingham opened officially on July 1, 1888 (Poor 1889).

Mississippians and the C & W

During the extension of the C & W, Captain Dabney boarded at the Florence Hotel in Birmingham, Alabama (*Weekly Iron Age* 1887b).

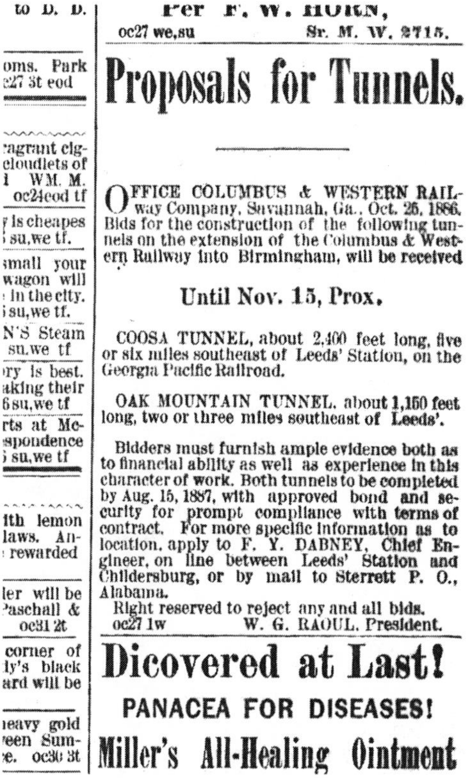

Per F. W. HORN,
oc27 we,su Sr. M. W. 2715.

Proposals for Tunnels.

OFFICE COLUMBUS & WESTERN RAILway Company, Savannah, Ga., Oct. 26, 1886. Bids for the construction of the following tunnels on the extension of the Columbus & Western Railway into Birmingham, will be received

Until Nov. 15, Prox.

COOSA TUNNEL, about 2,400 feet long, five or six miles southeast of Leeds' Station, on the Georgia Pacific Railroad.

OAK MOUNTAIN TUNNEL, about 1,150 feet long, two or three miles southeast of Leeds'.

Bidders must furnish ample evidence both as to financial ability as well as experience in this character of work. Both tunnels to be completed by Aug. 15, 1887, with approved bond and security for prompt compliance with terms of contract. For more specific information as to location, apply to F. Y. DABNEY, Chief Engineer, on line between Leeds' Station and Childersburg, or by mail to Sterrett P. O., Alabama.

Right reserved to reject any and all bids.
oc27 1w W. G. RAOUL, President.

Dicovered at Last!

PANACEA FOR DISEASES!

Miller's All-Healing Ointment

Figure 38. Advertisement from the *Daily American* of Nashville, Tennessee, November 2, 1886, which clearly identifies F.Y. Dabney as the Chief Engineer of the project to tunnel through Oak and Coosa Mountains near Leeds, Alabama. The ad also appeared in other regional newspapers and was intended to recruit workers in addition to those already known to the engineers. Among the latter was John Henry Dabney, former slave to F.Y. Dabney, and who C.C. Spencer, the most reliable witness to the John Henry race, said was "shipped" by the Chief Engineer to Coosa Mountain from Mississippi.

His wife's cousin, Edwin Conway "E.C." Moncure (1840–1917), was a right-of-way and title agent for the C & W. Like Captain Dabney, he maintained a household in Crystal Springs, Mississippi, where he was buried.

According to C.C. Spencer, John Henry Dabney ("Dabner") was "shipped" to Coosa Mountain from Mississippi (C.C. Spencer 1927b, Johnson 1929, 19). A similar idea is found in the ballad.

> When they brought John Henry to this country,
> They brought him through by land [Hazelhurst 1939]

I have not found this couplet elsewhere. It may be a survival from the original or a very early version of the ballad.

John Henry Dabney

John Henry Dabney, the steel-driving man, was one of Captain Dabney's Mississippi recruits. Judge Dabney owned a slave named Henry, about twenty-one years old in 1866. The 1870 census identifies him as Henry Page, so he was not John Henry (Miller 1926). Accordingly, Colonel Dabney must have owned John Henry, who must have been born and raised on Burleigh Plantation.

Henry Dabney, born in Mississippi in 1849–50, was enumerated in Copiah County, Mississippi, in 1870 and 1880. He is the best candidate in the census, and I accept him as John Henry Dabney.

In his youth, Captain Dabney spent considerable time at Burleigh. He was about fifteen years old when Henry Dabney was born, so he probably knew him from birth and saw him frequently.

General Troubles

The Civil War is said to be "unfinished" (Blackmon 2009, 115). By 1886 the North had given up on Reconstruction, and Southern whites were re-enslaving blacks through legislation, arrests and imprisonment, convict leasing, debt peonage, and terrorism (Blackmon 2009, Mancini 1996, Lewis 1987, Letwin 1998). All of this was prominent in the remote areas southeast of Birmingham, including Shelby and Coosa Counties.

The white Southern press was dramatically one-sided.

> The conduct of the negroes about the railroad camps, according to statements made to the reporter by persons living in their vicinity, has become almost unbearable. An instance is given where a white man was passing through a camp and a gang of negroes grossly insulted him. He attempted to resist, when the whole crowd pounced upon and beat him unmercifully. Another is told of how a short time ago two white men were passing in a wagon, and a gang, without any provocation, began using the most vile epithets toward them. The two dared not make a reply, but drove on home where their story was told. In a few hours seventy-two armed men had offered themselves to clean out the camp. No move was made then, but it is feared by many that very serious trouble will occur unless something is done to remove the cause of the indignation [*Weekly Iron Age* 1887a].

The language used by Southern politicians to get and keep their offices illustrates the attitudes of the majority of their white constituents.

In October 1901, President Theodore Roosevelt had Booker T. Washington to dinner. Ben Tillman, U.S. senator from South Carolina, said, "Now that Roosevelt has eaten with that nigger Washington, we shall have to kill a thousand niggers to get them back to their places" (Blackmon 2009, 166). In 1903 Roosevelt hosted a White House reception attended by several African Americans. James K. Vardaman, who would be elected governor of Mississippi the next year, reacted by saying that the White House was "so saturated with the odor of the nigger that the rats have taken refuge in the stable" (Ibid., 167).

Coosa Troubles

Trouble, some of it tragic, plagued Coosa Tunnel and Dunnavant. The plan to finish the C & W by the end of 1887 was "delayed by the Coosa Mountain Tunnel" (Belknap 1887).

> The Coosa Mountain tunnel on the Columbus and Western railroad has been driven into the mountain a distance of 1,300 feet. The contractors have encountered a peculiar hard granite in the tunnel, which has been extremely difficult to handle [*Alabama Sentinel* 1887].

In addition, there were "unprecedented floods" in July and additional heavy rains in August (Alexander 1887, *Weekly Iron Age* 1887a). According to the General Manager's Report of 1888, "The extremely hard character of rock encountered near the center of tunnels, bad weather and delay of contractors prevented the completion of the C&W within the contract time and for several months thereafter, and it was not opened to Birmingham until July 1st" (T.M.C. 1909).

Tragedy came in accidents and crimes. On May 4, 1887, a premature explosion at Coosa Tunnel killed twelve men. A spark was struck accidentally while ramming the powder into a drill hole with an iron bar (*Atlanta Constitution* 1887c). On June 7, 1887, a similar explosion, also at Coosa Tunnel, killed two men (Ibid. 1887d).

On Monday afternoon, March 7, 1887, timekeeper J.A. Pearce shot and killed William Mills, an English laborer, at Coosa Tunnel. Pearce had hit a drunken laborer "a severe blow with a rock." Mills and three others confronted him and asked why. Pearce replied, "I will answer with this," and fired his shotgun at Mills's head, killing him instantly (Ibid. 1887a). On March 9, a coroner's jury accepted Pearce's claim of self-defense and acquitted him (Ibid. 1887b).

On the night of August 31, 1887, a "negro gambler" named Monroe Johnson is said to have shot and killed a Mrs. Foster at Dunnavant's camp. Shortly thereafter, Johnson was found in Atlanta. "Special Officer Dabney" was sent to Atlanta to fetch the prisoner.

In the 1887 and 1888 Birmingham city directories, Captain Dabney is the only "Dabney" listed. This, his military experience, and his direct connection with Dunnavant's camp make it almost certain that he was Special Officer Dabney.

For the trip back to Birmingham, they took the night train on the Georgia Pacific, reaching a point near Leeds shortly before 4 a.m. on September 18. Fearing "interference" from citizens of Leeds, Dabney had chained Johnson to a seat. Near Leeds, more than a dozen armed men stopped the train and boarded.

> When they caught sight of the negro there was a shout and they seized him. They didn't wait to unlock the chain, but tore the seat from the floor and dragged it out with the negro. Two hundred yards from the depot a large walnut tree stood, and to this the mob hurried. A rope was already around the negro's neck and in a moment he was suspended in midair. The mob then moved off ten paces and with shotguns, rifles and pistols riddled the writhing body with bullets. The body remained hanging to the limb all day and was viewed by hundreds of people [*Atlanta Constitution* 1887e].

John Henry in Shelby County

Despite the danger of the job and location, John Henry survived everything but the steam drill. As Captain Dabney's friend and best steel driver, he would have been respected and protected.

To the youthful C.C. Spencer, he was a hero, "good old John Henry." He "lived for honor" and "died with his hammer in his hand," his head in the lap of his wife (Spencer 1927b).

The Captain—Later Life

In 1890 and '91, Captain Dabney appeared in the city directories of Savannah, Georgia, as chief engineer for the "S. & W. Ry," that is, the Savannah and Western. He boarded at Screven House, indicating that he maintained his home in Crystal Springs while working in the administration of the C of G, which owned the S & W, which in turn had absorbed the C & W. He does not appear in a Savannah directory after 1891.

According to an obituary, "ill health compelled him to retire from the field of active work to his home in Crystal Springs. There he passed his declining years with his family, enjoying general respect and admiration" (Dabney 1900b). He did not retire entirely from engineering, however, as he designed Lake Chautauqua, about a mile north of Crystal Springs, and supervised its construction in 1895–97 (Nelson-Easley 2007, Kiser 2012).

Agatha Ann Moncure Dabney died January 9, 1899. Captain Fred Y. Dabney died March 16, 1900, of a "bronchial affection" (Mississippi Department of Archives and History). His malady may have been acquired during his confinement on Johnson's Island.

⇒⊂ ⇒⊂ ⇒⊂

Cornelius S. "Neal" Miller misled Guy Johnson and Louis Chappell by fabricating testimony about John Henry at Big Bend Tunnel.

14

Just Another Negro

Mr. Miller is no apologist, and no hero-worshipper, for
John Henry or anyone else, as his testimony indicates.
—Louis W. Chappell

When Louis Chappell and Guy Johnson visited the vicinity of
Big Bend Tunnel in September 1925 and June 1927, respectively, each
of them interviewed C.S. "Neal" Miller, whose testimony has been
regarded as particularly important. Williams called him "by far the most
exciting witness" (1983, 39).

For Chappell, Miller did not claim to have seen John Henry race a
steam drill (Chappell 1933, 46–47). Even so, Chappell held his report
in high esteem, along with those of brothers George and John Hedrick.

These three witnesses are giving direct testimony, not popular or hearsay
reports. They are not ballad-singers and general repositories of oral tradition, but represent the stable citizenry of a conservative community. In a
court or forum of that locality, they would have the support of good character and general reliability in matters of dispute coming under their observa-
tion [Ibid. 48–49].

For Johnson, Miller claimed to have seen the contest between John
Henry and the steam drill at the east portal of Big Bend Tunnel, probably in 1870 (Johnson 1929, 40–42). It was Miller's testimony that per-
suaded Johnson to favor West Virginia as the John Henry site.

Just one man, Mr. C.S. Miller, among all those with whom I have come in
contact in my investigations, claims to have seen the contest.
One man against the mountain of negative evidence! Were it not for that
one man the question might not be so teasing [Ibid., 53].

Johnson corresponded with, but did not interview, another
self-proclaimed eyewitness to the contest, C.C. Spencer, who had seen
it in Alabama in 1882 (Ibid., 19–22). Chappell did not find anyone who
claimed to have witnessed the contest.

Any serious consideration of the evidence for the historical John Henry must evaluate Miller's and Spencer's testimonies. At least one of them was wrong.

The Contest at Big Bend Tunnel

Neal Miller testified as follows in 1925:

I saw John Henry drive steel in Big Bend Tunnel. He was a great singer, and always singing some old song when he was driving steel. He was a black, rawboned man, 30 years old, 6 feet high, and weighed near 200 pounds. He and Phil Henderson, another big Negro, but not so high, were pals, and said that they were from North Carolina.

Phil Henderson turned the steel for John Henry when he drove in the contest with the steam drill at the east end of the tunnel. John Henry beat the steam drill because it got hung up in the seam of the rock and lost time.

Dave Withrow, who lived with his wife at our home, was the foreman in charge of the work on the outside of the tunnel where John Henry beat the steam drill, and Mike Breen was the foreman on the inside of the tunnel there.

The steam drill was brought to Big Bend Tunnel as an experiment, and failed because it stayed broke all the time, or hung up in the rock, and it could be used only as a bench drill anyway. It was brought to the east end of the tunnel when work first commenced there, and was never carried in the tunnel. It was thrown aside, and the engine was taken from it and carried to shaft number one, where it took the place of a team of horses that pulled the bucket up in the shaft with a windlass.

John Henry used to go up Hungart's Creek to see a white woman,— or almost white. Sometimes this woman would go down to the tunnel to get John Henry, and they went back together. She was called John Henry's woman 'round the camps.

John Henry didn't die from getting too hot in the contest with the steam drill, like you say. He drove in the heading a long time after that. But he was later killed in the tunnel, but I didn't see him killed. He couldn't go away from the tunnel without letting his friends know about it, and his woman stayed 'round long after he disappeared.

He was killed all right, and I know the time. The boys 'round the tunnel told me that he was killed from a blast of rock in the heading, and he was put in a box with another Negro and buried at night under the big fill at the east end of the tunnel. A mule that had got killed in the tunnel was put under the big fill about the same time.

The bosses at the tunnel were afraid the death of John Henry would cause trouble among the Negroes, and they often got rid of dead Negroes in some way like that. All the Negroes left the tunnel once and wouldn't go in it for several days. Some of them won't go in it now because they've got the notion they can still hear John Henry driving steel in there. He's a regular ghost 'round this place.

His marks in the side of the rock where he drove steel with the steam drill stayed there awhile at the east end of the tunnel, but when the railroad bed was widened for double-tracking they destroyed them [Chappell 1933, 46–47].

Miller continued in 1927:

"I came here when I was seventeen," said Mr. Miller, "It was the spring of 1869. In the fall of that year I began work at Big Bend. I carried water and steel for the gang of drivers at the east end. I would take the drills to the shop and bring them back after they were sharpened. I often saw John Henry, as he was on the gang that I carried water and drills for.

"John Henry was a powerful man. He weighed about 200, was of medium height, was black, and was about thirty years old.

"The contest took place in 1870, as well as I remember. Jeff Davis, a white man, turned the drill for John Henry. There was a hundred dollar wager up between John Henry's foreman and the man who brought the steam drill.

"The steam drill wasn't very practical. It was operated by an eight horse-power steam engine. The drill was mounted on steel supports something like table legs, and it could be used only where there was a fairly level surface to set it on. The steam came through a pipe from the boiler to the engine. A belt ran from the engine shaft to a pulley on the drill. There was an apparatus to regulate the position of the drill. They would begin with a short drill and go down to its limit; then they would stop and insert a longer drill. The drill turned round and round instead of churning up and down, and this caused a lot of loose gravel around the top of the hole to slide down and pack the drill. Several times during the contest they had to take the drill out of the hole and clean the gravel out. John Henry outdid the power drill pretty easily, because they had so much trouble with it. After the test the steam drill was dismounted and the boiler was used to run a hoisting engine at shaft number one. The test took place at the east portal, and the steam drill was never taken inside the tunnel.

"Now some people say John Henry died because of this test. But he didn't. At least, he didn't drop dead. As well as I remember, though, he took sick and died from fever soon after that."

I asked Mr. Miller if the contest caused much excitement.

"No," he replied. "It was just considered a sort of test on the steam drill. There wasn't any big crowd around to see it. I was going and coming with water and steel, so I saw how they were getting along from time to time, but I didn't get excited over it especially. The test lasted over a part of two days, and the depth was twenty feet, more or less" [Johnson 1929, 40–41].

Both Chappell and Johnson were impressed by Miller's reputation. "In his neighborhood Neal Miller is regarded as having a good memory and being honest" (Chappell 1933, 46). "Mr. Miller's testimony was deliberate and restrained. Talcott people said, 'If Neal Miller says it happened, then it must have happened'" (Johnson 1929, 53).

Even so, the quality of his testimony is poor.

For Chappell, Miller was a native of the Talcott vicinity.
For Johnson, he "came here" in the spring of 1869.
For Chappell, he did not claim to have seen John Henry's contest.
For Johnson, he did.
For Chappell, he made no mention of a bet on the contest.
For Johnson, he said there was a hundred-dollar bet.
For Chappell, John Henry's shaker was Phil Henderson, a black man.
For Johnson, he was Jeff Davis, a white man.
For Chappell, John Henry was "6 feet high."
For Johnson, he was "of medium height."
For Chappell, the steam drill "got hung up in the seam of the rock and lost time."
For Johnson, the action of the steam drill "caused a lot of loose gravel around the top of the hole to slide down and pack the drill."
For Chappell, "the engine was taken from it and carried to shaft number one."
For Johnson, "the boiler was used to run a hoisting engine at shaft number one."
For Chappell, John Henry died "a long time after" the contest.
For Johnson, he died "soon after" the contest.
For Chappell, "he was killed from a blast of rock in the heading," according to the "boys 'round the tunnel."
For Johnson, he "took sick and died from fever."

Miller gave few details about John Henry's contest. For Johnson, he allowed, "There wasn't any big crowd around to see it. I was going and coming with water and steel, so I saw how they were getting along from time to time, but I didn't get excited over it especially." This is not the testimony of a convincing witness, nor is the scene he describes the kind that inspires legend.

Indeed, Miller didn't think much of John Henry.

Mr. Miller is no apologist, and no hero-worshipper, for John Henry or anyone else, as his testimony indicates. He has the characteristic mountaineer attitude toward the Negro, and regards the famous steel-driver as rather vicious, "just another Negro," superior of course and able to claim his woman when he was present, but remembers that he was not always present [Chappell 1933, 49].

Miller's testimony is impeached by inconsistencies, vagueness, and inappropriate characterization of John Henry and his contest with a steam drill. He is not a believable witness.

Up Hungart's Creek

Miller lived on a farm about a mile up Hungart's Creek, north from Talcott and the east portal of Big Bend Tunnel (Chappell 1933, 46, Johnson 1929, 40). "Hungart's Creek was named for the first settler whose identity, like others of the oldest pioneers, has been lost" (Miller 1908, 83). I'm not sure about this. Searches at Ancestry.com and elsewhere on the World Wide Web give no result for "Hungart" as a surname. The name of the creek is sometimes given as "Hungard Creek" or "Hungert's Creek." The German word "hungert" means "starves." Perhaps an original German name became garbled as it was passed on. In English, "Starvation Creek" seems to be a rather common name. A Google search for it returned about "64,300 results" (January 27, 2011). "Starving Creek" and "Starved Creek" are also extant, but less popular, English names.

According to Chappell, C.S. "Neal" Miller was a son of Andrew Jackson Miller (1933, 46). A Cornelius Miller lived in 1907 on Hungart's Creek in the Talcott District of Summers County (Miller 1908, 506). This suggests that C.S. "Neal" Miller was Cornelius S. Miller.

He appears in the federal censuses of 1870, 1880, 1910, and 1920. I have also found his death certificate and a citation of a record of his birth. In addition, considerable information about Brice Miller, Neal's grandfather, appears on the World Wide Web. Larry Palmer traces his ancestors through Ireland (about 1647–1753) to Scotland (as early as 1555) (Palmer 2007).

Neal Miller told Johnson that he was seventeen in the spring of 1869, implying that he was born in 1851 or '52. He also told Johnson that he was seventy-four in 1927, pointing to a birth in 1852 or '53. The censuses of 1910 and 1920 list his age as 56 and 66, respectively, consistent with one another and implying that he was born in 1853 or '54.

Small inconsistencies such as these are not rare. If Miller were born at any time from 1851 to 1854, he would have been old enough to have worked on the construction of Big Bend Tunnel beginning in the fall of 1869, even if he had not been exactly seventeen that spring.

Authoritative records challenge this picture. They also clarify his places of residence.

According to his death certificate, C.S. (Neil) Miller died on March 16, 1930, in Hinton, West Virginia, of bronchial pneumonia accompanying influenza (Miller 1930). In the space intended for the name of his father, *his* full name is given instead: "Cornelius Stratin Miller." Similarly, his wife's maiden name, "Cora Leota Wiseman," is given in the place intended for his mother's maiden name. In the 1910 census his wife is listed as "Cora," and in 1920 it is "Cora L.," making it clear that the death certificate and census records are for the same man.

In contrast to the information presented above, the death certificate gives his birth date as June 3, 1861. "Mrs. Cornelius Miller" signed it, thereby certifying that the information given was "true to the best of my knowledge." David Fridley provides similar information from original sources: "Cornelius S. Miller was born at Greenbrier Co, VA, on 25 Jun 1861. ... He married Cora L. Wiseman in Summers Co, WV, on 25 Dec 1888" (Fridley 1999). The date discrepancy between the death certificate and the birth record is of no concern here. They agree that Neal Miller was born in June 1861.

Census records for children are more likely to give accurate ages than those for adults. In the 1880 census, Cornelius S. Miller lives in the household of his father, A.J. Miller, in the Talcott District of Summers County, West Virginia. Cornelius is eighteen years old, consistent with a birth in June 1861. He had attended school within the census year (June 1, 1879–May 31, 1880).

In the 1870 census, Cornelius was eight years old, also consistent with a birth in June 1861. The Miller family lived in the "Bluesulpher Township" of Greenbrier County, West Virginia, with a post office at Lewisburg. Lewisburg is about twenty miles, as the crow flies, northeast of Talcott. The town of Blue Sulphur Springs is west of Lewisburg and about fifteen miles north-northeast of Talcott.

Miller was in no position to have watched John Henry's contest in 1870. Having recently had his eighth birthday, he was too young to carry water and tools in the fall of 1869. In addition, the boring of Big Bend Tunnel had not started at that time. It began in February 1870 (Lane 2010).

Miller told Johnson that he was seventeen years old when he moved to the Talcott area in the spring of 1869. The spring that he was seventeen was that of 1879, seven years after the tunnel was completed in 1872.

Neal Miller did not witness the contest between John Henry and a steam drill at Big Bend Tunnel. Perhaps he conflated memory with hearsay, fantasized, or pulled the legs of the learned professors who interviewed him, a time-honored sport of old farmers.

His testimony must be disregarded. The case for West Virginia as the John Henry site must rest on information other than the testimony of Miller.

———— ╡═ ╡═ ╡═ ————

Charles C. Spencer was a self-proclaimed eyewitness to John Henry's contest with a steam drill in Alabama.

15

We Called Him
John Henry

> I have reason to believe that I am the only living per-
> son who remembers these two persons, having worked
> with the both of them, and saw the end of them when
> they died.
>
> —C.C. Spencer

In responding to a query placed by Guy Johnson in the *Chicago
Defender* of February 12, 1927, C.C. Spencer wrote that he had seen John
Henry race the steam drill in Alabama in 1882 and that he seen John
Hardy hang in the 1890s. Spencer had carried water and tools for John
Henry in Alabama and had witnessed his contest with a steam drill and
subsequent death.

A New Suit of Clothes and Fifty Dollars

Spencer wrote two long letters (Johnson 1929, 19–22).

> 1400 East 21st South,
> Salt Lake City, Utah.
> February 24th, 1927.

Mr. Guy B. Johnson.
University of North Carolina,
Raleigh, N.C.

Dear Sir:

After seeing your request in the Chicago Defender asking for information about John Henry, or John Hardy, I am writing you as I have reason to
believe that I am the only living person who remembers these two persons,
having worked with both of them, and saw the end of them when they died.

John Henry was a native of Holly Springs, Mississippi, and was shipped

174

to the Cruzee mountain tunnel, Alabama, to work on the A.G.S. Railway in the year of 1880. In 1881 he had acquired such a skill as a hand driller that every one along the road was singing his praise. It happened that at about this time an agent for a steam drill company (drills used now are compressed air) came around trying to sell the contractor a steam drill. The contractor informed the agent that he had a Negro who could beat his damned old steam drill any day; as a result of this argument the company owning the drill offered to put it in for nothing if this man could drill more rock with the hammer than he could with his drill. And, so the contractor (Shea and Dabner) accepted the proposition.

This man John Henry, whose real name was John H. Dabner, was called to the office and they asked him if he could beat this steam drill. He said that he could, but the fact of the matter was he had never seen a steam drill and did not know what one could do. The contractor told him that if he could beat this steam drill he would give him a new suit of clothes and fifty dollars, which was a large amount for that day and time. John Henry accepted the proposition providing they would buy him a fourteen-pound hammer. This the contractor did.

Now the drills that we had in those days were nothing like the drills we have today. The drills they used then in hard rock could only drill a hole twenty-five feet deep in a day and the average man could only drill a hole about fifteen feet deep in a day working by hand.

Well—preparations were being made for the race for about three weeks, and on the 20th of September, 1882, the race took place, the agent from New York using steam, and the man from Mississippi, using a fourteen-pound hammer, in the hardest rock ever known in Alabama.

The agent had lots of trouble with his drill, but John Henry and his helper (Rubin Johnson) one turning the drill and the other striking, kept pecking away with that old fourteen-pound hammer. Of course the writer was only about fourteen years old at that time, but I remember there were about three or four hundred people present.

When the poor man with the hammer fell in the arms of his helper in a dead faint, they threw water on him and revived him, and his first words were: "send for my wife, I am blind and dying."

They made way for his wife, who took his head in her lap and the last words he said were: "Have I beat that old steam drill?" The record was twenty-seven and one half feet (27½"). The steam drill twenty-one (21'), and the agent lost his steam drill.

Now, Sir, this song has taken on such a versatile nature since the death of the subject, until it is very hard for any one to give the true version of it. As I believe all songs have some Hero as their subject, I would advise you to leave John Hardy out as an Honor to John Henry.

I do not think that you would like the history of John Hardy as the story of his life is different from that of good old John Henry. The one lived for honor, the other for dis-honor; the one died with his hammer in his hand, the other with his gun in his hand; the one with head in the lap of his wife, the other with his wife looking on while he swung from the gallows, and neither of them knew the other.

Hoping that this is the desired information, and that same will help you to meet your efforts, I am,

Very truly yours,
C.C. Spencer (1927a)

"Dabner" is a colloquial pronunciation of "Dabney."

Johnson responded with an encouraging letter dated March 1, 1927, in which he posed the following questions (Johnson 1927b).

1. Does the A.G.S. Railway mean the Alabama Great Southern? I am not certain, so would like your statement.
2. Was John Henry ordinarily called John Henry or was he known by his real name Dabner?
3. Was he, as far as you know, any relation to Dabner, the contractor whom you mentioned?
4. About how old would you say John Henry was at the time of the contest? Also if you could give me a brief description of him (his weight, height, degree of color, etc.) it would add to the value and interest of the history.
5. What county is the Cruzee Tunnel in? Or, better, what is the nearest town to the tunnel?

P.S.—I have seen a few songs about John Henry which say that he once worked in the Big Bend Tunnel on the C. & O. in West Virginia. Do you think this was true? As far as you know, did your friend John Henry ever work in W. Va.? Did you ever work in W.Va. yourself? If so, did you hear of any stories to the effect that John Henry worked there?

Spencer replied as follows.

1400 East 21st South,
Salt Lake City, Utah
March 10th, 1927

Mr. Guy B. Johnson.
Box 652.
Chapel Hill, N.C.

My Dear Mr. Johnson:

I have just received your letter and am indeed pleased to know that it was of some assistance to you in writing the history of John Henry.

Now, my Dear Sir, I feel sure that you do not expect one's mind to be clear concerning the minor things which were conected with this story forty four years after the Actor has passed from the stage. As I kept no diary in those days, I must quote from memory the facts as near as I can recall them.

No.1. The name of the railroad was the Alabama Great Southern.

No.2. His name was John Henry Dabner, but we called him John Henry.

No.3. I think he was born a slave in the Dabner family.

No.4. I should judge that he was at least 25 or 26 years old at the time of his death. His weight was near 180 lbs.; his color very dark; he was about 5'10 or 11 inches in height.

No.5. I do not recall the name of the County if I ever knew it, but the tunnel is near the line which devides Georgia and Alabama. I was told by the older men that there was a town on the Georgia side by the name of Risingforn. At that time I was under the care of a white man, the young Master of my people and I was never left to wander around very much, so I never went to this town in Georgia. There was, also, a town fifteen miles to the north in Alabama (in which was an Iron-Ore mine) by the name of "Red Mountain."

Now, Sir, as this Railroad was in the process of construction, there was no train's running upon it, so the names of these towns may have changed ere this time.

No, John Henry never was in West Virginia, but his wife stayed with the older men and cooked for many of them after we came to West Virginia, in 1886, for the purpose of working on the Narfork & Western Railroad in the Elkhorn tunnel.

The above is about all that I know of any importance about John Henry.

John Hardy was a native of South Carolina. He was brought to West Virginia on a transportation in the year of 89 to work on the N. & W. Railroad. He turned out to be a drunkard, gambler, gun man, and robber—and at last, a murder[er].

In 1891 this man killed a young man by the name of Read Drew for the sum of twenty dollars; he was arrested and convicted of murder, and he was the first man or person ever hanged in Welch, W.V., the County seat of McDowell County.

Now, if you will write to the County Clerk of McDowell County, Welch, W.V., I believe that he will be able to give the record of this trial, which was in the year of 1891 and 1892.

John Brown was the man of the "Big Ben tunnel fame." This man lived and probably died before this writer ever came upon the stage. In my younger days I saw old men who claimed to have worked with this man—but no two told me the same story.

This tunnel was put through with slaves, and if John Brown was one of the men who worked there as a slave, or in the Big Ben tunnel at any time, he never raced against a steam drill. There never was a steam drill in there. If you will write to any Railroad Journal you will find that the "C. &. O." road was put through in 59–69, long before the steam drill came into use.

This writer has seen many good men—but never one who could use a thirty pound hammer with any success.

This is a trend of the song about John Brown, sang when I was a boy some forty six years ago: "John Brown was a little boy, sitting upon his Mother's knee. He said the Big Ben tunnel on the C. &. O. Road will sure be the death of me."

Now, Sir, I was always counted one of the best Railroad men in my day, and my service was always in demand as a Foreman. Other than this, I will say nothing more about my-self at this time.

Hoping that the contents of this letter will prove of some assistance to you, and with all best wishes, I am,

Yours very truly,
C.C. Spencer [1927b]

Johnson's reply (March 17, 1927) expressed delight with Spencer's information and promised to keep in touch and let Spencer know his "final results" (1927c).

Spencer moved shortly after the correspondence quoted above. He never contacted Johnson with a new address.

⊒⊏-⊐⊏-⊐⊏

Charles C. Spencer, born John Matthews, led a colorful life. It is consistent with his testimony.

16

1400 East 21st South

...unlawfully, knowingly, willfully, feloniously, deliberately, premeditatedly, and of his malice aforethought...
—*State of Utah vs. Charles C. Spencer*, 1923

Charles C. Spencer is the star witness for John Henry in Alabama.
In February and March 1927, he wrote to Guy Johnson from 1400 East
21st South, Salt Lake City, Utah. Johnson didn't realize it, but that is a
famous address.

Sugar House

In 1853 Brigham Young selected a site for the territorial prison
some six miles south and east of the center of Salt Lake City (Strack
2000). It was near a sugar mill built in an unsuccessful attempt to grow
and process sugar beets. The mill was shut down in 1855 and replaced by
a succession of other ventures, but the community took the name Sugar
House and lent it to the prison.

In 1896, when Utah became a state, the prison became the Utah
State Prison but maintained its popular name (Figure 39). It remained in
use until 1951, when the prisoners were moved to the new prison at the
Point of the Mountain. Shortly thereafter the main prison building was
torn down and the site was converted to its present use as Sugar House
Park. Today, the only reminder of the prison is a plaque (ShopSugar-
House.org 2011).

Joe Hill

Sugar House prison is well known as the site of the imprisonment and execution of Wobbly labor activist and songwriter Joe Hill on

Figure 39. "Sugar House" prison, the old Utah State Prison, in 1903 (used by permission, Utah State Historical Society).

November 19, 1915 (Adler 2011). Hill was convicted of murder on circumstantial evidence after he refused to mount a substantial defense. Some believe him to have been innocent. Mormon leaders and the government of Utah regarded Wobblies, members of the Industrial Workers of the World (IWW), as extreme radicals. As he faced the firing squad, Hill's last word is said to have been "Fire!"

Murdering Minister

Guy Johnson never knew that C.C. Spencer was a prison inmate. He presented himself as follows: "Now, Sir, I was always counted one of the best Railroad men in my day, and my service was always in demand as a Foreman. Other than this, I will say nothing more about my-self at this time" (Spencer 1927a). My first clue to Spencer's reason for saying "nothing more" about himself came when I found online the parole application of Charles C. Spencer to the Board of Pardons of the State of Utah (Ibid. 1927, Application). Greg Walz, Cliff Ocheltree, and others helped me find Spencer's case file, a number of news articles, and other relevant documents (Utah State History 2010, Ocheltree 2008).

Mohrland, a mine and coal camp in Emery County, Utah, is now a ghost town. It was about eighty miles south-southeast of Salt Lake City and less than two miles south of the border between Emery and Carbon Counties. In 1920 C.C. Spencer lived there with his wife, "Luceal" (Lucile), and adopted son, Charles Pett (census). He and Pett were coal miners.

A newspaper headline, December 27, 1922, proclaimed "POSSES CONDUCT HUNT FOR SLAYER IN TWO COUNTIES" (*Salt Lake Telegram* 1922a). Authorities sought "D.C. Spencer," who had shot Pleasant Jackson after quarreling over Jackson's persistent winning, and Spencer's persistent losing, in a card game. The shooting was a few days earlier, but Jackson had just died when this article was sent to press on December 27, 1922 (Jackson 1922).

> Residents of Mohrland are considerably exercised over the murder, both because the men were gambling and also because it is the boast of the coal camp that there has been very little difficulty there in the past and the citizens desire to maintain a model town....
>
> Spencer is known to be a crack shot and deputies who are seeking him are heavily armed and have been cautioned to take no chances [*Salt Lake Telegram* 1922a].

Three days later the same newspaper carried the following.

> PRICE, Dec. 30.—C.C. Spencer, negro, who shot and killed Pleasant Jackson at Mohrland several days ago during a card game, was captured yesterday at Green River, brought here last night by Deputy Sheriff L.A. Pike and is now being held in the county jail. He will be taken to Emery county next week [Ibid. 1922b].

Also on December 30, 1922, the *Emery County Progress* noted that an informer had facilitated the arrest. "Spencer was said to have had two guns on him at the time of his arrest, but no resistance was reported by Deputy Pike."

On February 7, 1923, Spencer went to trial (*Emery County Progress* 1923b). The charge against him is interesting for its language.

> Charles C. Spencer ... is accused of said crime, committed as follows:
>
> That the said Charles C. Spencer on the 24th day of December, A.D. 1922, at and within Emery County, State of Utah, did unlawfully, knowingly, wilfully, feloniously, deliberately, premeditatedly, and of his malice afore thought, make an assault in and upon one Pleasant Jackson, with a certain gun, commonly called a revolver, then and there loaded with gun powder and leaden bullets and by him the said Charles C. Spencer then and there had and held in his hands and he, the said Charles C. Spencer then and there unlawfully, knowingly, wilfully, feloniously, deliberately, premeditatedly and of his malice aforethought, and with the specific intent to take

the life of him the said Pleasant Jackson, the said gun so loaded as aforesaid did shoot and discharge upon and against the body of him the said Pleasant Jackson, thereby and thus striking him the said Pleasant Jackson with one of said leaden bullets, inflicting upon and in the body of him, the said Pleasant Jackson one mortal wound, from which mortal wound the said Pleasant Jackson languished a short time, and on the 27th day of December, A.D. 1922, at and within the County of Salt Lake, State of Utah, did die.

And so the said Charles C. Spencer, did in the manner and form aforesaid wilfully, knowingly, unlawfully, feloniously, deliberately, premeditatedly and of his malice aforethought, kill and murder the said Pleasant Jackson, contrary to the form of the Statute in such case made and provided and against the peace and dignity of the State of Utah.

> B.W. Dalton [signature]
> District Attorney [State of Utah 1923, image 0081]

The *Emery County Progress* reported that a verdict was returned on the morning of February 11, 1923 (1923b).

Returning after some seventeen hours spent in discussion and deliberation, the jury in Emery County's first murder trial this (Sunday) morning about eight-thirty o'clock rendered a verdict of guilty in the first degree, including with the verdict a recommendation for life imprisonment instead of the infliction of the death penalty. The case at trial was that of the state against Charles C. Spencer, the Mohrland negro who was accused of mortally wounding Pleasant Jackson, another negro in an altercation over a card game last Christmas eve [Ibid.].

The defense was that Spencer thought Jackson was drawing his gun. When he drew his own in response, it went off accidentally (Ibid.).

According to reports, on the first ballot "six or seven" jurors were for "conviction without recommendation," while two jurors were for acquittal. A lone holdout for acquittal prolonged the deliberations (*Emery County Progress* 1923b).

The defendant bore himself well and betrayed no trace of the sullenness usual in so many defendants under similar circumstances. Asked what he would do if he were "sent up," he expressed the intention of doing everything he could to help his fellows in a moral and spiritual way. It seems that the defendant had done more or less missionary work among his race in the past, at one time holding the office of second degree minister in his faith. He is understood to have been an abstainer from both tobacco and drink until about a year before the shooting, but then commenced to have indulged in both and to take up gambling [Ibid.].

Judge Christensen followed the jury's recommendation. On Monday, February 19, 1923, he sentenced Spencer to life in the Utah State Prison (Ibid., 1923a).

Emery County was created in 1880 (Thomas 1880). Spencer was "the first man tried for first degree murder in the history of Emery Count" (*Emery County Progress* 1923a). While his lawyers appealed, Spencer was sent to the "state penitentiary at Salt Lake," to Sugar House prison, where mug shots were taken (Figure 40) (Utah State Prison 1923).

He was confined there on February 20, 1923, at age 52 (Ibid.). He had no previous convictions. On November 20, 1926, his sentence was commuted to five years "on the ground that the crime was not more serious than manslaughter" (*Salt Lake Tribune* 1926). He applied on April 22, 1927, for parole and early release, which was granted, and he was released on February 18, 1928 (Charles C. Spencer 1927, Utah State Prison 1923).

I was intrigued by the report that Spencer was a minister. In the prison registry there is a column headed "Religion," and something is scrawled there for Spencer, but neither I nor several others could decipher it. Then I noticed the term "second degree minister" in a news account (*Emery County Progress* 1923b). I found that the Church of the Brethren, Old German Baptist Brethren, Tunkers, Dunkards, etc., have this office, one among three degrees of ministers. In the light of this information, the scrawl became clear: "Dunkerd."

I had never thought of African Americans as Dunkards. However, reflection tells me that it is likely. The beliefs of the moral, peace-loving, anti-slavery Dunkards could be especially attractive to an African American. Evidently, such was the case for Charles C. Spencer, who abandoned the principles of his faith for about a year in 1922, when he drank, gambled, and killed. The coal-camp environment in which he had lived for several years could have promoted his lapse.

He probably lived up to his

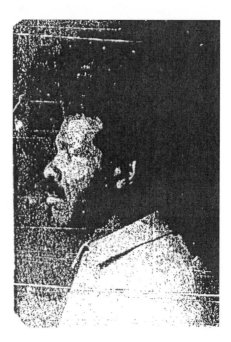

Figure 40. This badly degraded image of Charles C. Spencer is from a February 1923 mug shot taken at the Utah State Prison, Sugar House, Salt Lake City (Utah Department of Corrections).

commitment of "doing everything he could to help his fellows in a moral and spiritual way" while in prison. His piety may have impressed the parole board, inclining them toward leniency.

Castle Valley

The eastern side of Salt Lake City is nestled against the Wasatch Mountains. Castle Valley, east of the Wasatch Plateau, extends 80 miles south-southwest from the bluffs of the Book Cliffs, six miles north of Price, to the vicinity of Interstate 70. Most of the valley is less than 20 miles wide. Except along streams, it is a scrubby desert. Its elevation ranges around 6000 feet above sea level, and its annual rainfall averages about eight inches. The northernmost fourth of Castle Valley is in Carbon County, but most of it is in Emery County.

Brigham Young's 1877 call for the settling of Castle Valley was heeded slowly. In 1880 there were only 556 settlers there (Taniguchi 2004, 34, 44).

Things changed dramatically when the Denver & Rio Grande Western Railroad, "the Western," was completed in April 1883 (Ibid., 58). It provided Salt Lake City with rail access to northern Castle Valley. The railroad and its spurs brought farms, coal mines, livestock, other businesses, and thieves, including Butch Cassidy (Ibid., 76).

Butch Cassidy

Castle Gate was a coal camp in the Price River canyon, Book Cliffs, ten miles north of Price. At noon on Wednesday, April 21, 1897, the payroll of the Pleasant Valley Coal Company arrived in Castle Gate on a train from Salt Lake City and was unloaded in three sacks and a satchel. As the train pulled away, a man with a gun met the paymaster at the steps of the company store. Butch Cassidy and his accomplice, Elza Lay, got away with about $7,000 in gold coins (Ibid., 98–99, Weiser 2010). The money was never recovered.

Labor Troubles

The coal camps of Castle Valley were marked by frequent, if not continuous, labor disputes. They probably brought Charles C. Spencer to Mohrland.

Kenilworth is about three miles east of Helper, Carbon County, Utah. Kenilworth mine, also called Four Points, began its operations in 1907 (Pettit 1911, 20–24). An incident there in 1911 was described by the State Mine Inspector.

But one labor trouble was experienced during the past year. This occurred February 4th and 6th, when a number of Greek, Austrian and Italian miners, at Kenilworth, requested the mine superintendent to allow them to select a check-weighman, as they claimed they were not getting correct weights over the mine scales. This request was granted, but did not appease the lawless element, who refused to go to work and acted in a very boisterous and insulting manner, which resulted in fifteen of the ringleaders being discharged and escorted out of camp. On Sunday evening, the 5th, a number of the discharged men returned and incited about seventy of the dissatisfied miners to arm themselves, shoot up the town, and thus compel the Independent Coal & Coke Company to reinstate those discharged and remedy other grievances which they claimed existed.

Before daybreak on the morning of February 6th, several volleys were fired into the town by a party of armed miners, stationed on the Price road. They were driven from their position by Superintendent Bell and other mine officials. The miners then ran to the hills and joined their companions who had stationed themselves behind ledges of rock overlooking the town and were shooting at any mine official who showed himself in the opening. This firing was kept up nearly all day, or until an armed force of deputy sheriffs were rushed to the town. During the day, several Greeks were wounded and one killed. Thomas Jackson, a local watchman, was also killed, leaving a wife and four children.

The mine was idle four full days during this trouble, but worked with a decreased force for about two weeks [Pettit 1913, 5–6].

Italian immigrant miner Peter Aiello told a different story. The new superintendent was short-weighting the miners by 20–25 percent. About two days after the superintendent had agreed to allow a miner to check the weights, the company brought in "gunmen," who replaced some of the miners, thus precipitating the strife (Taniguchi 2004, 160–61).

Labor troubles did not begin or end in 1911. Among other things, miners were dissatisfied with unsafe conditions. In 1900 an explosion and fire at the Winter Quarters mine, in the Wasatch Mountains about twenty miles north northwest of Mohrland, killed 200 men (Ibid., 107–09).

Miners were dissatisfied with being paid in script. It could be used at full value only at the company store, where prices were generally inflated. They were also dissatisfied with wages and various forms of exploitation and corruption. Unions promised a solution.

During a strike in 1903–04, the legendary Mother Jones came to Castle Valley, where she narrowly escaped assassination. When she left for Salt Lake City to attend labor meetings there, the Western took her at no charge, glad to be rid of the troublemaker (Taniguchi 2004, 118–21).

A few African Americans were brought in as scabs, strike breakers, in Carbon County in 1903–04 (Ibid., 121). Other major strikes followed in 1919–20 and 1922 (Ibid., 171–72, 78–83).

Management brought in strikebreakers to mine coal and hired detectives to keep order alongside state and local lawmen. Striking miners hated the scabs, gun thugs, and lawmen. Violence was common and a gun was a necessity.

At the end of 1907 the "nationalities" of the 2778 men working in Utah coal and hydrocarbon mines were distributed as follows: "American" (1032) "Greeks" (614), "Italians" (429), "Austrians" (392), "Finns" (144), "Japs" (56), "Germans" (48), "Swedes" (23), "French" (20), "Belgians" (11), "Negroes" (8), and "Chinese" (1) (Pettit 1911, 17). In 1907–10, African Americans were no more than about 0.3 percent of the workers in the coal mines of Utah (Ibid., 17, 27, 69, 76). The fact that they were distinguished from "Americans" in official reports suggests that Utah coal camps may not have been hospitable to them.

Mohrland

Utah has considerable coal resources. In 2005, Utah coal fields produced over 24.5 million tons of coal, all from underground mines (BLM 2008). Coal is still being taken from the Emery Coal Field, which lies along the northwestern side of Emery County.

An entry in the diary of Albert F. "Bert" Potter for September 24, 1902, reads, "On Cedar Creek at Mr. Howard's mine there is a 17 ft. vein of coal at an elevation of 8,100 ft." (Potter 1902). Between 1896 and about 1908, men named Howard, Marshall, Gardner, and Grange conducted mining operations in Cedar Creek Canyon (Fauver 2010, Taff 1906, 299, Thomas 1899). The primary use of the coal produced, at that time, was heating nearby homes (Taniguchi 2004, 145–46). A coal seam thickness of seventeen feet allowed horse- or mule-drawn wagons to go into the mine and be loaded directly from the face being mined (Figure 41) (Savage 1895). Such mines were called "wagon mines," distinguishing them from "railroad mines," from which coal was sent out on trains.

In 1909 the Howard mine became the Mohrland mine, a property of the Castle Valley Coal Company. The Castle Valley Railroad Company

Figure 41. Wagon mine in Cedar Creek Canyon, Utah. This could be the Howard mine and is referred to as such by local residents in Emery County (used by permission, Utah State Historical Society).

built a spur to Mohrland in 1910, and the mine became a railroad mine. It was closed in 1938 when the U.S. Fuel Company decided to take coal out of that seam through tunnels connected to their Hiawatha mine in Carbon County, about three and a half miles north of Mohrland (Taniguchi 2004, 209).

The "Mohr" part of "Mohrland" is an acronym representing "Mays, Orem, Heiner, and Rice." Moroni Heiner was a leading businessman, coal developer, and politician. James H. Mays, Walter C. Orem, and Windsor V. Rice were his partners, investors in the Mohrland enterprise.

The town of Mohrland was established at the mouth of Cedar Creek Canyon. It was much like the coal camps of McDowell County, West Virginia, where John Hardy murdered Thomas Drews in 1893.

In 1920, Mohrland was a thriving community.

The town of Mohrland, like most mining towns in that era, was owned and controlled by the mining company for the benefit of the mine owner, the miners and their families....

A tram (a truck or car on rails for carrying loads in a mine) was installed to carry coal from inside the mine to the coal tipple (a structure used for loading coal into railroad cars) about a mile from the mine and East down the canyon. The tram used electricity and large electric motors and a large cable to move the coal from the mine to the tipple where it was loaded into railroad cars. The loaded tram cars going down the hill to the tipple helped pull the empty cars back up to the mine [Fauver 2010].

The tipple and end of the tram are shown in Figure 42.

A business district was established in Mohrland which included a hospital, boarding house, store, post office, and saloons. By 1920 Mohrland had over 200 houses, an amusement hall, and a school. The population was about 1000. The company worked to make it a pleasant place to live, despite its location at the edge of the desert. The streets were lined with shade trees, and a small stream ran along the canyon bottom. Mine employees' benefits included medical services, as well as regularly scheduled dances, films, and other social events. In the spring of 1915, as champions of the Carbon County league, they played an exhibition game at Price against the Chicago White Sox, drawing an audience of over 10,000, but losing by a score of 17 to 1 [Emery County 2011].

Living in Mohrland was segregated by "nationality." African Americans got the worst living quarters, up the canyon, close to the mine and

Figure 42. Tipple at the Mohrland Mine, 1911 (used by permission, Utah State Historical Society).

tipple and far from town, where Italians and Greeks lived (Taniguchi 2004).

In 1910 the Mohrland mine was just getting into operation (Pettit 1911, 132–35). It employed 145 men in 1911, 190 in 1912, and 357 in 1913 (Ibid. 1913, 65, 96, Lewis, R.S. 1914, 1732),

America's coal shortage of 1916 extended into the period of its participation in World War I, 1917–18 (Morrow 1918). Pressure for increased coal production, in the face of continuing labor problems, brought many miners to Castle Valley and Mohrland at this time. Circumstances suggest that Charles C. Spencer may have been one of them.

The nationalities of the miners at Mohrland seems to have been typical, as is shown by the 1920 census, except for the number of African Americans. Of the 691 individuals enumerated in the Mohrland Precinct in 1920, sixty (8.7 percent) are black. That is a considerably higher proportion than the approximately 0.3 percent that prevailed in Utah coal mines in 1907–10.

During the strike of 1922, African American scabs from the South were heavily recruited (Taniguchi 2004, 178). Pleasant Jackson was probably among them.

Strikers were driven out of Mohrland in April 1922 (Ibid., 179). When the strike ended in August, some found that scabs had taken their jobs. That Spencer was still there in late 1922 makes it almost certain that he was a scab.

Virginia

According to his death certificate, Charles C. Spencer "was born Matthews" at Spencer, Virginia (Spencer 1944). Spencer is in southwestern Henry County, Virginia, about thirty-five miles west of Danville and seven miles north of the North Carolina border. Prior to 1884 it was known as Spencer's Store (Pezzoni 2001). In that year, the Danville & New River Railroad was put through, bringing a station and a new name, Spencer (Brodsky 2011).

I am grateful to Beverly R. Millner for helping solve the mystery of Charles C. Spencer's name and parentage. He was born John Matthews, but by 1900, when he lived in Bell County, Kentucky, he had changed his name to Charles C. Spencer (census).

His mother, Jane Clanton, married Houston ("Hughes") Matthews on December 28, 1869, in Henry County, Virginia (Millner 2006, 40). John Matthews was born on December 5, 1870 (Spencer 1944,

Find-A-Grave 2000). His father died of consumption on November 7, 1879 (Spencer 1879, Hardis 1880).

We do not know when or why John Matthews changed his name to Charles C. Spencer. In so doing, he took a surname that was prominent in his community. Several other Spencers were named "Charles." Perhaps the middle initial "C" stood for "Clanton," his mother's family name. In any event, name changing was common among freed slaves (Killham 1870). The next generation may have inherited the tendency.

The family of David Harrison Spencer, a wealthy white tobacco farmer and producer of tobacco products, dominated the area. In the 1870 census, whites, blacks, and mulattoes named "Spencer" and "Matthews" (sometimes "Mathews") were enumerated in District 2 of the Ridgeway Township of Henry County. David H. Spencer is number 493 in order of residence visitation. Houston Matthews, a black tobacco prizer (packer), is number 500, indicating that he and Jane lived close to D.H. Spencer's Grassdale Farm home (Pezzoni 2001). In 1880, the recently widowed Jane Matthews and her five children still lived nearby. It is not clear who supported her family, but it is plausible that she would have had help from the white Spencers who controlled the community.

Figure 43. Gravestone of Charles C. Spencer, Mount Olivet Cemetery, Salt Lake City, Utah (courtesy Judie Huff).

In 1880, ten-year-old John Matthews could not read or write but was "at school," suggesting that he had just begun his education. Being sent to school suggests that the young John Matthews enjoyed a degree of privilege. That he was working at age sixteen at Dunnavant, Alabama, "under the care of a white man, the young Master of my people," is another such indication (Spencer 1927, March 10). The young Matthews seems to have impressed someone.

Alabama and West Virginia

At Dunnavant John Matthews / Charles C. Spencer witnessed John Henry's contest with a steam drill and subsequent death. Shortly thereafter, he went to West Virginia to work on the Norfolk & Western (N & W) at the Elkhorn Tunnel, in Mercer County at its western border with McDowell County. While in West Virginia, he witnessed the hanging of John Hardy at Welch, McDowell County, in January 1894.

It was probably his work in West Virginia that allowed Spencer to represent himself to Johnson as a railroad worker. Recall his boast, "Now, Sir, I was always counted one of the best Railroad men in my day, and my service was always in demand as a Foreman" (Ibid.).

Spencer would have related his extraordinary story about John Henry's contest and death in Alabama frequently. He must have been a source of the John Henry legend in West Virginia. Subsequent relocalization from the Columbus and Western and the Dunnavant tunnels to the Chesapeake and Ohio and its Big Bend Tunnel reflects the normal workings of folk tradition.

Kentucky

The 1900 census for Bell County, in Kentucky's eastern coal field, lists a black Charles Spencer who was single, was born in December 1873, was a miner, and could read and write. The name, race, marital status, birth month, occupation, and literacy are all matches for Charles C. Spencer, and the year is close enough, given that Spencer was frequently uncertain with years.

Birthplaces do not match. Charles Spencer, his father, and his mother were all born in North Carolina, according to the Bell County census of 1900. Charles C. Spencer was born in Virginia, his father in North Carolina, and his mother in Virginia.

Because census takers were casual with such details as birthplaces, and because so many other details match, I accept Charles Spencer of Bell County in 1900 as Charles C. Spencer, the former John Matthews.

Bell County, the southeasternmost county in the state, borders Virginia (Lee County) and Tennessee (Claiborne County). Cumberland Gap is at the intersection of Kentucky, Virginia, and Tennessee.

> Cumberland Gap's a noted place,
> Three kinds o' water to wash your face.
> —"Cumberland Gap" [folk song]

Bell County is the locale of Elbert McDonald's 1934 John Henry tale (Chapter 2). According to McDonald, legend has it that John Henry died at the Seven Sisters, on the Cumberland River near Varilla, Kentucky, near Pineville. McDonald himself believed that it had been at nearby Ewing, Virginia.

If Spencer brought his John Henry story to Bell County, McDonald's tale, containing elements of truth, is just the sort of thing that would be expected to have survived some thirty-odd years later. McDonald's John Henry was a "tall, gaunt, Alabama negro," "the most powerful steel driver of the crew, who was loved by his 'foreman, his name long since lost to the ages.'"

Colorado

In 1910, ten years after he had been a coal miner in Kentucky, Charles C. Spencer lived with his wife "Lessie" ("Lucy," Lucille) at 3115 Walnut Street, Denver, Colorado, and he worked as a hodcarrier (census). They had been married for nine years.

Also in 1910, he became a minister of the Second Church of the Brethren of Denver, a "Negro Mission" (Dumbaugh 1983, 377, Frantz 1958, 27–28, 35–39). I am grateful to Pastor Jack Lowe, Peters Creek Church of the Brethren, Roanoke, Virginia, for information about Spencer as a Dunkard minister.

The Second Church had its origin in the establishment in 1903 of an orphanage and home for the elderly by William Rhodes, an African American. In 1908 Brethren pastor A.C. Root, his wife, and A.C. Daggett began to minister to Rhodes' group, and in 1909 Root baptized Rhodes and seven others. Shortly thereafter, he baptized thirteen additional blacks. Charles C. Spencer was probably among these twenty new Dunkards.

The Second Church was established in early 1910 with Rhodes as the pastor and Charles C. Spencer as a first-degree minister. When

Rhodes was disfellowshipped over improprieties involving the matron of the orphanage, he was succeeded as pastor by Spencer, who was then elevated to second-degree minister (Dumbaugh 1983, 377, 1107, 209, Frantz 1958, 27–28).

It is not clear just when Spencer became pastor or how long the Second Church lasted. It appears to have dissolved in about 1914 (Frantz 1958, 35). However, it is listed in a 1916 Brethren publication (Dumbaugh 1983, 377). Spencer is listed in the Denver city directories for 1910 (laborer), 1911 (laborer), and 1915 (miner) (Callaway 2011).

Later Life

I have found no record of Lucile Spencer after Charles' release from prison. In 1930 he was a boarder in the household of Mrs. Lula V. Stevens at 661 East 4th South, Salt Lake City (census), where he lived until she died. He was 60 years old in 1930 (46 in the census), worked as a "crane man" in a factory, and was married but not living with his wife. In 1934 he worked at the Griffin Wheel Company (Salt Lake City directory). By 1936 he and Lula had married (city directory).

Figure 44. Second Church of the Brethren, "colored" mission, 300 block of Yuma Street, Denver, Colorado, circa 1910. William Rhodes, pastor, is standing at the far right. The tall man standing at the far left is probably Charles C. Spencer, first-degree minister (Brethren Historical Library and Archives, Elgin, Illinois).

Lula V. Stevens Spencer died in 1940 (Spencer 1940). When Charles C. Spencer died from a stroke in 1944, he lived at 561 East 7th South and still worked at the Griffin Wheel Company (Ibid. 1944). Charles' and Lula's gravestones in Mt. Olivet Cemetery, Salt Lake City, are headed "Father" and "Mother." Charles was the step-father of Lula's daughter, Elect.

Lula's obituary states that she "came to Salt Lake City 13 years ago," which would have been about 1927, just as Charles Spencer was about to be released from prison (*Salt Lake Tribune* 1940).

In the directories of 1936, 1939, 1940–41, the Rev. Charles C. Spencer is listed as the pastor of Calvary Baptist Church, a position he held for twelve years, according to his obituary, ending in 1941 (Ibid. 1944b). Church records indicate that his pastorate at Calvary began in 1932 (Davis 1997). I am grateful to Pastor France A. Davis, Calvary Baptist Church, for information about the Reverend Spencer and his life in Salt Lake City.

In October 1929, less than two years after his release from prison, "Rev. Mr. Spencer" conducted at an evening service of Pilgrim Baptist Church (*Salt Lake Tribune* 1929). In August 1931, Mrs. L.V. Stevens, her daughter, and her son-in-law sang for a service of Pilgrim Baptist (Ibid. 1931). The Rev. C.C. Spencer was the principal speaker at the annual meeting of the Salt Lake branch of the NAACP, held at Calvary Baptist Church, in November 1932 (Ibid. 1932). From 1932 through much of 1941, *The Salt Lake Tribune* contains notices of church services, funerals, and other meetings conducted by or featuring the Rev. C.C. Spencer. In 1937 he established a free employment bureau for African Americans (*Salt Lake Tribune* 1944a, Davis 1999, 1997, 40).

Testimonial Integrity

Charles C. Spencer's life can be summarized as follows.

He was sixteen years old on September 20, 1887, when John Henry died at Dunnavant, Alabama. That is old enough for him to have carried water and steel for steel drivers, as he claimed, and it is tolerably consistent with his statement that he "was only about fourteen years old at that time" (Chapter 15).

He was "under the care of a white man, the young Master of my people." The "young Master" was probably from Spencer, Henry County, Virginia, where Spencer was born and raised.

After John Henry's death, the crew moved to West Virginia to work on the N & W "in the Elkhorn tunnel." Spencer was in West Virginia long enough to have known John Hardy there and to have witnessed his death by hanging in January 1894.

In 1900, he was mining coal in Bell County, Kentucky. In 1910, he became a Brethren minister in Denver, Colorado. At some time between 1915 and 1920, he moved to Mohrland, Utah, to mine coal. In 1922, he shot and killed a man during a card game. From February 1923 until February 1928, he was held in the Utah State Prison in Salt Lake City.

On his release from prison, he remained in Salt Lake City, where he became a Baptist minister. For ten years or more, through most of 1941, he served Calvary Baptist Church. During this period he was a social activist. He died in 1944 at age seventy-three.

His year of smoking, drinking, and gambling in 1922, culminating in a Christmas Eve killing, is a blot on his record, which is otherwise admirable. He was an intelligent and industrious man, a servant of Christ, African Americans, and all people.

Nothing we know of Spencer's life casts doubt on his testimony. We are fortunate to have it.

⹶⹶⹶

Identifying the historical John Henry site is a matter of inference from evidence. Theories must be formulated and tested. A simple method derived from Bayes' Rule meets our needs.

17

Trying to Get Things Right

> "I see that you are professionally very busy just now," said he, glancing very keenly across at me.
>
> "Yes, I've had a busy day," I answered. "It may seem very foolish in your eyes," I added, "but really I don't know how you deduced it."
>
> "I have the advantage of knowing your habits, my dear Watson," said he. "When your round is a short one you walk, and when it is a long one you use a hansom. As I perceive that your boots, although used, are by no means dirty, I cannot doubt that you are at present busy enough to justify the hansom."
>
> "Excellent!" I cried.
>
> "Elementary," said he. "It is one of those instances where the reasoner can produce an effect which seems remarkable to his neighbour, because the latter has missed the one little point which is the basis of the deduction."
>
> —A. Conan Doyle

Holmes' conclusion that Watson rode a hansom is an induction, not a deduction (Rocha 2011, 147–48). Given that the premises are true, a deduction is definitely true, whereas an induction is only probably true (IEP 2003).

Nothing that Holmes says makes it certain that Watson had a busy day. It is impossible to be certain about the past because it cannot be examined. The best anyone can do is to formulate a theory.

Evidence

Evidence can be anything with a logical impact on an inference. Evidence includes persistent artifacts, things that were generated in the past and that still exist. Lipstick on the face of a man is a persistent artifact that is evidence of a recent kiss by a woman. Evidence also includes the absence of persistent artifacts that would be expected under certain circumstances. The absence of dirt on Dr. Watson's shoes is evidence that he did not walk on his round that day. Evidence also includes accepted principles. The principle that no human lives to an age past 123 is evidence that a woman born in 1820 has died.

Theories

A theory is an inductive inference from evidence. It is constructed so that it accounts for at least some of the evidence and does not contradict any. It is not an unguided guess.

A theory cannot be certain because inductive reasoning cannot rule out every possible alternative. The man might have put lipstick on his own face. Watson could have cleaned his boots before Holmes arrived. The woman could be the first person to live for 192 years. There is always the possibility of a valid theory that has not been thought of.

Inference from Evidence

A recent book on inference from evidence, by twenty authors, consists of 483 pages of dense words, dense ideas, dense diagrams, and dense mathematics (Dawid 2011). We take a less dense approach, based on the scientific method:

Find evidence.
Formulate viable theories.
Think of new evidence that could discriminate among these theories.
Find some of that evidence.
Test the theories against the new evidence, ruling out some.
Continue in this fashion until only one theory remains [ideally].

In general, there is no systematic method of generating theories. They must be imagined.

An algebraic relationship, bearing the name of Thomas Bayes (1702–61), tells how the probability that a theory is true changes in the light of new evidence (1763, Dawid 2011, McGrayne 2011). We use a simplification of Bayes' Rule.

Two Tests

Gardner-Medwin drew attention to two propositions, based on Bayes' Rule, that are critical in deciding whether or not evidence supports a theory (2005). They are cast here as questions.

Confirmation: Given that the theory is true, is the evidence plausible?
Discrimination: Given that the theory is false, is the evidence plausible?

If the answers to the confirmation and discrimination questions are "Yes" and "No," respectively, then the evidence supports the theory. Good evidence must confirm the theory *and* militate against alternatives.

History

A history is a theory of the past.

No history is complete. There are always issues for which no evidence can be found. How many insects were in the room with the players in the poker game you watched on television last night?

No history is certain. Every history is a more or less probable inference from evidence.

When the evidence is sufficiently strong, uncertainty is unimportant. No sane person doubts that John F. Kennedy was President of the United States of America or that he was assassinated. The evidence makes the probabilities of these things very high. In contrast, there are many uncertainties in the history of any individual. There are aspects of President Kennedy's life that we know little or nothing about.

Cherry Picking

The "confirmation bias" is the tendency to accept evidence in favor of a theory and to neglect evidence against it (Nickerson 1998). Selecting evidence is called "cherry picking."

A historian finds evidence for a novel theory. He ignores opposing evidence because he thinks its implications are wrong. He seeks and finds additional evidence for his theory, which helps build a good story. In publishing that story, he includes only cherry-picked evidence.

Nelson's evidence for John Henry in Virginia is cherry picked (Nelson 2005, 2006). "We [historians] are suspicious of other people's narratives, but we always assemble our own stories out of the flotsam and jetsam we find" (Ibid. 2006, 24).

Long Shots

New evidence is not the only factor relevant to the truth of a theory. Another is its probability before the new evidence is taken into account. A less likely theory requires stronger evidence: "the more extraordinary the event, the greater the need of its being supported by strong proofs" (Laplace 1902). This principle is embodied in Bayes' Rule.

For example, consider John Henry in Jamaica. The John Henry tradition is strong in the American Southeast and weak in Jamaica. Because Jamaica is the more unlikely John Henry site, it should require stronger evidence.

———

Some witnesses are better than others.

18

Witnesses
Good and Bad

A witness who is probably telling the truth can still
come across as a liar.—Douglas D. Connah

With Neal Miller discredited (Chapter 14), we are left with C.C.
Spencer as the only self-proclaimed eyewitness to John Henry's contest
with a steam drill who could be credible (Chapter 15). We begin our
scrutiny of Spencer by asking, "Was he a good witness?"

Here are some trial lawyers' responses to the question, "What
makes a good witness?" (McElhaney 2005, 94–98) We apply them to
Spencer and Miller.

A good witness answers the question.
—William Pannill, Houston, Texas

Spencer passes with flying colors. Johnson asked for specific information about John Henry and John Hardy, and Spencer addressed each
question. He did not get off track or throw in extraneous material. By
this criterion, his testimony is excellent.

In contrast, Miller gave a small core of relevant information and
then rambled. His testimony suffers from a lack of focus.

A good witness is comfortable with not knowing the
answer.—Steve Miller, Cleveland, Ohio

Spencer implied the possibility of error: "I must quote from memory the facts as near as I can recall them." He was comfortable with not
knowing the answer.

Miller said that he went about his regular work and "saw how they
were getting along from time to time," but he "didn't get excited over

it especially." Despite the casual nature of his observations of the contest between John Henry and the steam drill, he knew all the answers. His testimony for Chappell contains no qualifications (Chappell 1933, 46–47). For Johnson, he qualified on just two points: "The contest took place in 1870, as well as I remember" and "As well as I remember, though, he took sick and died from fever soon after that" (Johnson 1929, 40–41).

> A good witness doesn't play the advocate and try to argue the case.—Gerald Messerman, Cleveland, Ohio

Spencer and Miller both claimed to be giving recollections.

> A good witness is willing to spend time to prepare.
> —David Schaefer, Cleveland, Ohio

The lengths and forms of Spencer's letters show that he put considerable effort into them.

The criterion does not apply to Miller, who was interviewed personally.

> A good witness grasps the big picture.—Miriam Kass, Houston, Texas

Spencer's view spans John Henry and John Hardy, several railroad tunnels, several other places, and several other people.

Miller lived his whole life on farms in a small area of West Virginia. He might have known a great deal about the construction of Big Bend Tunnel, but it was hearsay. He was too young for personal experience.

> A good witness tells the jury the same thing he told you.—Mark F. McCarthy, Cleveland, Ohio

Consistency is the hallmark here. Spencer wrote two letters, and there are no inconsistencies between them.

In contrast, Miller was remarkably inconsistent in his testimonies for Chappell and Johnson (Chapter 14).

> A witness who is probably telling the truth can still come across as a liar. All he has to do is exaggerate and fill in the blanks with assumptions.
> —Douglas D. Connah, Baltimore, Maryland

Spencer may have "come across as a liar" to Johnson. Perhaps he filled in some blanks with assumptions in his testimony about John Brown. Johnson commented, "he merely enlarges the mystery when he speaks of 'John Brown, the man of Big Ben tunnel fame'" (1929, 22). Spencer had no personal experience with Big Bend Tunnel. Whatever he believed about it was hearsay.

Miller's self-contradictions make it clear that he was not truthful. Johnson didn't know about them, but Chappell did. Perhaps the confirmation bias was at work with Chappell (Nickerson 1998).

> A good witness has the right demeanor.
> —Nancy Vecchiarelli, Assistant U.S. Attorney,
> Cleveland, Ohio

Surely a lawyer's view of the "right demeanor" is a demeanor that will be persuasive to a jury. Unfortunately, demeanor can persuade people of things that are wrong.

We can't detect Spencer's demeanor and body language in his letters. The letters themselves leave an impression of honesty.

Of his interview with Neal Miller, Johnson wrote, "Mr. Miller told me all this in a quiet and casual way as we sat on his porch at dusk. He seemed to see John Henry and the steam drill as clearly as if it were only a few years since he had seen them." This explains how Johnson could dismiss the logically stronger Alabama claims and believe Miller. According to studies, "Vivid interviews with people have profound effects on judgment," often leading them to irrational decisions (Schwartz 2004).

> A good witness is believable.—Robin Weaver,
> Cleveland, Ohio

The very first time I read Johnson's book, I was disturbed that he took Spencer's testimony lightly. "In view of the absence of any sort of objective evidence to support these Alabama claims, they must be dismissed as unproved" (1929, 25). To Johnson, Spencer was not a believable witness.

Of his interview with Neal Miller, Johnson noted, "I made a rough pen sketch of the drill as he described it, and later I found a striking resemblance between this drill and illustrations of early steam drills as shown in *Scientific American* and other magazines in the latter part of the last century.... I could not bring out by questions any evidence that he had ever had an opportunity to observe one unless it were at Big Bend Tunnel" (Ibid., 53–54).

The drill was mounted on steel supports something like table legs.... The steam came through a pipe from the boiler to the engine. A belt ran from the engine shaft to a pulley on the drill.... The drill turned round and round instead of churning up and down... [Ibid., 41].

Miller described a rotary drill mounted on legs and driven by a belt running from the steam engine shaft to a pulley on the drill. I found no illustration or description of such an apparatus in Drinker, who described and illustrated drills as extensions of engine shafts and drills driven by systems of gears but not drills driven by belts from an engine shaft (Drinker 1883, 222–32). For a drill mounted on a table or tripod, the belt system Miller described would probably be unstable.

> A good witness is sincere.—Cyril McIlhargie, Chicago, Illinois

"And that is the way the best witnesses are—with no effort to appear perfect or better than they are; with all the flaws, wrinkles and warts that make them human" (McElhaney 2005, 98).

Spencer's sincerity shines through. He made a great effort to tell his story to Johnson.

Chappell and Johnson were deceived by Miller's show of knowledge and sincerity.

Challenges

Spencer responded to every question; gave considerable detail, all of it relevant; and admitted the possibility of errors of memory. These are marks of someone who is trying to be truthful and helpful. He was an excellent witness.

Even so, he has been ridiculed in the popular press.

Spencer's memories were so confused that he mixed up John Henry—not with John Hardy—but with John Brown, the abolitionist who led the 1859 raid on Harpers Ferry. At least Spencer had a general feeling that someone named John had done something to help black people in the Mountain State, but he certainly didn't prove an Alabama source for the legend... [Douglas 2004].

Douglas, "a Berkeley Springs [West Virginia] novelist and newspaper editor," put his faith in John Henry at Big Bend Tunnel. He cherry picked the evidence and seized on Spencer's apparent confusion to reject Alabama without giving consideration to all of Spencer's testimony or to other evidence.

"John Brown" is such a common name that Douglas could be wrong in assuming that the famed abolitionist was Spencer's source for it. John Brown the abolitionist was not even the original subject of "John Brown's Body" (Fuld 2000, 133).

Knowing that John Henry died in Alabama, Spencer would have rejected his association with West Virginia. In versions of the ballad that made this association, he could have substituted "John Brown" for "John Henry." He would have had plenty of versions of "John Henry" left to accommodate Alabama. About sixty percent of those extant by 1933 make no mention of Big Bend Tunnel or the C & O.

Spencer's testimony is quite coherent.

Spencer and John Hardy

Spencer denied that John Henry was ever in West Virginia, but he said that John Henry's wife went there after leaving Alabama, along with Spencer himself and some older men. He could have seen John Hardy hanged in Welch, West Virginia, in January 1894, as he claimed.

Spencer was clear and correct about John Hardy at a time when some scholars were still confused. This is further evidence of the high quality of his testimony.

Common Sense

In late 1927, after his June visit to Big Bend Tunnel, Johnson wrote, "Personally, I am pretty well convinced that John Henry existed in the flesh and beat a steam drill at Big Bend Tunnel, but I confess that my belief is based on a sort of common-sense logic and not on what historians call documentary evidence" (1927g, 51).

What people call common sense is fascinating. Johnson and Chappell saw the abundant presence of Big Bend Tunnel and the C & O in tradition as strong evidence that John Henry was there. They failed to take adequate account of the fact that ballads and legends relocate. Common sense tells me that the incoherence of the evidence gathered by Johnson and Chappell militates strongly *against* John Henry at Big Bend Tunnel.

━━ ━━ ━━

Without Neal Miller's testimony, the case for John Henry in West Virginia collapses.

19

The Case
for West Virginia

> Perhaps the wisest thing would be to suspend judg-
> ment on this question, but, after weighing all of the
> evidence, I prefer to believe that (1) there was a Negro
> steel driver named John Henry at Big Bend Tunnel,
> that (2) he competed with a steam drill in a test of the
> practicability of the device, and that (3) he probably
> died soon after the contest, perhaps from fever.
> —Guy B. Johnson

> At all events, it is no longer necessary, or possible, to
> regard "John Henry" as made up of whole cloth. The
> energy and variety of the Big Bend community will not
> allow it.
> —Louis W. Chappell

With the publication of a series of articles and books during the period 1919–33, especially those of Guy Johnson and Louis Chappell, it became the conventional wisdom that John Henry worked on the construction of "Big Bend Tunnel on the C & O road" in West Virginia, where he raced a steam drill and died (Cox 1919, 1925, Johnson 1929, Chappell 1933). Construction began in February 1870 and ended in September 1872 (Lane 2010).

Evidence

The West Virginia Archives and History site lists over fifty local news articles, dated 1955–96, from its John Henry clippings file (WVA&H 2011). I have examined this material and found only one item of evidentiary value, a 1957 press release written by Kyle McCormick,

Director, West Virginia Department Archives and History, that militates *against* West Virginia as the John Henry site. Otherwise, Chappell's 1933 book made the last significant contribution to the evidence.

Here are the important points.

There is a long-standing tradition around Big Bend Tunnel that it is the John Henry site. It is uncertain when this tradition began. In the 1920s, some local residents promoted it, and others rejected it.

The earliest known version of "John Henry" that places the steel driver on the C & O was collected in 1912 (Perrow 1913, 163–64). He is at "that big tunnel." Another version, ca. 1913, places John Henry on the C & O at "tunnel number nine" (Lomax 1915, 13–14). The first collected reference to John Henry at Big Bend Tunnel may be from 1909 (Combs 1967, 164–65, 211).

About 40 percent of versions of "John Henry" collected by 1933 say that John Henry was at Big Bend Tunnel, on the C & O, or both (Perrow 1913, Lomax 1915, Cox 1919, 1925, Combs 1925, Scarborough 1925, Odum 1926, White 1928, Johnson 1929, Chappell 1933). Two versions place John Henry on the Central of Georgia or the "Georgia Line" (Crawford 1930, Johnson 1929, 124).

Numerous people with no personal connection with Big Bend Tunnel have stated that they had heard that it was the John Henry site. Numerous others have stated that they had heard that some place other than Big Bend Tunnel was the John Henry site (Johnson 1929, Chappell 1933).

Of eleven people who claimed to have had direct personal knowledge of the construction of Big Bend Tunnel, five believed that Big Bend Tunnel was the John Henry site and six believed that it was not (Johnson 1929, 16, 34–41, Chappell 1933, 35–36, 46–55). The believers were the Rev. J.F. Glaze, George Hedrick, John Hedrick, C.S. "Neal" Miller, and J.M. Logan. Sam Wallace, Agnes Wyant, W.H. Cottle, William Wimmer, George Jenkins, and D.R. Gilpin were nonbelievers.

Glaze, the Hedrick brothers, and Logan had only hearsay knowledge of John Henry. Wallace was about fifteen years old at the time, lived near Big Bend Tunnel, was there frequently during its construction, "knew personally most of the foremen and the leading steel drivers," and "never heard of John Henry until two years ago," that is, 1925 (Johnson 1929, 34–35).

Steam drills were not used in boring Big Bend Tunnel (Johnson 1929, 48–52, Chappell 1933, 43–60, McCormick 1957, Nelson 2006, 17–19, 81, 185n22). Johnson and Chappell assumed that one had been brought in for a trial.

Neal Miller stated that a "steam drill was brought to Big Bend

Tunnel as an experiment" (Johnson 1929, 41, Chappell 1933, 47). He said that he witnessed John Henry's contest with a steam drill, probably in 1870, outside the east portal of Big Bend Tunnel (Johnson 1929, 40–41). He is the only person known to have made this claim.

According to a 1957 press release by Kyle McCormick, Director, West Virginia Department Archives and History, James Twohig, contractor's foreman at the construction of Big Bend Tunnel, wrote of his knowledge of John Henry there as follows (McCormick 1957).

> There was a strapping big Negro named John Henry who weighed 275 pounds. He was a very valuable man and the contractor paid him $1.50 a day instead of the usual $1.25. His father came directly from Africa. He did not use 20-pound hammers (as stated in the ballad) as there were no 20-pound hammers in use at Big Bend. No such contest (between John Henry and a steam drill) as described in the ballad ever took place.
>
> John Henry died from old age near Gap Mills in Monroe County years later (and not from exhaustion as implied in the ballad). He had a son who became a prominent Negro educator.

Neal Miller described John Henry as black, medium height or 6 feet tall, 200 pounds, and 30 years old. George Hedrick described him as black, 6 feet tall, 200 pounds, and 30–35 years old. John Hedrick described him as yellow, 5 feet 8 inches tall or less, 160–70 pounds, and about 30 years old.

Argument

The evidence does not support the conclusion that the John Henry site is in West Virginia. Neal Miller, who claimed to have witnessed John Henry's contest with a steam drill, fabricated his story, and the remaining evidence is contradictory.

Chappell founded his conviction that Big Bend Tunnel was the John Henry site on the local tradition, but if that tradition had been strong, Johnson would not have been able to gather a "mountain of negative evidence" (Johnson 1929, 53). The Big Bend tradition is most likely a result of relocalization.

The frequent occurrences of "Big Bend Tunnel" and "C & O" show that these are attractive phrases. The fact that about 60 percent of versions of "John Henry" collected by 1933 fail to mention a site suggests that the earliest versions did not contain "Big Bend Tunnel" or "C & O." If they had been present, these phrases would have had better staying power.

The contradictory testimonies of those who had heard of a John

Henry site, but who had had no direct connection to it, have no evidentiary value. Neal Miller's fabricated testimony must be discarded (Chapter 14).

The accounts of the eleven people who claimed to have been at Big Bend Tunnel during its construction are also contradictory. When James Twohig is added to this list and Neal Miller removed, the majority, seven of eleven, deny that John Henry raced a steam drill at Big Bend Tunnel.

Guy Johnson wrote, "Just one man, Mr. C.S. Miller, among all those with whom I have come in contact in my investigation, claims to have seen the contest.... One man against a mountain of negative evidence. Were it not for that one man the question might not be so teasing" (1929, 53). If Johnson had known that Miller's testimony was false, he would have been left with his "mountain of negative evidence."

Two men other than Miller, the Hedrick brothers, gave descriptions of John Henry from their knowledge of him at Big Bend Tunnel. George's John Henry was black, six feet tall, and weighed more than 200 pounds, while John's John Henry was yellow, not over five feet eight inches tall, and weighed 160–70 pounds.

Johnson and Chappell considered Miller and the Hedrick brothers to be the most important witnesses for John Henry at Big Bend Tunnel. Throwing out Miller's testimony leaves only that of the Hedrick brothers, who contradicted one another.

The evidence for John Henry in West Virginia is incoherent.

Confirmation and Discrimination

> Theory: John Henry raced a steam drill at Big Bend Tunnel during its construction in 1870–72
> Confirmation: Given that the theory is true, is the evidence plausible?
> Discrimination: Given that the theory is false, is the evidence plausible?

The confirmation question must be answered, "No." If John Henry's contest and death had been at Big Bend Tunnel ca. 1871, the surviving tradition there in the 1920s, especially among men who had worked on the construction of the tunnel, would have been more coherent. In addition, the occurrence of "Big Bend Tunnel" and "C & O" would have been more prevalent in the ballad.

The discrimination question must be answered, "Yes." The evidence could have arisen through relocalization and embellishment. It is consistent with a John Henry site other than Big Bend Tunnel.

West Virginia is not the John Henry site.

⇒⇐ ⇒⇐ ⇒⇐

The case for John Henry in Jamaica rests on a weak, aberrant, and localized tradition.

20

The Case for Jamaica

> The fact remains that we have no sure evidence beyond
> the songs that place John Henry as a steel driver on the
> C. & O. or any other American railroad.... The oldest
> objective data concerning John Henry are the Jamai-
> can songs.
>
> —MacEdward Leach

MacEdward Leach

MacEdward Leach (1892–1967) was the first scholar to challenge the conventional wisdom that John Henry was at Big Bend Tunnel, West Virginia (1966). Finding the evidence for Big Bend Tunnel to
be inadequate, he proposed an alternative, Jamaica, where he found a
John Henry work-song tradition in the Blue Mountains near Kingston.
Jamaica had been investigated previously by Chappell, who dismissed it
(1933, 40–42).

Leach suggested three theories (1966, 104–5).

1. The Jamaican and American are two separate stories, growing out
   of two different, but similar, situations. John Henry is a common
   nickname, as one of Johnson's informants points out. Two
   different men named John Henry engaged in manual labor of a
   construction job is certainly not impossible.
2. John Hardy was the original hero of the C & O Tunnel. (We know
   that John Hardy was employed by one of the contractors on the
   tunnel.) John Henry from Jamaica supplanted him in the United
   States about 1900.
3. The John Henry story traveling solely in oral tradition from
   the Big Bend Tunnel on the C. and O. in 1872 was carried by
   laborers to Jamaica, there to be stripped of all its distinguishing

characteristics except the name, John Henry, and the fact of his death, and furthermore translated into a different poetic, and narrative form.

The first theory is unnecessary because there is a better way to account for the data. The second and third theories are wrong because neither John Hardy nor John Henry was ever at Big Bend Tunnel. Leach was cautious about John Henry but gullible about John Hardy (Williams 1983, 65–67).

Evidence

Jekyll reported a Jamaican work song that was sung before 1906 to a tune that bears some resemblance to Lead Belly's "Take This Hammer" (Jekyll 1907, Ledbetter 1944).

> Them Gar'n Town people them call me follow-line, (3×)
> Sombody dying here ev-'ry day.

According to Jekyll, the tune was used for dancing a Schottische or the Fourth Figure of a Quadrille (1907). John Henry is not mentioned, but the text contains the lines "A ten pound order him kill me pardner" and "Den number nine tunnel I would not work dé," similar to lines of work songs that do mention John Henry. Jekyll recovered the following story (Ibid.):

> An incident, or perhaps it were better to say an accident, in the making of the road to Newcastle. A man who undertook a piece of contract work for £10 was killed by a falling stone. The so-called tunnels are cuttings. Number nine had a very bad reputation.

This was a road, not a railroad. It is probably present-day road B1, which goes from north from Kingston through the Blue Mountains to Buff Bay by way of New Castle (a military training base about nine miles northeast of Kingston harbor).

H.R. Fox, Chief Engineer of the Jamaica Government Railway, and C.S. Farquharson, Public Works Department (Jamaica), recounted for Chappell a story that "a Jamaican labourer named John Henry is said to have died" during the construction of the No. 9 tunnel on the extension of the railway from Bog Walk to Port Antonio (Chappell 1933, 41–42). Farquharson included a list of names.

> Dabner, in charge of blasting operations.
> John Henry, checking up cuts and embankments.
> Shea, Engineer in charge.
> Tommy Walters, Assistant Pay Master.

Perrow published a 1905 hammer song, "This ole hammer killed John Henry" (1913). Leach considered this to be the oldest reference to John Henry in America (1966, 96).

John Henry was known in Jamaica eleven years earlier. In 1894, Reginald Murry copied the text of what was known as the "John Henry Song" "from the singing of a muleteer who was guiding him up Blue Mountain from Irish Town" (Leach 1966, 98–99). It is a typical hammer song. John Henry is not mentioned in the text.

> Ten pound Hammer it crush me pardner (3×)
> Somebody dyin' every day [plus two more stanzas]

Leach's final example of this song is a text obtained by Chappell from Martin Barrow, Public Works Department of Jamaica, in 1932 (Chappell 1933, 99–101). No title is given, but the first line mentions John Henry.

> Ten pound hammer kill John Henry (3×)
> Somebody dying every day [plus thirteen more stanzas].

Two other lines are "I come wid Mexican to put this tunnel through" and "Going buddy to my country." At least two American construction companies were building railroads in Jamaica during the 1890s, suggesting that American contractors and laborers were not rare in Jamaica (Ibid., 41–42).

Leach noted that "Somebody dying every day" is from a spiritual "found throughout the Caribbean" and given "wide distribution" by the Salvation Army.

In 1957, when he was collecting folklore in Jamaica, Leach looked "all over" for information about John Henry, but he found it only in the mountain region near Irish Town, a few miles into the Blue Mountains northeast of Kingston along present-day road B1 to New Castle. There, in a typical statement, Arthur Miles told Leach, "John Henrdy, he was a man killed on makin' dis road; de rocks mash him up" (Leach 1966, 102). Leach found the "Somebody dying" song with the line, "Old hammer, him kill John Henry," and a couple of unrelated songs that included the name "John Henry." Leach commented, "At the time of these songs, before the middle of the 1890's no vehicular road penetrated the mountains" (Ibid., 101).

Piecing the story from the statements of these songs, one would say that a man named John Henry was killed during construction work on the Garden Town-Newcastle road and specifically at Number 9 tunnel, and that his fellow worker (workers) improvised these songs about him, using the well-known "Somebody dying every day" spiritual and the already widely existent form of line thrice repeated followed by a bobbin or refrain line [Leach 1966].

Argument

There is no evidence of John Henry in Jamaica before 1894, the date of the Murry manuscript. In contrast, there is considerable evidence of John Henry in America before then.

Leach's assertion that Jamaican John Henry songs are "older than any in the United States" requires him to reject testimony collected by Johnson and Chappell. That of R.H. Pope, Clinton, North Carolina, is especially significant (Chappell 1933, 31).

> Well I know of the song 41 years. I went to Georgia 1888, and that song was being sung by all the young men ... he would die with the hammer in his hand before he would be beat driving steel.... He was a negro and a real man so I was told.

Pope's testimony is hard to dismiss because it is self-documenting. He surely recalled correctly when he moved to Georgia, and he associated that move with finding young men singing a song that was new to him, a ballad about John Henry, who "would die with his hammer in his hand before he would be beat driving steel" (Ibid.). Perhaps Leach was thinking of this when he wrote, "of course, it may be earlier in uncollected oral tradition," referring to the possibility that "John Henry" was extant in America before "the 1910s or early '20s" (1966, 104).

There are differences between Jamaican and American John Henry lore. In Jamaica, there is no contest with a steam drill. Sometimes, as in Leach's theory, there is no railroad either, although some informants say that John Henry died in the construction of the railroad between Bog Walk and Port Antonio.

John Henry work songs are similar in Jamaica and America. Leach thought it "evident from an examination of John Henry texts that the work songs, hammer songs, digging songs, spiritual-blues ditties are chronologically and culturally older than the ballads of John Henry." There is no agreement on this. Johnson agreed with Leach, positing that John Henry work songs "probably antedated the ballad" (1929, 69). Combs and White took the opposite position, and Chappell ridiculed Johnson on the subject (Combs 1967, 80, 166, White 1928, 189, Chappell 1933, 80).

As Chappell noted, American contractors brought laborers to Jamaica (1933, 42). It is likely that John Henry lore came with them.

Farquharson's testimony makes this explicit. In connection with

John Henry, he named Dabner (Dabney), Shea, and Tommy Walters, all three of whom are associated with John Henry in America. John Henry lore survived in Jamaica in a desiccated form.

Confirmation and Discrimination

> Theory: John Henry died in Jamaica in an accident during the construction of a road in the Blue Mountains, a few miles northeast of Kingston, in the early 1890s.
>
> Confirmation: Given that the theory is true, is the evidence plausible?
>
> Discrimination: Given that the theory is false, is the evidence plausible?

The confirmation question must be answered, "No." There is good evidence that the ballad existed by 1888. The Jamaica theory contradicts a date this early.

The discrimination question must be answered, "Yes." The Jamaican John Henry lore is just the kind that would be expected if John Henry had died in America before 1890 and American workers had taken his story to Jamaica. The evidence is consistent with a John Henry site in America.

Jamaica is not the John Henry site.

❊❊❊

The case for John Henry in Virginia consists of a few simple coincidences.

21

The Case for Virginia

> Unlike wills, diaries, census records, and the other
> documents historians tend to find in archives, songs
> continue to change after their creation. Yet African
> American trackliners' songs were not so different
> from documents at all. They *had* been passed down,
> documents without paper.
>
> —Scott R. Nelson

Scott R. Nelson placed John Henry on the C & O at Lewis Tunnel, Virginia, ca. 1871 (2005, 2006). Part of the evidence is a stanza of the ballad "John Henry," which he treated as if it were an archival document: "As a skeptical historian, I distrusted the story and clung to the documents, to the bitter and mournful songs" (2006, 35).

Evidence

John William Henry came to the Virginia State Penitentiary in Richmond on November 16, 1866, to serve a ten-year term (Nelson 2006, 39). He was black, nineteen years old, and five feet one and a quarter inches tall. On at least one page of the prison register, he appears as "William Henry" (Virginia State Penitentiary 1866).

On December 1, 1868, John William Henry was taken to work under C.R. Mason, railroad construction contractor for the C & O, to whom he was leased by the State of Virginia (Nelson 2006, 39, 78). Work on the C & O was progressing westward toward the site where Lewis Tunnel would be bored, which is in Virginia less than two miles east of its border with West Virginia and something over five miles southeast of White Sulphur Springs, West Virginia.

Work on Lewis Tunnel started before the Civil War. Post-war work there was underway by March 1870 (Ibid., 82). Between August 1870 and the summer of 1871, under the direction of contractor J.J. Gordon, free laborers operated steam drills while convicts did hand drilling (Ibid., 85–88).

Gordon had trouble with boilers. In October 1871, he wrote to Chief Engineer Henry Whitcomb, "I am very anxious to get that boiler to run Burleigh Drill in East approach. If you have done anything in regards to furnishing it please inform me, if not I will have to double on it with hammers" (Nelson 2006, 87).

By 1874 John William Henry had disappeared from prison records (Ibid., 92). The penciled word "Transferred" appears in the prison register in the space allotted for the date that John William Henry was pensioned, discharged, or died (Ibid., 39).

A provision of the lease contract stipulated that contractors "would have to post a bond that guaranteed the safe return of prisoners and pay all the expenses for the state's attempts at recapture, should it be necessary. Governor Wells wrote that contracts have 'stipulated damages of one hundred dollars for each *prisoner not returned*'" (italics in original) (Ibid., 78).

In the ballad "John Henry," a stanza like the following occurs occasionally.

> They took John Henry to the White House,
> And buried him in the san,'
> And every locomotive come roarin' by,
> Say there lays that steel drivin' man. [Johnson 1929, 99].
> —Onah L. Spencer, ca. 1927

Of fifty-eight version of "John Henry" given by Johnson and Chappell, twenty-one mention John Henry's burial (Johnson 1929, Chappell 1933). Eight have him buried at the white house; three at the burying ground; three, the graveyard; one, by the river; and one at his father's house. In one version, they put John Henry "on that long white road" (Chappell 1933, 117).

A workhouse, made white by lime plaster, once stood on the grounds of the Virginia Penitentiary. In 1992 an old burying ground was found "right next to the old white house, near the tracks of the Richmond, Fredericksburg & Potomac Railroad" (Nelson 2006, 36–38). "Each box was separated from the other by a small layer of sand" (Ibid., 38).

It is not clear when burials there began. It might have been in or after 1874, the year after John William Henry's name last appeared in the prison register (Thompson 2010).

Nelson's Scenario

Nelson constructed a scenario in which John William Henry was a steel driver at Lewis Tunnel (2006, 85–92). During Gordon's trials with steam drills, August 1870 to summer 1871, he was one of the convicts who "worked alongside the drill" (Ibid., 86). From Gordon's comment of October 1871, "if [I don't get a boiler] I will have to double on it with hammers," Nelson construed that Gordon had been "drilling two sets of holes on the rock face of the east approach, one with convicts, one with the Burleigh drill. If the steam drill failed that day, he would have to do the work with two teams of hammer men. Before the boiler failed, Gordon would have run a steam drill on one side and a hammer team on the other" (Ibid., 87–88).

According to Nelson, John William Henry "raced a steam drill at the Lewis Tunnel in the late summer of 1871. He beat the steam drill, but he and dozens of other railroad men died doing it," many from lung disease (Ibid., 92).

The contractor avoided the hundred-dollar damage fee by returning John William Henry's body to the Virginia Penitentiary (Ibid., 78–79).

> The biggest problem, as the superintendent saw it, was what to do with the bodies. They were taken to the white house that lay along the track of the Richmond, Fredericksburg & Potomac Railroad and buried in the sand, and no one was the wiser. Only a song, stubbornly sung by railroad men, convicts, and miners, kept the story alive [Ibid., 92].

This accounts for John Henry's burial in the sand near a white house and a railroad in a stanza of "John Henry."

Nelson supposed that Cal Evans, a cook, carried the John Henry story from Lewis to Big Bend Tunnel, to which it was relocalized (Nelson 2006, 89).

Argument

At the outset, the Virginia theory faces three significant obstacles. (1) There is no tradition of John Henry at Lewis Tunnel. (2) John William Henry was a long-term convict. (3) John William Henry had no wife.

Nelson accounted for (1), the absence of a tradition of John Henry at Lewis Tunnel, by supposing that the convict laborers there were so sickened and killed by silicosis that they could not tell the John Henry story. There is simpler and better explanation: Lewis Tunnel is not the John Henry site.

To account for the legend at Big Bend Tunnel, Nelson gave Cal Evans a pivotal role.

> It was up to free workers on the nearby Big Bend Tunnel to report what had happened. One man, an African American roundhouse cook named Cal Evans, traveled from the Lewis Tunnel to the Big Bend Tunnel in 1875.... He and others immortalized John Henry in an old-fashioned ballad... [Ibid.].

Cal Evans did not take the John Henry story from Lewis Tunnel to Big Bend Tunnel. According to Chappell, he was never at Lewis Tunnel. He first worked on the C & O near White Sulphur Springs, then near Huntington, then around 1875 at the roundhouse in Hinton, all in West Virginia. In the 1880s he moved to the Big Bend community at Talcott, where he heard "reports of John Henry's connections there" (Chappell 1933, 36). He was living at Talcott in 1925 and in 1927, when he was interviewed by Chappell and Johnson (Ibid., 13–14, Johnson 1929, 37).

The problem with (2), that John William Henry was a leased convict laborer, is that long-term convicts lose self-worth and become lethargic (Haney 2001). John William Henry was serving a ten-year sentence and had been a convict for about five years before he is supposed to have died at Lewis Tunnel in about 1871. Douglas Galbi, who studies history through the lens of psychology, wrote:

> John Henry obviously had great respect for himself and for his work. That's the sort of attitude I could easily imagine in a freed black slave owning little but his own muscle. Being in prison is hugely demoralizing. A convict in a work gang probably wouldn't have the sense of professional pride and motivation to do what John Henry did. It's unlikely, in my opinion, that John Henry was a convict laborer [2012].

The legendary John Henry is indeed proud and confident. He said to the Captain, "A man ain't nothing but a man / But before I'll let that steam drill beat me down / I'll die with my hammer in my hand." John Henry's pride in his ability is the psychological core of the ballad and legend. Convict John William Henry is a poor candidate for the proud John Henry of legend.

The problem with (3), that John William Henry had no wife, is that John Henry's wife is important in both C.C. Spencer's eyewitness account and the ballad (Yronwode 2007). When John Henry was sick and could not work, "Polly drove steel like a man" (Johnson 1929, 107). Accepting John William Henry as the steel-driving man would require that John Henry had no wife.

Other vital points in Nelson's scenario lack evidentiary support.

(a) There is no evidence that John William Henry was ever at Lewis Tunnel. All we know is that he was leased to the C & O and left the penitentiary on December 1, 1868. According to Nelson, contracts for drilling at Lewis Tunnel went out by March 1870 (2006, 82).

(b) There is no evidence that John William Henry was a steel driver, that he was an exceptional steel driver, or that he raced a steam drill. These are essential aspects of the John Henry legend.

(c) There is no evidence that John William Henry died at Lewis Tunnel. He disappeared from prison records with no mention of death, pardon, parole, or release (Ibid., 39, 92). The word "Transferred" in the records does not suggest death. It doesn't suggest escape, either, but a number of convict workers did escape (Ibid., 83, 86). John William Henry could have been one of them.

(d) There is no evidence that John William Henry was buried at the Virginia Penitentiary in Richmond. From Lewis Tunnel to Richmond is over 150 miles as the crow flies, further by rail or road. Nelson imagined that the return of a dead body would satisfy the requirement of the "safe return" of a prisoner and avoid the "stipulated damages of one hundred dollars for each *prisoner not returned*" (Nelson 2006, 78–79). Surely "each prisoner not returned" referred to living prisoners. Returning bodies makes no sense.

(e) There is no evidence that John William Henry was "buried in the sand." Nelson posits that he was buried in the mass grave by the white house at the Virginia Penitentiary. According to Katherine Beidleman Thompson, the archeologist who examined the site, layers of the soil in which the grave was dug separated the boxes of body parts. That soil is not sand (Thompson 2010).

The evidence for John Henry's burial at the Virginia penitentiary consists of a stanza of "John Henry" and a few facts that agree with it. There is no reason to believe that this stanza is historically correct, but even if we assume that it is, the evidence does not necessarily point to the Virginia Penitentiary. "John Henry," either as a given name-surname combination or as a pair of given names, was very common, as were white houses, burying grounds, and railroads.

It is doubtful that anyone who sang, "They took John Henry to the White House," would pass the ballad on with John Henry being buried somewhere else. Even so, about half of "John Henry" versions that mention his burial have him buried in a "burying ground," "graveyard," etc. It is unlikely, therefore, that John Henry's burial at a white house appeared in the earliest versions of "John Henry."

According to a prison record, John William Henry went by "William," not "John." This is further evidence against his being the legendary John Henry.

Nelson described his method of research this way: "Beginning on the day I discovered the man I *thought* was John Henry, I set out to confirm the story" (2006, 38). *Steel Drivin' Man* omits a considerable body of contradictory evidence.

Confirmation and Discrimination

> Theory: John Henry raced a steam drill at Lewis Tunnel during its construction ca 1871.
>
> Confirmation: Given that the theory is true, is the evidence plausible?
>
> Discrimination: Given that the theory is false, is the evidence plausible?

The confirmation question must be answered, "No." If John Henry had been at Lewis Tunnel, the evidence would be stronger.

The discrimination question must be answered, "Yes." Plausible coincidences account for the evidence.

Virginia is not the John Henry site.

≡⊏ ≡⊏ ≡⊏

The case for John Henry in Alabama is compelling.

22

The Case for Alabama

His name was John Henry Dabner, but we called him
John Henry.—C.C. Spencer

Charles C. Spencer was the most important informant on John
Henry. His testimony is given in Chapter 15. A self-proclaimed eyewitness to John Henry's contest with a steam drill, he was good witness and
a reliable informant. Additional evidence supports his testimony.

Evidence

F.P. Barker wrote to Guy Johnson in 1927 (Barker 1927a, Johnson
1929, 22).

> #723 7th St. Thomas Ala
> Aurgust 10 1927
>
> Professor G.B. Johnson
>
> I take great Peasur to write and informing you that there was a real Man
> John Henry. Brown skin Colored 147 lb a steel driver He drive against a
> steam drill and beate it down a shaft avancin He song before He wowld let it
> beat him down that He wowld die with his Hammer in his Hand and He did
> it. I F.P. Barker I was driving steel on Red Mountain at that time This Happen about 45 yeors ago sown where about that time. Just as true as you see
> the sun. There was a real man John Henry. He was the champan of wowld
> with a Hammer. I could drive from Both Shoulders myself and I was as for
> behind John Henry as the Moon is behind the Sun. The wowld Has Not yet
> Produce a Man to Whip steel like John Henry
>
> Yours ???
> F.P. Barker

Red Mountain lies along the southeastern edge of Birmingham. The
Thomas community is west of downtown Birmingham and east of Pratt.

A second letter from Barker provided encouragement and a little more information (1927b, Johnson 1929, 22).

723 7 St. Thomas Ala
Aurgust 30 1927

Mr Prof. B. Johnson

Dear Sir I received your and was glad to Hear from you Sir I write to Keep you in good Heart you will gaive Me a little time and I think I can gaive you a full recrord Thear a man in this vin.?.cey that has His Picure. and then some of His Songs When I see I will write you I was Driving Steel on Red Mountain at the time of the Contest. John Henry was on Cursey Mountain—Tunnel in His Song He told His Shaker to shak. that drill and turn it around John Henry is Bound to Beat the steem Drill down The steem Drill Beat men of Every other Race down to the sand. Now Iil gaive my lile before I let it beat the Negro Man I tell you more a bout it when see some more of my old Meetes I am 73 years old and it been Nerley a Half a Cenerery When I write the Next letter I will mail it your envelop

Han..? yours
F.P. Barker

Barker wrote that he was 73 years old in August 1927. Census records for Frank Percy Barker for 1880–1930 indicate that he was born in Tennessee between 1851 and 1856.

Glendora Cannon Cummings wrote as follows (1927, Johnson 1929, 22–23).

September 6, 1927
1017 S. Birch St.
Lansing, Mich.

My Dear Professor Johnson:

I am writing you concerning the history of John Henry. This is my story:
My Uncle Gus (the man who raised my father) was working by John Henry and saw him when he beat the steam drill and fell dead. This was in the year of 1887. It was at Oak Mountain, Alabama. They were working for Shay and Dabney, the meanest white contractors at that time.

The steel drivers were the highest salaried men. But John Henry's salary was higher than theirs. Nobody ever drove steel as well as him. I mean when I say the steel drivers were the highest paid; that for a negro in those days in South.

John Henry wielded a nine pound hammer Hammer. So the words of one of the songs: Is: "A nine pound hammer killed John Henry but this old hammer wont kill me." Both my Uncle Gus and my father were steel drivers. So I have heard several different kinds of the John Henry songs. In one John Henry song a man named Lazarus is mentioned, and also George Collins. These people are not myths. They all lived in the camp with my Uncle Gus and my father. My father arrived after John Henry dropped dead, but my

Uncle Gus and John Henry were friends. Lazarus had been a steel driver but he turned to a gambler. So they ordered him to stay away from camp. But he stayed on anyhow. One day while in the woods he saw Shay and Dabney with a searching party; he jumped and ran, they shot him, but accidentally for they were searching for George Collins, he was a negro gambler and bad man. He carried two guns on him. However a year later my father and Uncle went to driving steel for Thompson Brothers and one of the Thompson Brothers caught George Collins with his guns off, and killed him. Thompson Brothers then always kept his skull on their desk where the men could see it when they came to draw their pay.

Both my father and Uncle Gus are living. But as my Uncle Gus knew John Henry personally, I will be able to write you more in November as I am taking a trip to my home town and will see Uncle Gus. Also be able to send you a copy of one of the songs.

Yours truly,
Glendora Cannon Cummings

Glendora Cannon was born in February 1899, in Joliet, Illinois, to Edward and Mamie Cannon (census, 1900). In the 1930 census, she is a divorcee living with her parents and other family at 1017 Birch Street, Lansing, Michigan.

A 1930 article placed John Henry's death at the east portal of Oak Mountain Tunnel. "'Jawn Henry' is no mere fiction hero, for in the mountain side near Leeds, at the east end of our Oak Mountain tunnel, there stands a monument to him—the last steel he drove before he fell dead, standing in the hole into which he pounded it with his twelve pound hammer" (Figure 24) (Crawford 1930). The article goes on to describe the local John Henry legend around Leeds, Alabama, as reported by Road Supervisor J. Morgan, and to identify the railroad for which Oak Mountain Tunnel was bored as the Columbus and Western, a subsidiary of the Central of Georgia (Clemons 2007, Cline 1997). This legend persists to the present. It is widespread along the tracks of the old Columbus and Western (now Norfolk Southern) from Birmingham east and south.

The extension of the Columbus and Western from Goodwater, Alabama, to Birmingham began in late 1886. The road was opened for traffic on July 1, 1888. In the process, tunnels were bored through Oak and Coosa Mountains. These are the only tunnels on the line.

Oak and Coosa Mountains are parallel southwest-to-northeast trending ridges. The Dunnavant Valley and the community of Dunnavant lie between them.

Oak and Coosa Mountain Tunnels are two and four miles, respectively, south of Leeds and fifteen miles east of Birmingham. Locals call them the "short" (or "little") and "long" (or "big") tunnels. The short tunnel, 1198 feet, is through Oak Mountain, and the long tunnel, 2431 feet, is through Coosa Mountain (Borkowski 2008).

Captain Fred Y. Dabney, chief engineer for the Columbus and Western, was in charge of construction of its extension in 1886–88 (Chapter 13). Captain Dabney gained his rank in the Confederate engineers (Chapter 12). From about 1875 until his death in 1900, he lived in Crystal Springs, Copiah County, Mississippi.

Thomas Dabney, Captain Dabney's uncle, owned Burleigh Plantation, Hinds County, Mississippi, about twelve miles northwest of Crystal Springs. The plantation was established in 1835, when Thomas, his lawyer brother Gus, and Gus's son Fred, then six months old, moved from tidewater Virginia to Mississippi. Gus settled in Raymond, Hinds County, about eleven miles north-northeast of Burleigh.

In 1955, Mrs. C.T. Davis said that "John Henry's boss man killed him in Mississippi after he left here" (Musgrove 1955).

In 2008, Robert Moore, 87, said that he had learned from his father, Julius Moore, b ca. 1877, that John Henry was from Mississippi (R. Moore 2008, G. Moore 2008). Julius got his information

Figure 45. Coosa Tunnel, near Dunnavant, Alabama (photograph by the author).

from two older men, Sam Angle and Hilliard Holly, who had worked on the construction of the extension of the C & W in 1886–88, had known John Henry, and had witnessed his contest and death. Hilliard Holly appears in the 1920 census as sixty-three years old and a worker in a cement plant in Leeds, Alabama. He was about thirty years old in 1887.

Harry Hicks sang, "John Henry died on a Tuesday" (Chappell 1933, 105–6). September 20, 1887, the date of John Henry's death, as construed from information given by C.C. Spencer, fell on a Tuesday. No other version of "John Henry" names a day.

A stanza Leon R. Harris learned in 1909–11, in Virginia or West Virginia, includes "Cap' Tommy" and Virginia (Johnson 1929, 92, Harris 1927 [23 Mar]).

> John Henry's cap'n Tommy,—
> V'ginny gave him birth;
> Loved John Henry like his only son,
> And Cap' Tommy was the whitest man on earth.

In another version, John Henry's boss is "cap'n Monday," and John Henry brags, "I drill all way from Rome / To Decatur in one day" (Odum 1926, 234–35).

Uncle Dave Macon sang the following (1926, Johnson 1929, 117).

> People out West heard of John Henry's death,
> Couldn' hardly stay in bed,
> Monday morning' caught that East-bound train,
> Goin' where John Henry's dead.

Onah L. Spencer sent Guy Johnson a similar stanza (Spencer, Onah ca. 1927, Johnson 1929, 99).

> All the women in the West
> That heard of John Henry's death,
> Stood in the rain, flagged the east bound train,
> Goin' where John Henry dropped dead.

The Blankenship broadside contains the following lines (stanza eleven) (Chapter 9).

> John Henry's woman heard he was dead,
> She could not rest on her bed,
> She got up at midnight, caught that No. 4 train,
> "I am going where John Henry fell dead."

"Number four" also appears in the version of "John Henry" published by John A. Lomax in 1915 (stanza ten).

> If I die a railroad man
> Go bury me under the tie,
> So I can hear old number four
> As she goes rolling by.

Rich Amerson sang the following lines (1956).

> When Henry was 'tween them mountains,
> His wife couldn't hear him a-cryin'.
> When she went out 'tween them-a mountains,
> Tried to git 'im to lay the irons down....

From an informant in Pigeon Forge, Tennessee, Niles collected a version of "John Henry" in which he is buried between "two mountains" (1936).

> When John Henry died, they wasn't no box
> Big enough to hold his bones,
> So they buried him in a box-car deep in the ground,
> And let two mountains be his grave-stones.

In the same version, "A man in Chatanooga, two hundred miles away / Heard an awful rumbling sound."

In 1916, ex-governor MacCorkle, of West Virginia, described John Henry but called him John Hardy: "he was a steel-driver, and was famous in the beginning of the building of the C. & O. [Chesapeake and Ohio] Railroad. He was also a steel-driver in the beginning of the extension of the N. & W. [Norfolk and Western] Railroad. It was about 1872 that he was in this section" (Chapter 2).

The name of John Henry's wife or woman is given most frequently as "Polly Ann." Johnson and Chappell collected "Julie Ann," "Mary Ann," "Martha Ann," "Sary Ann," "Mary Magdalene," and "Lucy" as well (Johnson 1929, 89–135, Chappell 1933, 103–28). Neal Pattman sang "Maggadee," and Furry Lewis sang "Neva Lee" (Pattman 2002, 2003, Lewis 1968b). "Julia Ann," "Nellie Ann," "Lizzie Ann" are also known (Odum 1926, 228, 32, 35).

John Henry was first noticed in a scholarly or popular publication in 1909.

Argument

Spencer, Barker, Cummings, Davis, and Moore put John Henry and his contest with a steam drill on the Columbus and Western during its extension. So do a host of others who live or have lived along the old Columbus and Western line from Birmingham east and south.

The rest of the evidence affirms and expands the testimonies of these informants.

According to Spencer and Barker, John Henry drove steel at "Cruzee" / "Cursey" Mountain in about 1882. These names sound like "Koosee," the old spelling and pronunciation of "Coosa" (Cornelius 1818). The year had to be 1887 or 1888, when the extension of the Columbus and Western was under construction.

Cummings placed John Henry's contest with a steam drill at Oak Mountain in 1887. So do locals, who say it was outside the east portal, as described by Morgan.

Cummings confirmed Spencer's statement that John Henry worked for a Dabney. Spencer gave it as "Dabner," reflecting a colloquial pronunciation. In Jamaica, Farquharson gave "Dabner" as one of John Henry's bosses (Chapter 20).

According to Spencer, the steel-driving man was John Henry Dabney ("Dabner"), probably born a slave in the Dabney family in Mississippi. In her memoir, Letitia Dabney, Captain Dabney's sister, describes the family's faithful servant, Henry (Miller 1926). He was probably the Henry Page of the 1870 census of the Gus Dabney household. Henry Dabney of the census of 1870 for Copiah County, Mississippi, was probably John Henry Dabney, then twenty years old and probably born a slave on Thomas Dabney's Burleigh Plantation.

Census records show that the frequency of the surname "Dabney" in the United States has been nearly constant over the years from 1880 at about 3 per 100,000, or 3×10^{-5}. This is an estimate of the probability that someone would report "Dabney" as a random choice for the name of John Henry's boss. Given that one person had already reported it, the probability that a second person would report it as a random choice would be 3×10^{-5}. The probability that two additional people would report it randomly would be $(3 \times 10^{-5})^2$, or 9×10^{-10}, which is about one in a billion.

These very low probabilities guarantee that "Dabney" was not a random choice for Spencer, Cummings, and Farquharson. Each of them had a link with John Henry and Captain Dabney. They are either eyewitnesses to John Henry's contest or recipients of accurate information transmitted orally.

The probability that two others would confirm by simple coincidence Spencer's statement that John Henry was from Mississippi is estimated as $(\frac{1}{13})^2$, or 0.006, by assigning the thirteen former Confederate states equal probabilities of being John Henry's home. Again, the sensible conclusion is that Spencer, Davis, and Moore were either eyewitnesses to John Henry's contest or recipients of accurate information transmitted orally.

Similarly, if Hicks had picked a day at random, the probability of his confirming Spencer's information that John Henry died on a Tuesday would be ⅙, or 0.17, assuming a six-day workweek. It is more likely that Spencer and Hicks were eyewitnesses to John Henry's contest or recipients of accurate information.

Captains "Tommy" and "Monday," found in the ballad, are plausible mutations of "Dabney," which could not have lasted long in oral tradition.

"V'ginny gave him birth," sung of Captain Tommy by Leon Harris, is true of Captain Dabney.

It is plausible that Captain Dabney "Loved John Henry like his only son." Captain Dabney had probably known John Henry Dabney since his birth on Burleigh Plantation in 1849–50, when Captain Dabney was about fifteen years old.

Drilling "all way from Rome to Decatur in one day" gives John Henry a Georgia connection, perhaps reflecting his employment by the Central of Georgia.

John Henry's friends and relatives in Mississippi would have been "People out West." The overall trip from Crystal Springs, Mississippi, to Leeds, Alabama, would be east, so in a broad sense they would have taken an "east-bound train" to go "where John Henry dropped dead," as the ballad states.

There was no eastbound train through Crystal Springs in 1887. The Illinois Central Railroad (IC) ran north and south, so a trip from Crystal Springs to northern Alabama would have begun with a northbound leg. The ballad says, "She got up at midnight, caught that No. 4 train." I have no timetable information for 1887, but in December 1885, IC No. 4 was the "Fast Express" going north from New Orleans to Chicago with a scheduled time for Crystal Springs of 11:57 p.m. (jackf66 2008). The train number and time match the ballad. To travel from Crystal Springs to Leeds, Alabama, one could have gone north to Jackson on IC No. 4, east to Meridian on the Vicksburg & Meridian, northeast to Birmingham on the Alabama Great Southern, and east to Leeds on the Georgia Pacific (University of Alabama 2012).

Amerson's ballad puts John Henry "'tween them mountains." The John Henry site outside the east portal of Oak Mountain Tunnel is between Oak and Coosa Mountains. Niles' informant sang, "And let two mountains be his grave-stones," which may also refer to Oak and Coosa Mountains. These lines don't make sense for West Virginia. At Big Bend Tunnel, there are mountains all around, and no two are distinctive.

Chattanooga, Tennessee, is about 130 miles from Dunnavant, Alabama, not quite as far as the 200 miles Niles' informant gave but in the same ballpark. That the rumbling sound John Henry's hammering could be heard 130 or 200 miles away is, of course, hyperbole. Chattanooga is more than 300 miles from Big Bend Tunnel, Summers County, West Virginia, and Lewis Tunnel, Alleghany County, Virginia, an even greater auditory stretch.

Governor MacCorkle placed John Henry (as John Hardy) on an extension of the "N & W" (Norfolk and Western) after he had been a steel driver for the "C & O" (Chesapeake and Ohio) at Big Bend Tunnel. The Norfolk and Western had several extensions. The Clinch Valley extension from Bluefield, West Virginia, to Norton, Virginia (1887–1890), overlapped in time the construction of the "C & W" (Columbus and Western) extension from Goodwater, Alabama, to Birmingham (1886–88). "C & W" shares something with both railroads mentioned by MacCorkle. In his story, both "C &" of "C & O" and "& W" of "N & W" could have been borrowed from "C & W."

In the 1870 and 1880 censuses of Copiah County, Mississippi, Henry Dabney's wife is Margaret. "Polly Ann," the most common name for John Henry's wife/woman in the ballad, can be obtained from "Margaret Dabney" through a plausible sequence of mutations.

Margaret Dabney was called "Maggie D."

"Maggie D" was understood as "Maggadee."

"Maggie D" or "Maggadee" suggests "Magdalene," which was provided with "Mary" to make the familiar "Mary Magdalene."

"Mary Magdalene" is cumbersome and does not provide a rhyme for "drove steel like a man," so it became "Mary Ann."

"Polly," a common nickname for "Mary," replaced "Mary" to give "Polly Ann."

Margaret Dabney → Maggie D → Maggadee → Mary Magdalene → Mary Ann → Polly Ann

"Maggadee," "Mary Magdalene," "Mary Ann," and "Polly Ann" are all found in tradition. Variants such as "Julie Ann," "Sary Ann," "Martha Ann," etc., could follow from "Mary Ann" or "Polly Ann." "Neva Lee," sung by Furry Lewis, is a fairly common name and a natural reconstruction of "Maggadee." Perhaps "Lucy," the only name Leon Harris had heard, was once "Lucy Ann."

The first mention of John Henry in print was in 1909, thirty-eight years after 1871 and twenty-two years after 1887. It is more probable that twenty-two years would elapse before publication than thirty-eight.

Nothing about Charles C. Spencer's life contradicts his testimony that he had worked with John Henry in Alabama (Chapter 15).

As he warned, his memory was not perfect. He gave the year as 1882, but it was 1887; he gave the railroad as the AGS (Alabama Great

Southern), but it was the C & W; and he gave John Henry's and the Captain's home as Holly Springs, Mississippi, but it was Crystal Springs.

These are understandable memory lapses. Spencer tended to date everything from the mid- to late nineteenth century a few years too early. Parts of the AGS were under construction in the Birmingham area at the same time as the C & W, 1886–88, and AGS was a more prominent name than C & W. Spencer could have worked on both railroads. Holly Springs, Mississippi, exists. It is easy to see how it and Crystal Springs could be confused. "Springs" sticks in the memory better than "Crystal Springs."

Spencer gave 1869 as the completion date of Big Bend Tunnel, but it was 1872, and it is not true that slaves built it, as he wrote. He cannot be faulted for such errors because he had only hearsay knowledge of Big Bend Tunnel.

He got a number of things right, as judged by documentation or agreement with other informants.

1. John Henry was from Mississippi. (Spencer, Davis, Moore, and extant legend)
2. He worked for a Dabney (Captain Fred Y. Dabney). (Spencer, Cummings, and Farquharson)
3. Captain Dabney was from Mississippi. (He moved there as an infant.)
4. Captain Dabney was from a town with "Springs" in its name. (Crystal Springs)
5. John Henry worked at Coosa Mountain Tunnel, Alabama. (Spencer and Barker)
6. He raced a steam drill and died near there. (Spencer and Barker; Cummings, Morgan, and extant legend put it two miles north at Oak Mountain Tunnel)
7. It was on a Tuesday. (Spencer and ballad)
8. Coosa Mountain is about fifteen miles from Red Mountain. (True)
9. Coosa Mountain is a reasonable traveling distance from Rising Fawn, Georgia. (About a hundred miles)
10. The Norfolk & Western built the old Elkhorn (Coaldale) Tunnel in West Virginia. (Completed in about 1888)
11. John Hardy and John Henry were different. John Hardy killed a man in McDowell County, West Virginia, and was hanged there. (Facts about John Hardy are correct except for small errors in years and the name of the victim: Thomas Drews, not Read Drew)

Documentation or other informants confirm the most important aspects of Charles C. Spencer's testimony. There is no reason to reject his testimony and every reason to accept it. He *was* the eyewitness that he claimed to be.

Confirmation and Discrimination

> Theory: John Henry raced a steam drill near Dunnavant, Alabama, during the extension of the C & W in 1886–88.
> Confirmation: Given that the theory is true, is the evidence plausible?
> Discrimination: Given that the theory is false, is the evidence plausible?

The confirmation question must be answered, "Yes." The facts tell a complete, consistent story. The evidence is abundant. It is what would be expected if the theory were true.

The discrimination question must be answered, "No." It is inconceivable that the body of evidence for Alabama could have arisen if John Henry had not raced a steam drill there. That evidence has to have a source. No fictional story about John Henry and his death, published before 1925, has ever been found. An orally circulating story with no foundation in fact would be very unlikely to include rare names such as "Cruzee" Mountain and "Dabney." The only plausible ultimate source of the evidence is historical fact.

Alabama is the John Henry site.

⸎ ⸎ ⸎

John Henry in legend and reality.

23

Legend and Reality

...good old John Henry ... lived for honor...
—C.C. Spencer

The legendary John Henry died at various times in various places, all over the American South and in Jamaica. The real John Henry died in Alabama.

The Real John Henry

One thread of John Henry's story begins in Africa. Born a slave, he inherited African genes and what was left of African culture in that of his owner's slaves.

Another thread begins in Scandinavia. In the ninth century AD, Vikings invaded and settled Normandy, the northwestern district of France. Among the Normans were knights with surnames such as D'Aubigny, D'Aubigné, and D'Albini. Some of them came to England with William the Conqueror in 1066. There they acquired estates and became aristocrats. A descendant, Cornelius Dabney, established the Dabney family in tidewater Virginia, where he was living by 1664.

The Dabney family has consistently emphasized character. Having been aristocrats in England, they became aristocrats in Virginia.

Benjamin Dabney (1757–1806) was a wealthy lawyer moved in the highest social and political circles. Benjamin's sons, Thomas (1798–1885) and Gus Dabney (1800–1878), had different temperaments. Thomas was robust and active. Gus was sickly and scholarly. Thomas protected him. When their father died and their mother remarried, Thomas dropped out of school to manage the family estate, Elmington, while Gus continued his studies at the College of William and Mary.

In 1835, they moved their families to Hinds County, Mississippi.

Gus became a lawyer and probate judge in Raymond. More interested in literature and flowers than law and money, his means were modest. Thomas established Burleigh Plantation, nearly 4000 acres eleven miles south-southwest of Raymond. Burleigh provided part of the food for both families.

John Henry was born a slave at Burleigh in 1849–50. Thomas Dabney thought of himself as a kind master whose "servants" were part of his family. He motivated them through rewards instead of punishment and gave them an unusual amount of freedom in their daily activities. Life at Burleigh was probably as good as it ever got for a slave.

The Dabneys were role models for John Henry. It is not surprising that he took "Dabney" as his surname and that he "lived for honor."

Frederick Yeamans Dabney, a son of Gus Dabney, was born in Virginia about six months before the move to Mississippi in 1835. According to his younger sister, Mary, Fred's "heart and soul and mind were all built on a big scale."

Fred admired his uncle and was a frequent visitor to Burleigh. He probably knew John Henry from birth, and it is possible that an emotional bond between them developed over the years. One version of the ballad says that the Captain "loved John Henry like his only son." According to Elbert McDonald, the Captain wept when John Henry died.

With financial assistance from Thomas for his education at Rensselaer, Fred became a civil engineer and railroad builder. During the Civil War, he designed and supervised the Confederate defenses at Port Hudson, on the Mississippi River in Louisiana. When Port Hudson fell to a siege on July 9, 1863, First Lieutenant Dabney was captured and sent to the prison for Confederate Officers on Johnson's Island, Ohio. In March 1864, he was promoted to the rank of captain in the Confederate engineers. His health broken, he was released in desperate condition in late September 1864. A bronchial condition plagued him for the rest of his life.

Captain Dabney married Agatha Ann Moncure in 1865. When his health permitted, he resumed his career in railroad construction. In about 1875, he moved his family to Crystal Springs, Copiah County, twelve miles southeast of Burleigh.

In 1869, John Henry Dabney married Margaret Boston. They settled in Copiah County, near Crystal Springs, and farmed.

In 1886, Captain Dabney became the chief engineer for the Columbus & Western, a wholly owned subsidiary of the Central of Georgia. He designed and supervised the construction of the extension of the Columbus and Western from Goodwater, Alabama, to Birmingham in

1886–88. For that project, he recruited some friends and neighbors, including John Henry. In John Henry lore, Captain Dabney is usually called "the Captain."

John Henry drove steel at Coosa Mountain Tunnel, fifteen miles east of Birmingham. By the summer of 1887, he had developed such skill that he was winning all the steel-driving contests. Also that summer, the miners at Coosa Mountain Tunnel struck a layer of exceedingly hard rock, the excavation of which delayed the project by six months.

Charles C. Spencer was there as a sixteen-year-old carrier of water and tools for John Henry and other laborers. According to his account, a steam-drill salesman approached the Captain, who declared that he had "a Negro who could beat his damned old drill any day." The company offered to "put it in for nothing" if this man could beat its drill.

The Captain asked John Henry if he could beat the steam drill. He replied that he could, if he could use a fourteen-pound hammer. The Captain bought the hammer and promised John Henry a new suit of clothes and fifty dollars if he won the contest.

The contest took place outside the east portal of Oak Mountain Tunnel, two miles north of Coosa Mountain, on September 20. Before a crowd of several hundred, John Henry drilled twenty-seven and one-half feet, while the steam drill made only twenty-one feet. John Henry won a steam drill for the Captain.

At the end of the contest, John Henry collapsed into the arms of his shaker. Water revived him, and he said, "Send for my wife. I am blind and dying." As his wife cradled his head in her lap, he asked, "Have I beat that old steam drill?" He died shortly thereafter.

The salesman had been confident that a man could not beat his steam drill, but he had "lots of trouble," according to Spencer. The ballad agrees.

> John Henry said to his Captain,
> "Captain, can't you see,
> Your hole is choked and your steel is broke
> And your hammer can't go down with me?"

John Henry's usual hammer was lighter than the fourteen-pounder he used in the contest. The extra weight added to his exertion and could have been a factor contributing to his death, which could have been from bleeding from ventricular or some other rupture. His fainting, going blind, and having a roaring in his head, as reported in narrative or song, are all symptoms of low blood volume. (Other causes of death, such as sickle cell anemia, are possible.)

> He drove so hard that he broke his heart

John Henry's size was not extraordinary. Spencer gave his height and weight as 5 feet 10 or 11 inches and "near" 180 pounds. Mrs. Davis reported that her father, who had known John Henry, described him as "common sized."

The ballad says that John Henry was "buried in the sand." Sand Ridge Cemetery is about two miles from the site of the contest. It is said in the locality that a black man is buried there.

The Captain continued in railroad construction until about 1892, when he retired to his home on West Railroad Avenue in Crystal Springs. In 1895–97, he designed and supervised the construction of Chautaqua Lake as a water supply for trains.

Agatha Ann Moncure Dabney died in January 1899. The Captain died of a "bronchial affection" in March 1900.

After his youth in Virginia and Alabama, Charles C. Spencer lived in West Virginia, Kentucky, Colorado, and Utah. Wherever he went, he told his story of John Henry.

For about ten years, the Reverend Spencer was the pastor of Calvary Baptist Church in Salt Lake City. He died there in 1944.

The Legendary John Henry

Legend may begin with historical truth, but it is free to reinterpret, expand, and elaborate. It elevates heroes by adding wondrous, often miraculous, events to their lives.

Shortly after John Henry's death, someone wrote a ballad, and people began to tell his story. As the story spread, it was embellished to include miracles and dialog.

The infant John Henry miraculously predicted that the hammer would "be the death of me" and that he would die at the Big Bend Tunnel on the C. & O. road. It came true.

As an adult, John Henry asserted his humanity, "A man ain't nothin' but a man," but vowed to give his all, "Before I'd let that steam drill beat me down / I'd die with my hammer in my hand," "I will hammer my fool self to death."

His hammer weighed "nigh fo'ty poun.'"
He used two hammers.
He swung his hammer so hard that it caught fire.
John Henry was very large.
He drilled from Rome, Georgia, to Decatur in one day.
"Polly Ann drove steel like a man."
He had more than a thousand women.
He was taken to the White House for burial.
He uttered various last words:

And I was the best, but I am going home to rest,
That steam hammer is done broke me down

Captain, I've hammered my insides in two

I've beat him to the' bottom but I'm dead

Fix me a place I want-a lay down,
Got a mighty roaring in my head

Give me a cool drink of water before I die

Take my hammer and wrap it in gold
And give it to the girl I love

Take care of my wife and child

Julie, do the best you can

Be true to me when I'm dead

O son, do the best you can

Son, you must be a steel driving man

Son, don't be a steel-drivin' man

In the ballad, many of John Henry's last words are addressed to his wife and son. Spencer's eyewitness account includes his wife but not his son. The ballad features both and mentions as many as three children.

It is unlikely that "Polly Ann drove steel like a man." Even so, this is a fine tribute to John Henry's wife. According to Spencer, she stayed with the crew after John Henry's death and cooked for some of the older men in West Virginia.

Last Words

An eyewitness is a better authority for John Henry's last words than the ballad. According to Charles C. Spencer, John Henry's last words were "Have I beat that old steam drill?"

＝＝ ＝＝ ＝＝

Many have suggested "meanings" for "John Henry."

24

Meaning of John Henry

> It is [the] family context that gives John Henry his
> human dignity and complexity, renders his most pro-
> found statement, "A man ain't nothin' but a man," so
> proud and sad, and makes fictional parodies of him so
> often offensive.
>
> —Brett Williams

John Henry was a tragic hero. His story invites analysis.

Does anyone know what "John Henry" is really about? Its first impression
is of the power of the human spirit and the often inspiring nature of tragedy. This interpretation makes us take the song at its word. But I've heard
it argued that we should be more skeptical in interpreting the lyrics, that
the song actually works in favor of the railroad bosses and against the men
who work for them. In this view, it justifies the torturous labor the men are
asked to do, and it creates a situation in which a man being worked to death
is a hero. It is, in fact, not a song that many politically conscious rail workers would enjoy. There are all sorts of possibilities it never allows, like John
Henry resenting being overburdened, or John Henry refusing to work himself to death. Especially helpful would be if someone can trace the history
of the song for me, but any thoughts at all would be appreciated, enjoyed
[Turner 1998].

There is no shortage of opinions on what "John Henry" is "really
about."

Race

Guy Johnson opened his book as follows:

This volume offers as its reason for being its attempt to describe in some
detail one of the most fascinating legends native to America—the legend of
John Henry, the Negro steel driver. Whatever the origin of the first beliefs and

237

ballads about John Henry, Negro folk have been almost solely responsible for the preservation and diffusion of the legend, and this work is offered as a sympathetic study of a significant element of their folklore [1929 Preface].

Even though Johnson believed that John Henry lore was to be found mainly among blacks, many of those he interviewed were white. According to Louis W. Chappell, Johnson "does not take properly into account the frequency of ... white people [singing] 'John Henry'" (1933, 11).

For many whites, John Henry is a hero whose race is incidental. For others, John Henry did as his white bosses expected. Even the most racially prejudiced white can sing praises of such a "good nigger."

Blacks can see John Henry as proof of racial superiority. According to F.P. Barker, "the steem Drill Beat men of every other Race ... the wourld Has Not yet Produced a Man to Whip steel like John Henry" (1927a, 1927b, Johnson 1929, 22, 143). Given the outstanding records of white steel drivers such as Fred Dopp (Chapter 5) and the absence of any means of comparing them with John Henry, Barker's racial claim must be regarded as unjustified.

According to Williams, "The song is a wonderful reaffirmation of the worth of a human life—a worker's in a workplace which denies it, a black man's in a context reminiscent of slavery, a southerner's during a time of bitter humiliation and drastic change—and, ultimately, of every ordinary person who through dignity and strength of will can be great" (1983, 124).

Race is not what this book is about. It is about a "natural" man who became a legendary hero.

Overexertion

"John Henry" died from overexertion. In a common hammer-song stanza, a laborer declares that he will not follow John Henry's example.

> This old hammer / Killed John Henry (3×)
> But it won't kill me, boys / It won't kill me [Johnson 1929, 72].
> —Willa P. Wood, ca 1927, Norfolk, Virginia

Dedication

In the ballad, John Henry vows, "And if I don't beat your steam drill down / I'll die with a hammer in my hand" and "Before I'll let the steam drill beat me down / I'll hammer my fool self to death" (Chappell 1933, 104). These are commonplace statements of dedication, not predictions. People often say that they would die before they would let something happen. To refer to "my fool self" is a common way of poking gentle fun at yourself for having done something you wished you hadn't.

John Henry did not predict his own death.

Saving Jobs

John Henry beat a machine intended to replace steel drivers. It is often said that he was trying to save the jobs of steel drivers by showing that a man is better than a steam drill (Williams 1983, 3, 111). If this were so, John Henry would have been a fool, "for, surely, the next man couldn't beat the steam drill—John Henry himself couldn't beat it over a protracted period, and no one would be able to vanquish the next generation of the machine" (Mamet 1999, xv, 131).

Retraining

The "saving jobs" idea is "too narrow a view" (Cohen 2000, 74).

For each John Henry left unemployed there will be a job for a steam-drill operator—not to mention for the factory worker who makes the steam drill and the mechanic who repairs it.... The tragedy is not that the old ways of performing tasks are superannuated by newer ones, but that society finds it more convenient to discharge the old laborer than retrain him, or at least retire him in dignity [Ibid., 74–75].

America and other industrialized nations still struggle with this problem. Robots continue to replace workers.

Family Tragedy

The John Henry story is that of a family tragedy.

It explores life and death and human purpose, generational continuity, parents and children, hopes and prophecies. It is this family context that gives John Henry his human dignity and complexity, renders his most profound statement, "A man ain't nothin' but a man," so proud and sad, and makes fictional parodies of him so often offensive. The song is a wonderful reaffirmation of the worth of a human life—a worker's in a workplace which denies it, a black man's in a context reminiscent of slavery, a southerner's during a time of bitter humiliation and drastic change—and, ultimately, of every ordinary person who through dignity and strength of will can be great. The ballad not only praises John Henry's courage and skill, but it also reminds us that the details of his personal life matter. Like all of us, he is a member of a family [Williams 1983, 124].

The reference to "a time of bitter humiliation and drastic change" reflects Williams' belief that John Henry died in West Virginia in about 1871, in the midst of Reconstruction. Instead, he died in Alabama in 1887–88, but the characterization of the times remains appropriate. Southerners still felt humiliated, and it was still a time of drastic change. Jim Crow laws that would send southern blacks into conditions resembling slavery were being enacted (Blackmon 2009).

Rich Amerson's "John Henry" emphasizes the family tragedy (Chapter 3) (1956). John Henry's woman's eyes "turned red with blood" as "she came a-screamin' and a-cryin' that day" down the railroad track, "goin' where my man fell dead." Her brother and father promised to help her and her three little children, but neither brother nor papa could replace her man. Amerson made especially effective use of lines from the "Lass of Roch Royal" (Child 76).

> Who goin' to shoe my children's feet?
> Who goin' to glove my children's hands?
> Who goin' to shoe my lovin' feet?
> Who goin' to glove my lovin' hands?
> Papa looked 'round in his daughter's face,
> Tried to pacify his daughter's mind.
> Daughter, I'll shoe your lovin' feet,
> Daughter, I'll shoe your children's feet,
> Daugher, I'll shoe your children's feet.
> Brother, he looked in his sister's face,
> Tried to pacify his sister's mind,
> Sister, I'll kiss your rosy cheeks.
> But you can't be my lovin' man,
> Brother can't be my lovin' man.
> Papa can't be my lovin' man,
> Papa can't be my lovin' man.
> 'Cause you can't file the whole deal down,
> Brother can't file the whole deal down.
> Papa can't file the whole deal down,
> Papa can't file the whole deal down [Amerson 1956].

Useless Resistance

The triumph of the machine is inevitable.

But, of course, the meaning of the song was not that he won but that he died—that the one person capable of defeating the machine is no more. The song, seemingly a paean to resistance, is, I think, more an assertion of its uselessness—"The hero died in the attempts: what do you think you could do?" [Mamet 1999, 131–32].

Mamet's thesis is not plausible. John Henry was not resisting the onslaught of machinery. Quite the opposite, he embraced machines. He was trying to win a steam drill for the Captain.

Charles C. Spencer's eyewitness account suggests that John Henry had these motives (1927b, Johnson 1929, 19–20):

1. To win a steam drill for the Captain.
2. To win prizes offered by the Captain.
3. To live up to the Captain's boast that John Henry could beat the steam drill.
4. To justify his own pride.

Spencer must have told about John Henry in his home in Henry County, Virginia, and in places he lived later: Mercer and McDowell Counties, West Virginia; Bell County, Kentucky; Denver, Colorado; and Salt Lake City, Utah. Other eyewitnesses to John Henry's contest and death in Alabama would also have spread the story all over the American South and taken it to other parts of the nation.

Wherever it went, it inspired. John Henry was a poor, black laborer in North Alabama in 1887, a terrible place and time for black people. If he could be a hero, then anyone could.

Appendix

The following is an article that appeared in the October 1930 issue of *Central of Georgia Magazine* (for a close-up of the photo of the drill see Figure 24). It clearly shows that the Central of Georgia Railroad had no doubt that the "Jawn Henry" story was not fiction and that the event the ballad celebrated took place on "our line" in the tunneling through the Oak and Coosa mountains near Leeds, Alabama.

Note that the title contains a not-uncommon error: John Henry was not a "spike driver"—a worker who drives spikes to attach rails to ties— but rather a "steel driver" who drives steel into rock to drill holes for explosives that blast tunnels through mountains.

Eight   CENTRAL OF GEORGIA MAGAZINE   *October, 1930*

Old Negro Folk Song Commemorates Colored
Spike-Driver On Our Line

RAILROAD building and operating have inspired more than their share of legends and ballads, celebrating the prowess or ability of some worker. "Casey Jones" is of course best known of all railroad ballads, but many another song has been chanted in honor of the bravery or devotion of some otherwise obscure worker on the railroad. And most of these songs or legends have been based on actuality, somewhat elaborated perhaps in the telling and retelling but describing some heroic or near heroic deed that actually happened.

Such a song, based on an actual happening, was recently sent to the magazine by Mr. Peter A. Brannon of the Alabama Anthropological Society of Montgomery, Ala. The song celebrates the prowess of one "Jawn Henry," a colored steel driver who helped build Oak Mountain Tunnel on our Columbus-Birmingham line in 1888. Jawn Henry was a mighty man who had made his living on other railroads as well as ours by the strength of two good arms. Like Ajax defying the lightning he hurled his challenge against a power greater than he, the steam drill which was to do by steam what he had done by brawn. But Jawn Henry died without admitting the mastery of his rival.

As sent to us by Mr. Brannon, the song goes:

A CLOSE UP VIEW OF DRILL

Steel drill standing for more than forty years in mountain side at east end of our Oak Mountain Tunnel near Leeds, Ala. on our Columbus-Birmingham main line. This is the steel drill referred to in the accompanying folk song.

"JAWN HENRY"

When Jawn Henry was a baby
  Sat on his granddaddy's knee;
Said 'The Central o' Georgia Rail Road
  Gonna be th' death o' me,
  Gonna be th' death o' me.

Jawn Henry hammered in th' mountains,
  And blows from his shoulder did rain.
Hung his hammer on a little blue point,
  Sayin' 'Lord, I'se a steel drivin' man.'

Jawn Henry hammered in the mountains,
  Hammer from his shoulder did rain;
His hammer hung on a little blue place
  Cried, 'I b'lieve these mount'ns cavin' in!'

Cap'n said to Jawn Henry,
  'Gonna bring me a steam drill 'round';
Take that steam drill out on the job,
  Gonna whop that steel on down.'

Jawn Henry said to de Captin,
  'A man ain't nothin' but a man,
'Fore I let yore steam drill beat me down
  I'd die with th' hammer in m' han'.'

Jawn Henry said to de Captin
  'A man ain't nothin' but a man,
If I let yore steam drill beat me down,
  Lay five hundred dollars in yore han'.'

Jawn Henry said to the Captin,
  Send me a twelve pound hammer erround,
Er twelve poun' hammer wid a fore foot handle
  An' I beat yore steam drill down.'

Jawn Henry said to his shaker,
  'Nigger, why don' you sing?
I'm throwin' twelve poun' fum my hips on down,
  Jes lissen to de col' steel ring.'

Jawn Henry went down d' rail rode
  Wid er twelve poun' hammer by his side,
He walked down d' track but he didn't come back
  'Cause he laid down his hammer an' he died.

Jawn Henry hammered in de mountains
  De mountains were so high,
Th' las' I heard de pore boy say,
  'Gimme a cole drink of water 'fore I die.'

Jawn Henry had a little baby,
  Hel' him in th' pa'm uv his han'.
An' the las' words I heard th' pore boy say,
  'Son, yore gonna be a steel drivin' man.'

Figure 46. (*above and opposite*) The 1930 *Central of Georgia Magazine* article about John Henry and Alabama (*Central of Georgia Magazine*, October 1930, pp. 8–9).

October, 1930   CENTRAL OF GEORGIA MAGAZINE   *Nine*

Jawn Henry had er little woman,
    Dress she wore wuz blue,
Las' word I heard de pore gal say
    'Jawn Henry I been Tru' to you.'

Jawn Henry had er little woman,
    Th' dress she wore wuz brown;
Th' las' word I heard de pore gal say,
    'I'm goin' whur m' man went down.'

Jawn Henry had ernother woman,
    Dress she wore wuz red;
Las' word I heard de pore gal say,
    'I'm goin' whur m' man drapt dead.'

Jawn Henry had er little woman,
    Her name wuz Polly Ann,
On th' day Jawn Henry drapt dead,
    Polly Ann hammered steel like a man.

'Where did you get tat dress,
    Where'd you get t'ose shoes so fine?'
'Got tat dress fum a railroad man,
    An' shoes fum er driver in er mine.'

"Jawn Henry" is no mere fiction hero, for in the mountain side near Leeds, at the east end of our Oak Mountain tunnel, there stands a monument to him—the last steel he drove before he fell dead, standing in the hole into which he pounded it with his twelve pound hammer.

As reported by our Road Supervisor J. Morgan of Leeds, Ala., the legend about Jawn Henry is as follows. He was a giant, standing 6 feet 4 inches in his sox feet. He had made himself famous in reconstruction days when the "Big Bend" tunnel was cut through the Alleghany Mountains on the road built from Richmond to Cincinnati, now the Chesapeake & Ohio. Among his race in the Virginia mountains he was known as the greatest steel driver in history. Hearing of work on another railroad farther south, (the old Columbus & Western, now a part of our line) he came to Oak Mountain tunnel and whipped steel there. Here too he won the fame and admiration of his race, and one day, so legend has it, while whipping down a steel at the east end of the tunnel he worked so hard and fast that the steel melted at the point and stuck. This is reputed to have had something to do with Old Jawn Henry's death, for he dropped dead with hammer in hand at the side of this drill which still sticks in the hole he was driving. And around Leeds his race claim that if you bother that drill still standing there after forty-two years or more, that the spirit of old Jawn Henry will come and put a spell on you.

The Oak Mountain Tunnel is 1,198 feet long, and was opened for traffic July 1, 1888 when first regularly scheduled passenger trains passed through.

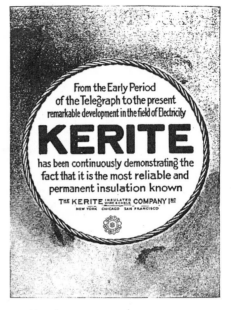

Bibliography

Abbott, Lynn, and Doug Seroff. 2007. *Ragged but Right: Black Traveling Shows, "Coon Songs," and the Dark Pathway to Blues and Jazz.* American Made Music Series. Jackson: University Press of Mississippi.

Adler, William M. 2011. *The Man Who Never Died: The Life, Times, and Legacy of Joe Hill, American Labor Icon.* First U.S. ed. New York: Bloomsbury USA.

Alabama Sentinel. 1887. The Official Organ of the State Assembly of Knights of Labor. Birmingham, Alabama. October 8.

Alexander, E.P. 1887. *Report of President and Directors.* Savannah, Georgia. *Fifty-Second Report of the President and Directors of the Central Railroad and Banking Company of Georgia.* September 1: 16.

Allen, C. Frank. 1920. *Railroad Curves and Earthwork.* 6th ed. New York: McGraw-Hill Book Company. Google Books.

The American Engineer. 1885. May 8: 228. Google Books.

The American Folklife Center. 2010. "Alan Lomax Collection: Britain, Ireland and Scotland." Washington, D.C. Library of Congress. April 20, 2011. http://www.loc.gov/folklife/lomax/britain/photos/04.html.

American Society of Civil Engineers. 1882. "List of Members. Additions. Members." *Proceedings of the American Society of Civil Engineers* 8 (November): 116. Frederick Y. Dabney, Chief Engineer and Superintendent, Vicksburg, Shreveport and Pacific R.R., Monroe, Louisiana; election to membership effective November 1, 1882. Google Books.

Amerson, Rich. 1956. "John Henry." Sound recording. LP record. *Negro Folk Music of Alabama, Volume III: Rich Amerson, 1.* New York: Ethnic Folkways Library, FE 4471. Recorded in January-February 1950. "John Henry" is side 1, band 3.

Amick, Kay, et al. 2008. "Dabney Line." November 19. November 23, 2008. http://www.milleralbum.com//dabney-line/.

———. 2011a. "Burleigh Plantation." November 3. http://milleralbum.com/wp-content/uploads/links/Burleigh/index.php. This site provides links for overlays of a map of Burleigh Plantation on Google Earth.

———. 2011b. "Autobiography of Thomas Gregory Dabney." December 8. http://milleralbum.com/tmm/docs/ThomasGregoryDabney.html. Notes following the autobiography.

ARC. 2011. "Appalachia Regional Commission." Washington, D.C. August 30, 2011. http://www.arc.gov/index.asp. Links found here provide maps, data, and other information.

Armstrong, L.K., ed. 1901. "Rock Drilling Contest." *Mining* VIII.3 (September): 72.

Association of Defenders of Port Hudson, M.J. Smith, and James Freret. 1886. "Fortification and Siege of Port Hudson." *Southern Historical Society Papers* XIV: 305–48. Google Books.

The Atlanta Constitution. 1887a. "The Answer Given." March 9: 1. Atlanta, Georgia. ProQuest Historical Newspapers Atlanta Constitution (1868–1945).

_____. 1887b. "Done in Self-Defense." March 10: 5. Atlanta, Georgia. ProQuest Historical Newspapers Atlanta Constitution (1868–1945).

_____. 1887c. "Twelve Men Killed." May 5: 1. Atlanta, Georgia. ProQuest Historical Newspapers Atlanta Constitution (1868–1945).

_____. 1887d. "Two Men Killed." June 8: 5. Atlanta, Georgia. ProQuest Historical Newspapers Atlanta Constitution (1868–1945).

_____. 1887e. "Hanged to a Tree." September 19: 1. Atlanta, Georgia. ProQuest Historical Newspapers Atlanta Constitution (1868–1945).

_____. 1913. "Sings 'John Henry' in Court to Prove He Was Wronged." September 2: 14. Atlanta, Georgia. ProQuest Historical Newspapers Atlanta Constitution (1868–1945).

Austen, Jane. 1813. *Pride and Prejudice.* London: T. Egerton. 1995. New York: Modern Library (Random House). The quote given in the main text is an out-of-context paraphrase of what Austen wrote, "Elizabeth could never address her without feeling that all the comfort of intimacy was over, and though determined not to slacken as a correspondent, it was for the sake of what had been, rather than what was." This found on pp. 107–08 of the Modern Library reprint. It describes Elizabeth Bennet's altered feelings toward her friend Charlotte Lucas, who had recently married, for security rather than love, the officious Rev. Mr. Collins.

Baker, Etta. 1956. "John Henry." New York: Tradition Records. Side 2, Track 6 of the LP *Instrumental Music of the Southern Appalachians,* Tradition TLP 1007, edited by Diane Hamilton, Liam Clancy, and Paul Clayton. Recorded in the summer of 1956 at Morganton, North Carolina.

Baker, J.A. 1888. "Railroads: Southern: Central R.R. of Georgia." *Engineering News-Record* 19 (March 10): 192. Google Books.

Baldwin, James Mark. 1901. *Dictionary of Philosophy and Psychology.* New York: Macmillan, 387. The "Folk-lore" entry, p. 387, is by Professor Joseph Jastrow, University of Wisconsin. Jastrow was an eminent psychologist who often dealt with folklore. February 5, 2009. http://books.google.com/books?id=YFNqAAAAMAAJ&printsec=frontc over&dq=%22dictionary+of+philosophy+and+psychology%22+baldwin.

Bales, Mary Virginia. 1928. "Some Negro Folk-Songs of Texas." *Publications of the Texas Folklore Society* 7: 85–112. Quoted in Doyle, Charles Clay, and Charles Greg Kelley. 1991. "Moses Platt and the Regeneration of 'Barbara Allen.'" *Western Folklore* 50: 151–69.

Barker, F.P. 1927a. Guy B. Johnson Papers (#3826), Southern Historical Collection, Manuscripts Department, Wilson Library, University of North Carolina at Chapel Hill, Chapel Hill, North Carolina. Letter to Guy B. Johnson, August 10.

_____. 1927b. Guy B. Johnson Papers (#3826), Southern Historical Collection, Manuscripts Department, Wilson Library, University of North Carolina at Chapel Hill, Chapel Hill, North Carolina. Letter to Guy B. Johnson, August 30.

Barry, Phillips. 1934. "John Henry: A Folk-Lore Study. By Louis W. Chappell." *Bulletin of the Folk Song Society of the North East* 8: 24–26. Book review.

Barton, William E. 1899. "Recent Negro Melodies." *New England Magazine* XIX (February): 707–19. Boston: Warren F. Kellogg. <http://books.google.com/books?id=ArEVA AAAYAAJ&pg=PP8&dq=%22recent+negro+melodies%22+%22new+england+magaz ine%22>. Reprinted in Bruce Jackson, ed. 1967. *The Negro and His Folklore.* Austin: University of Texas Press (for the American Folklore Society).

Bascom, Louise Rand. 1909. "Ballads and Songs of Western North Carolina." *Journal of American Folklore* 22 (April–June): 238–50.

Baskin, Andrew. 2008. "Berea College and Interracial Education: The First 150 Years." Berea, Kentucky: Berea College. Essay written for Berea College Course GSTR 210: Identity and Diversity in the United States. http://www.berea.edu/bereadigital/ gstr210/default.asp.

Bayes, Thomas, and Richard Price. 1763. "An Essay Towards Solving a Problem in the Doctrine of Chances." *Philosophical Transactions of the Royal Society of London* 53: 370–418. Available online, as a PDF file, through a link at http://www.science.uva. nl/~seop/entries/bayes-theorem/.

Belknap, M.S. 1887. *General Manager's Report*. Savannah, Georgia. *Fifty-Second Report of the President and Directors of the Central Railroad and Banking Company of Georgia*. September 1: 29.

Berea College. 1910. "John Hardy." *The Berea Quarterly* 14.3: 26.

Birmingham Public Library. 2009. "Alabama Coal Mine Fatalities, 1898–1938." Birmingham, Alabama. December 5, 2009. http://bpldb.bplonline.org/db/coalmine. Using these databases, the author tallied the causes of mine deaths for the years 1898–1902.

_____. 2010. "Government Documents: Birmingham's Population, 1880–2000." Birmingham, Alabama. October 12, 2012. http://www.bham.lib.al.us/resources/government/ BirminghamPopulation.aspx.

Blackmon, Douglas A. 2008. *Slavery by Another Name: The Re-Enslavement of Black Americans from the Civil War to World War II*. New York: Doubleday. 2009. 1st Anchor Books ed. New York: Anchor Books.

Blankenship, Don. 2005. "Blankenship Origins." October 28, 2010. http://www.blankenshipweb.com. A PDF file is available at this URL.

Blankenship, James W. 2001. "Blankenship-Lossing Family Databases." Fairgrove, Michigan. James W. Blankenship. September 19, 2010. http://blankenshipweb.com/. Over 750 researchers have contributed. A link to the file at RootsWeb (Ancestry.com) is given at this URL.

Blankenship, Pat. 2008. Personal communication: e-mail, March 31. DeSoto, Texas.

Blankenship, Rollie, Jr., and Pat Blankenship. 2008. Recorded interview with John Garst, July 30. About two and a half hours in three segments. DeSoto, Texas.

Blankenship, Rollie, Jr., and Pat Blankenship. 2010. Personal communication: genealogical data. DeSoto, Texas.

Blankenship, W.T. 1912. "The Great Titanic." Broadside. W.T. Blankenship. Sold on eBay to an anonymous buyer in about 2002.

_____. "Our President." 1917. Broadside. Huntsville, Alabama: W.T. Blankenship. I am grateful to Mrs. Ruby L. Mooney, Madison, Alabama, for providing a photocopy of this broadside in 2002.

_____. n.d. "John Henry, the Steel Driving Man." Broadside. W.T. Blankenship. The only known copy is in the Guy Benton Johnson Papers, Manuscripts Department, Wilson Library, University of North Carolina, Chapel Hill, North Carolina. Two other known Blankenship broadsides are "The Great Titanic" (which sold on eBay a few years ago) and "Our President" (of which I have obtained a photocopy). "Our President" is about World War I. The *Titanic* and World War I are both topics from the 1910s. Unlike the other two Blankenship broadsides, "Our President" specifies a place of publication: Huntsville, Alabama.

BLM. 2008. "Coal." U.S. Department of the Interior, Bureau of Land Management, Utah State Office, 440 West 200 South, Suite 500, Salt Lake City, Utah 84145–0155, April 30. February 12, 2011. http://www.blm.gov/ut/st/en/prog/energy/coal.html.

Blue Ridge Music Makers Guild, Inc. 2008. *Music Makers of the Blue Ridge Plateau*. Images of America. Charleston, SC: Arcadia.

Bluefield Daily Telegraph. 1925. "John Henry Won Over Steam Drill." Sunday, September 6: 5.

Boette, Marie, John Laflin, and Marcia Ogilvie. 1971. *Singa Hipsy Doodle and Other Folk Songs of West Virginia*. Parkersburg, WV: Junior League of Parkersburg.

Borkowski, Richard C. 2008. *Norfolk Southern Railway*. Minneapolis: MBI Publishing Company and Voyageur Press, 59.

Bradbury, Joseph T. 1986. "John Robinson Circus. Season of 1927. Part One." *Bandwagon: The Journal of the Circus Historical Society* 30.3 (May-June): 8.

Bradford, Roark. 1931a. *John Henry*. New York: Harper & Brothers/The Literary Guild.

_____. 1931b. "The Latest News About John Henry." *Wings* 5: 6–10, 26. Official publication of the Literary Guild of America.

Bradley, Jaime Marie. 2011. Personal communication: e-mail, August 31. Bradley is a Berea College archivist.

Bradley, William Aspenwall. 1915. "Song-Ballets and Devil's Ditties." *Harper's Magazine* (May): 901–14. Reprinted in the *Berea Quarterly* later in 1915.

Brinson, Betsy, Arthur Rouse, and Joan Brannon. 2011. "A Kentucky Civil Rights Timeline." Lexington, Kentucky. *Living the Story: The Civil Rights Movement in Kentucky.* Ed. Betsy Brinson. KET. July 16, 2011. http://www.ket.org/civilrights/timeline.htm.

Brodsky, Marc. 2011. Personal communications: e-mail, May 17–18. Blacksburg, Virginia.

Brown, Richard "Rabbit." 1927. *Mystery of the Dunbar's Child.* Victor 35840 (12-inch 78 rpm record). Recorded March 11 in New Orleans.

Brown, Zak. 2007. "Boulder's Pow Wow Past: Rodeo, Rock Drilling and Pig Catching Were Once the Biggest Event in Boulder." *Boulder Daily Camera*, July 26. http://www.dailycamera.com/news/2007/jul/26/no-headline---26gcen/.

Burroughs, Nannie Helen, et al. 1932. *Negro Housing.* Washington, D.C.: The President's Conference on Home Building and Home Ownership. Leon R. Harris was a member of the Rural Section of the Group on Physical Aspects of Negro Housing (p. vi).

Byron, Carl R. 1995. *A Pinprick of Light: The Troy and Greenfield Railroad and Its Hoosac Tunnel.* Expanded and revised ed. Shelburne, VT: New England Press. Originally published 1978.

The California Eagle. "1957. Writer Recites Vows." November 21: 8.

Callaway, Jennifer. 2011. Reference Librarian, Denver Public Library, Denver, Colorado. Personal communication: e-mail, June 6, with attached copies of pages of Denver city directories for 1910, 1911, and 1915, listing Charles Spencer (1910) or Charles C. Spencer (1911, 1915).

Cameron, Kenneth Walter. 1988. "WVU Sixty Years Ago and Memories of Louis Watson Chappell." *Newsletter, West Virginia Regional History Collection, West Virginia University Library* 4.2 (Summer), 4.3 (Fall/Winter): 3–9, 3–6. Available as PDF files at www.libraries.wvu.edu/wvcollection/newsletter/1985–1994/v4n2.pdf and www.libraries.wvu.edu/wvcollection/newsletter/1985–1994/v4n3.pdf.

Campbell, Olive Dame, and Cecil J. Sharp. 1917. *English Folk Songs from the Southern Appalachians, Comprising 122 Songs and Ballads, and 323 Tunes.* New York: G.P. Putnam's Sons.

Carpenter, H. [Horace]. 1891. "Plain Living at Johnson's Island. Described by a Confederate Officer." *Century Illustrated Monthly Magazine* 41.5 (March): 705–18.

Chamberlayne, John Hampden, and C.G. Chamberlayne. 1932. *Ham Chamberlayne— Virginian: Letters and Papers of an Artillery Officer in the War for Southern Independence, 1861–1865.* Richmond, Virginia: Press of the Dietz Printing Co. Reprint 1992, Wilmington, North Carolina: Broadfoot.

Chappell, L. 1927. *Letter 1.* Howard Washington Odum Papers, 1908–1982 (#3167), Southern Historical Collection, Manuscripts Department, Wilson Library, University of North Carolina at Chapel Hill, Chapel Hill, North Carolina. Letter to Howard M. Jones, Acting Editor of Studies in Philology, dated February 15.

Chappell, Louis W. 1930a. "John Hardy." *Philological Quarterly* IX.3 (July): 260–72.

_____. 1930b. "*John Henry.* By Dr. Guy B. Johnson." *American Speech* 6.2 (December): 144–46. Book review.

_____. 1931. "Ben Hardin." *Philological Quarterly* X.1 (January): 27–35.

_____. 1933. *John Henry; a Folk-Lore Study.* Jena: Frommannsche Verlag, W. Biedermann.

Chase, Richard, and Joshua Tolford. 1971. *American Folk Tales and Songs, and Other Examples of English-American Tradition as Preserved in the Appalachian Mountains and Elsewhere in the United States.* New York: Dover.

Child, Francis James. 1882–98. *The English and Scottish Popular Ballads.* 10 vols. Boston: Houghton Mifflin.

Clemons, Marvin, and Lyle Key. 2007. *Birmingham Rails: The Last Golden Era: From World War Ii to Amtrak.* Birmingham, Alabama: Red Mountain Press, 15–36. "Rattlesnake Tunnel" through Coosa Mountain, p. 15.

Clinard, John Alan. 2008. *Ancestors of Taylor Nicole Natale.* A PDF file is available at johnandlil.com/images/pdf%20files/TaylorRoyal.pdf.

Cline, Wayne. 1997. *Alabama Railroads.* Tuscaloosa: University of Alabama Press.

Cobb, Ty. 1999. "Hitting Tips." 3D4LIFE Internet Ventures. June 18. http://www. beabetterhitter.com/text/funstuff/Ty%20Cobb%20Hitting%20tips/TyCobbsHittingTips. htm.

Coffin, Tristram Potter. 1950. *The British Traditional Ballad in North America.* Philadelphia: American Folklore Society.

Cohen, Norm. 2000. *Long Steel Rail: The Railroad in American Folksong.* Second ed. Urbana: University of Illinois Press. First edition, 1981. "John Henry": 61–89.

_____. 2005. *Folk Music: A Regional Exploration.* Greenwood Guides to American Roots Music. Westport, CT: Greenwood Press.

Combs, Josiah Henry. 1925. *Folk-Songs Du Midi Des États-Unis.* Paris: Les Presses Universitaires de France.

_____. 1967. *Folk-Songs of the Southern United States.* Trans. and ed. D.K. Wilgus. Austin: University of Texas Press for the American Folklore Society. French edition, 1925.

The Community Builder. 1923. "Mrs. William Blankenship Died of Cancer." February 8. Huntsville, Alabama. Copy provided October 12, 2010, by Thomas Hutchens, Huntsville Public Library.

Comstock, Jim. 1968. *West Virginia Hillbilly.* "The Comstock Load: The Professor and the Watch Trader." September 7. Reprinted in Cameron, Kenneth Walter. 1988. "WVU Sixty Years Ago and Memories of Louis Watson Chappell." *Newsletter, West Virginia Regional History Collection, West Virginia University Library* 4, no. 3 (Fall/Winter).

Conan Doyle, A. 1893. "The Adventures of Sherlock Holmes: XX. The Adventure of the Crooked Man." *The Strand Magazine: An Illustrated Monthly,* Vol. 6. 22–32. London: George Newnes. Google Books.

Conque, Sheila Parker. 2009. "Civil War (CSA) Military Record: Charles Chaney." *Newton County, Mississippi.* Ed. LeFloris Lyon. June 21. December 15, 2011. http://newton. msgen.info/military/charles_csa_mil_rec.txt.

Cornelius. 1818. *Panoplist and the Missionary Herald* 148: 67. Boston: Samuel T. Armstrong. Google Books.

Courlander, Harold. 1956. *Negro Folk Music of Alabama, Volume III: Rich Amerson, 1.* Sound recording, LP record. Ethnic Folkways Library, FE 4471. Notes by Harold Courlander.

_____. 1963. *Negro Folk Music U.S.A.* New York: Columbia University Press, 1963.

_____. 1976. *A Treasury of Afro-American Folklore: The Oral Literature, Traditions, Recollections, Legends, Tales, Songs, Religious Beliefs, Customs, Sayings, and Humor of Peoples of African Descent in the Americas.* New York: Crown. 1996. New York: Marlowe.

Courlander, Harold, and John Benson Brooks. 1960. *Negro Songs from Alabama.* New York: Harold Courlander. Published with the assistance of the Wenner-Gren Foundation for Anthropological Research.

Cowles, Teresa Harbin. 1999. "George Webb Morring (1793–1874)." Provo, Utah. *Morring Family Genealogy Forum* (December 10): Ancestry.com, GenForum. October 21, 2010. http://genforum.genealogy.com/morring/messages/1.html.

Cowley, John. 2000. "Ella Speed." Unpublished. England. John A. Lomax papers. Archive of Folk Song, Library of Congress. "Written Down from the Singing of a Negro Girl at Prairie View About 1909." Ballad text consisting of five stanzas of four lines each.

Cowley, John, and John Garst. 2001. "Behind the Song (Ella Speed)." *Sing Out!* 45.1: 69–70.

Cox, John Harrington. 1919. "John Hardy." *Journal of American Folklore* 32 (October–December): 505–20.

_____. 1925. *Folk-Songs of the South.* Cambridge: Harvard University Press (West Virginia Folk-lore Society).

_____. 1927. "'The Yew Pine Mountains': A 'John Hardy' Ballad." *American Speech* 2.5 (February): 226–27.

_____. 1929. "American Negro Folk-Songs." *American Literature* 1.1 (March): 106–07. A review of White, Newman I. 1928. *American Negro Folk-Songs.* Cambridge: Harvard University Press.

Crampton, Frank A. 1993. *Deep Enough: A Working Stiff in the Western Mine Camps.*

Norman: University of Oklahoma Press. Previous editions were published in 1956 and 1982.

Crawford, Captain Jack. 1904. *Lariattes; a Book of Poems and Favorite Recitations.* Sigourney, IA: William A. Bell, 25. archive.org.

Crawford, Jack. 1879. *The Poet Scout; Being a Selection of Incidental and Illustrative Verses and Songs.* San Francisco: H. Keller & Co.

Crawford, William A., ed. 1930. "Old Negro Folk Song Commemorates Colored Spike-Driver on Our Line." *Central of Georgia Magazine* 20 (October): 8–9.

Cray, Ed. 1992. *The Erotic Muse: American Bawdy Songs.* 2nd ed. Music in American Life. Urbana: University of Illinois Press.

_____. 2005a. "Re: Bawdy Song Census." E-mail message to BALLAD-L (BALLAD-L@ LISTSERV.INDIANA.EDU), July 11.

_____. 2005b. "Re: Red River Valley." E-mail message to BALLAD-L (BALLAD-L@LIST-SERV.INDIANA.EDU), July 17.

Cummings, Glendora Cannon. 1927. Guy B. Johnson Papers (#3826), Southern Historical Collection, Manuscripts Department, Wilson Library, University of North Carolina at Chapel Hill, Chapel Hill, NC. Letter to Guy B. Johnson, September 6.

Cunningham, Edward. 1994. *The Port Hudson Campaign, 1862–1863.* Louisiana paperback ed. Baton Rouge: Louisiana State University Press.

Currie, Jefferson, II. 2005. "With Deliberate Speed: North Carolina and School Desegregation." *Tar Heel Junior Historian* 44.1 (Fall). Publication of the North Carolina Museum of History, 5 East Edenton St., Raleigh, North Carolina, Office of Archives and History, North Carolina Department of Cultural Resources. PDF at www. ncmuseumofhistory.org/collateral/articles/F04.deliberate.speed.pdf.

Dabney, Charles William. 1937. "The Origin of the Dabney Family of Virginia." *Virginia Magazine of History and Biography* XLV, no. 2 (April): 121–43.

Dabney, Fred Y. 1860. "Map of the Plantation and Lands of Col. Thos. S. Dabney of Hinds County, Mississippi." Dry Grove, Mississippi. December 24, 2010. http://milleralbum. com//links/Burleigh/BurleighMapUVA.jpg. Original at the University of Virginia, Albert and Shirley Small Special Collections Library, Papers of Virginius Dabney, Second Series (1901–), Charlottesville, Virginia. See finding aid at http://ead.lib.virginia. edu/vivaead/published/uva-sc/viu03179.scopecontent.

_____. 1861. Dabney (Fred Y.) letters. Folder 1. Mississippi Department of Archives & History, Jackson, Mississippi. Letter, handwritten from "Evansport Batteries" (Virginia), to Dr. Jno. E. Moncure, Dry Grove, Mississippi. December 3.

_____. 1862. Dabney (Fred Y.) letters. Folder 1. Mississippi Department of Archives & History, Jackson, Mississippi. Letter, handwritten from "Evansport Va." to Dr. Jno. E. Moncure, Dry Grove, Mississippi. January 20.

_____. 1863. Dabney (Fred Y.) letters. Folder 1. Mississippi Department of Archives & History, Jackson, Mississippi. Letter, handwritten from "Port Hudson, La.," to "My Dear Doctor" (John E. Moncure). February 24.

_____. 1873. *Plat of Lands Belonging to Dr. J.E. Moncure of Hinds Co., Miss.* Natchez Trace Collection. Natchez Trace Map Collection. The Dolph Briscoe Center for American History, University of Texas at Austin. Box 2.325/V48. Item 14. http://www.lib.utexas. edu/taro/utcah/00115/cah-00115.html.

_____. 1887. "Anecdotes of the Peninsular Campaign. I. General Johnston to the Rescue." *Battles and Leaders of the Civil War.* Eds. Robert Underwood Johnson and Clarence Clough Buel. Vol. 2. New York: The Century Company, 275–76.

_____. 1900a. *Vicksburg Evening Post*, March 17. Vicksburg, Mississippi. Name given erroneously as "Capt. F.G. Dabney."

_____. 1900b. Obituary. *Confederate Veteran.* May: 230. A photograph, "Capt. F.Y. Dabney, C.S.A.," appears on p. 284 of the June 1900 (8.6) issue. http://www.archive.org/ stream/confederatevete08conf#page/230/mode/2up, http://www.archive.org/ stream/confederatevete08conf#page/284/mode/2up.

Dabney, Lucius B., Jr. 2008. Vicksburg, Mississippi. July 29. Personal communication. Interview in the law offices of Lucius B. Dabney, Jr.

Dabney, Richard L., Jr. 2000. "The Dabneys of Virginia." November 9. December 3, 2008. http://www.genealogy.com/genealogy/users/d/a/b/Richard-L-Dabney-jr/?Welcome=1001861092.

Dabney, Thomas Gregory. 1922. "Autobiography of Thomas Gregory Dabney." Accessed December 11, 2008. http://milleralbum.com/tmm/docs/ThomasGregoryDabney.html.

Dabney, William H. 1888. *Sketch of the Dabneys of Virginia*. Chicago: Press of S.D. Childs & Company.

Darling, Charles W. 1983. *The New American Songster: Traditional Ballads and Songs of North America*. Lanham, Maryland: University Press of America.

Davis, France. 1997. *Light in the Midst of Zion: A History of Black Baptists in Utah*. Salt Lake City: University Publishing, LLC.

_____. 1999. "Calvary Baptist Church: A Brief History." Salt Lake City, Utah. *Utah's African American Voices*. Ed. Kathleen Weiler. KUED. July 7, 2011. http://www.kued.org/productions/voices/articles/calvary.htm.

Dawid, Philip, William L. Twining, and Mimi Vasilaki. 2011. *Evidence, Inference and Enquiry*. Oxford: Published for the British Academy by Oxford University Press.

de Gournay, P.F. 2011. *New Orleans Weekly Times*. "The Siege of Port Hudson." *The Louisiana Native Guards*. Ed. Jim Hollandsworth. USGenWeb Archives. December 11. http://files.usgwarchives.net/la/state/military/afriamer/natguard.txt.

Denver Public Library. (1900–1910?) "Fred Dopp—Once Held World Champion Rock Drilling Title." Denver, Colorado. *Photographs—Western History*. November 21, 2013. http://cdm16079.contentdm.oclc.org/cdm/singleitem/collection/p15330coll22/id/25618/rec/1. Call No. X-60049.

Derickson, Alan. 1998. *Black Lung: Anatomy of a Public Health Disaster*. Ithaca: Cornell University Press.

Dixon, Robert M.W., John Godrich, and Howard Rye. 1997. *Blues & Gospel Records, 1890–1943*. 4th ed. Oxford and New York: Clarendon Press and Oxford University Press.

Douglas, Davison M. 1997. "The Limits of Law in Accomplishing Racial Change: School Segregation in the Pre-Brown North." *UCLA Law Review* 44: 677–744.

Douglas, John. 2004. "John Henry: A West Virginia Legend." *People & Mountains*. Charleston West Virginia Humanities Council, Summer, 1, 3–4.

Drake, Rebecca Blackwell. 1990. "Dabney, the Model Master and Planter: Dry Grove." *Hinds County Gazette*. February.

Drinker, Henry S. 1883. *A Treatise on Explosive Compounds, Machine Rock Drills and Blasting*. New York: Wiley. Google Books.

Drinker, Henry Sturgis. 1878. *Tunneling, Explosive Compounds, and Rock Drills*. New York: John Wiley. Later editions include those of 1882, 1888, and 1893.

du Bellet, Louise Pecquet. 1907. *Some Prominent Virginia Families*. Vol. 3. 4 vols. Lynchburg, Virginia: J.P. Bell Company.

Du Bois, W.E.B. 1919. "The Looking Glass." *The Crisis: A Record of the Darker Races* 17.3, 127–28. Published monthly and copyrighted by the National Association for the Advancement of Colored People, at 70 Fifth Avenue, New York City. Conducted by W.E. Burghardt Du Bois; Augustus Granville Dill, Business Manager. Google Books.

Dumbaugh, Donald F., ed. 1983. *The Brethren Encyclopedia*. Philadelphia: Brethren Encyclopedia.

Dundes, Alan. 1973. *Mother Wit from the Laughing Barrel: Readings in the Interpretation of Afro-American Folklore*. Englewood Cliffs, N.J.: Prentice-Hall.

Dunford, Alexander W. 1918. "Registration Card." Galax, Grayson County, Virginia: Local Board in the County of Grayson, State of Virginia, Independence, Virginia. Draft registration card. September 12.

Emery County. 2011. "San Rafael Swell Mohrland Ghost Town." Castle Dale, Utah. *San Rafael Country*. Emery County Travel Bureau. http://www.emerycounty.com/Travel/Images/MohrlandGhostTownPhotos/index.html.

Emery County Progress. 1922. "Mohrland Shooting Results in Death." December 30.

_____. 1923a. "Change-of-Venue Begins Trial Tuesday."

_____. 1923b. "First Degree Murder Is Jury's Verdict." February 10.

Engels, Friedrich. 1892. *The Condition of the Working-Class in England in 1844*. Trans. Florence Kelley Wischnewetzky. London: S. Sonnenschein & Co. Written in German by Friedrich Engels. First published in Germany in 1845. English translation first published 1887, New York: J.W. Lovell Co.

Engle, David G. 2008. "Re: What Is a Ballad? Folk Song?" E-mail message to BALLAD-L (BALLAD-L@LISTSERV.INDIANA.EDU), March 25.

_____. 2009. "Re: Herrschaft Des Volkes." Personal communications, e-mail, February 12 and February 25.

Evans, Wilma. 2010. Digitally recorded interview by John Garst, November 23, near Somerville, Alabama. About 37 minutes in two segments.

Farkas, David K. 2009a. "Re: John Henry." Personal communication, e-mail to John Garst, September 29.

_____. 2009b. "HCDE 510—Information Design—Syllabus." Seattle, Washington. Department of Human-Centered Design & Engineering, University of Washington, Seattle. November 24, 2009. http://faculty.washington.edu/farkas/TC510/syllabus. htm. This page contains a link for downloading the John Henry hypertext exercise in PDF format.

Fauver, Phil. 2010. "Remembering the Historic Mining Town of Mohrland." *Emery County Progress*. October 19: 1. February 15, 2011. http://www.ecprogress.com/index. php?tier=1&article_id=9931.

Ferguson, Cheryl. 2011. "Re: Leon R. Harris." Tuskegee, Alabama. Personal communications, August 24. Two e-mail messages summarizing some Tuskegee records for Leon R. Harris, with attached excerpts from a 1902 Tuskegee catalog.

Find-A-Grave. 2000. "Charles C. Spencer." Salt Lake City, Utah. http://www.findagrave. com/cgi-bin/fg.cgi?page=gr&GRid=167523. The photograph of Spencer's gravestone was added by Judy Huff, August 11, 2010.

Fisk University. 2001. "Rosenwald Fund Card File Database." Nashville, Tennessee, July 31. 2011. http://rosenwald.fisk.edu/. This URL represents a search page. Searching "Guilford County" and "North Carolina" returns a list of schools. The pre–1918 school is one of those at Florence.

Fowke, Edith. 1964. "The Red River Valley Re-Examined." *Western Folklore* 23: 163–71.

Frantz, Blanche B. 1958. *History of the Churches of the Brethren in Colorado*. Rocky Ford, Colorado: B.B. Frantz. Mimeographed. 338 pp. My copy is bound, but others may be in loose leaf binders, as suggested by the holes punched in the unbound edges of my copy. This work is undated. Most sources give 1958, the date of the drawings, but the Brethren Encyclopedia gives 1963.

Frémaux, Léon J. 1862. *Map of the Battlefield of Shiloh*. Shiloh, Tennessee: G.T. Beauregard, Provisional Army of the Confederate States. http://www.civilwar.org/battlefields/ shiloh/maps/shilohfremauxmap.html.

Frémaux, Léon Joseph, and Patrick J. Geary. 1987. *Leon Fremaux's New Orleans Characters*. Gretna, Louisiana: Pelican Publishing Company. *New Orleans Characters* was first published in 1876.

Fridley, David. 2012. "Descendants of Abraham Dehart (C1755 - Aft 1833): Cornelius S. Miller." San Francisco, 1999 (June 21). November 1. http://www.fridley.net/dehart/ p1454.htm.

Fuld, James J. 2000. *The Book of World-Famous Music: Classical, Popular, and Folk*. 5th ed. New York: Dover.

Galbi, Douglas A. 2012. Washington, D.C. Personal communication: e-mail.

Garcia, Céline Frémaux, and Patrick J. Geary. 1987. *Céline Remembering Louisiana, 1850–1871*. Athens, Georgia: University of Georgia Press.

Gardner-Medwin, Tony. 2005. "What Probability Should a Jury Address?" *Significance* 2.1: 9–12.

Garst, John. 2002. "Chasing John Henry in Alabama and Mississippi: A Personal Memoir of Work in Progress." *Tributaries: Journal of the Alabama Folklife Association* 5: 92–129.

_____. 2004. "'Delia.'" *Blues & Rhythm* 189 (May): 8–10.

Garst, John, et al. 2002. "Hammer Ringing." June 25, 2009. http://groups.google.com/group/sci.physics/browse_thread/thread/ff7e9506ff608f23/725c77fcb99134c2?hl=en&ie=UTF-8&q=ringing+hammer#725c77fcb99134c2.

Gillette, Halbert Powers. 1904. *Rock Excavation: Methods and Cost.* New York: M.C. Clark. Google Books.

_____. 1916. *Handbook of Rock Excavation, Methods and Cost.* New York: Clark Book Company.

Goldsborough, William Worthington. 1900. *The Maryland Line in the Confederate Army, 1861–1865.* Baltimore: Board of Governors of the Association of the Maryland Line; Press of Guggenheimer, Weil & Co. Google Books.

Google. 2010. "Google Maps." Mountain View, California. Google. July 6. http://maps.google.com/maps.

Gordon, R.W. 1927. "American Folksongs: Outlaw Ballads." *The New York Times* June 5: Sunday Magazine, 13, 19. Available through ProQuest.

Green, Archie. 1972. *Only a Miner: Studies in Recorded Coal-Mining Songs.* Urbana: University of Illinois Press.

Green, Fletcher M. 1965. "Editor's Introduction." *Memorials of a Southern Planter*: ix-xlvii, plus a two-page chart of the Dabney family tree. Reprint of the 1887 book by Susan Dabney Smedes.

Guida, Nick. 2009. "Instrumental Music of the Southern Appalachians." *The Clancy Brothers and Tommy Makem.* March 18, 2011. http://clancybrothersandtommymakem.com/trad_1007_appalachians.htm.

Hall, Delaney. 2011. "Lights and Shadows: Dewey Roscoe Jones and the *Chicago Defender*'s Poetic Legacy." Chicago, Illinois. Poetry Foundation. August 16, 2012. http://www.poetryfoundation.org/article/243478.

Haney, Craig. 2001. "The Psychological Impact of Incarceration: Implications for Post-Prison Adjustment." *From Prison to Home: The Effect of Incarceration and Reentry on Children, Families, and Communities.* Washington, D.C.: U S Department of Health and Human Services. August 16, 2012. http://aspe.hhs.gov/hsp/prison2home02/Haney.htm. Available in PDF format.

Hardis, John A., Enumerator. 1880. "U.S. Federal Census Mortality Schedule." Horse Pasture Magisterial District, Henry County, Virginia: U.S. Government, Page 1, Supervisor's Dist. No. 2, Enumeration Dist. No. 128. Hueston Matthews, age 35, died of consumption. Attended by R.A. Read, physician.

Hardy, Gary. 2011. "The Battle of Port Hudson." Garland, Texas. May 2. December 15, 2011. http://pth.thehardyparty.com/. To find F.Y. and T.G. Dabney records, search "Dabney" at http://pth.thehardyparty.com/soldiers.htm.

Harris, Leon R. 1918. *The Steel Makers and Other War Poems.* Portsmouth, Ohio: T.C. McConnell Printery.

_____. 1925. "The Steel-Drivin' Man." *The Messenger* 7: 386–87, 402. Reprinted in Dundes, *Mother Wit from the Laughing Barrel* (1973), 561–67. Published with variations as "That Steel Drivin' Ma," in *The Phylon Quarterly* 18.4, 402–06 (1957).

_____. 1927. Guy B. Johnson Papers (#3826), Southern Historical Collection, Manuscripts Department, Wilson Library, University of North Carolina at Chapel Hill, Chapel Hill, North Carolina. Letter to Dewey R. (Jones), dated March 23, in response to Johnson's and Jones' request in the *Chicago Defender*, February 12, 1927, p. A2, for information about John Henry. Twenty-two stanzas of "John Henry" enclosed.

_____. 1946. *Locomotive Puffs from the Back Shop.* Boston: B. Humphries.

_____. 1948. *I'm a Railroad Man: Original American Railroad Songs, Including First Version of "John Henry."* Pamphlet. Title on cover: *The Chicago Railroad Fair, 1848–1948. Special Edition.*

_____.1956. Obituary. *Greensboro* (North Carolina) *Daily News.* "Man Who Had Never Been Teacher Tells How He Founded Florence School Forty-Five Years Ago." April 15: Sunday Feature Section, 1. An inset describing Harris, titled "He Had to Eat—So Leon Harris Worked at Many Jobs," appears on the page with Harris' article.

_____. 1957. "That Steel Drivin' Man." *The Phylon Quarterly* 18.4: 402–06.

_____. 1959. *Run, Zebra, Run! A Story of American Race Conflict.* New York, New York: Exposition Press.

_____. 1960. *Rock Island Argus.* January 23. Rock Island, Illinois. Photocopy provided by Carol Kroeger, Rock Island County Historical Society.

Hartland, Edwin Sidney. 1904. *Folklore: What Is It and What Is the Good of It?* Second ed. London: David Nutt. Hartland was president of the Folklore Society (London) from 1899 to 1901. February 5, 2009. http://books.google.com/books?hl=en&lr=&id=ilcSA AAAYAAJ&oi=fnd&pg=PA3&dq="handbook+of+folk-lore"+gomme&ots=3o2TSTU PBb&sig=nIIsjtndAYpbqYcKdHvpK295m0c.

Hazelhurst, Harold B. 1939. "John Henry." Jacksonville, Florida. June 18. Sound recording by Herbert Halpert. http://memory.loc.gov/diglib/ihas/loc.afc.afc9999005.6923/default.html.

Hewitt, Lawrence Lee. 1987. *Port Hudson, Confederate Bastion on the Mississippi.* Baton Rouge: Louisiana State University Press.

_____. 2002. "An Ironic Route to Glory: Louisiana's Native Guards at Port Hudson." *Black Soldiers in Blue: African American Troops in the Civil War Era.* Ed. John David Smith. Chapel Hill: University of North Carolina Press. 78–106.

Hinds County MSGHN. 2012. "Hinds County Marriages." *Mississippi Genealogy and History Network (MSGHN).* April 19, 2012. http://hinds.msghn.org/marriages.html.

Hoffman, Larry C. 1999. "The Rock Drill and Civilization." July 2, 2009. http://www.americanheritage.com/articles/magazine/it/1999/1/1999_1_56.shtml. Article from *Invention and Technology Magazine* 15.1 (Summer).

Hope, John, II. 1940. "Rochdale Cooperation among Negroes." *Phylon* 1.1: 39–52.

Hubbard, Freeman H. 1945. *Railroad Avenue; Great Stories and Legends of American Railroading.* New York, London: Whittlesey House McGraw-Hill Book Company. Chapter 4, pp. 58–64, is about "The Mighty Jawn Henry."

IEP. 2003. "Deductive and Inductive Arguments." Martin, Tennessee. *Internet Encyclopedia of Philosophy.* Eds. James Fieser and Bradley Dowden. January 27. Computer Center, University of Tennessee at Martin. June 5, 2011. http://www.iep.utm.edu/ded-ind/.

Ingersoll Rand. 2009. "Our Company History." http://company.ingersollrand.com/aboutus/Pages/History.aspx.

The Ingersoll Rock Drill. 1874. *The Manufacturer and Builder* 6.4 (April): 78–79. Western & Company, Publishers, 37 Park Row, New York.

_____. 1879. *The Manufacturer and Builder* 11.7 (July): 153–54. Western & Company, Publishers, 37 Park Row, New York.

Jackf66. 2008. E-mail. October 16. Jack's information is from published timetables in his possession.

Jackson, Pleasant. 1922. "State of Utah—Death Certificate." Salt Lake City, Utah. March 4, 2011. http://images.archives.utah.gov/data/81448/2259288/2259288_0000925.jpg.

Jacobs, David, and Anthony E. Neville. 1968. *Bridges, Canals & Tunnels.* New York: American Heritage Publishing Company. The illustration on page 48 is from *Frank Leslie's Illustrated Journal,* December 20, 1873.

Jekyll, Walter, et al. 1907. *Jamaican Song and Story: Annancy Stories, Digging Sings, Ring Tunes, and Dancing Tunes.* London: Published for the Folk-lore Society by D. Nutt. 268–69. Google Books.

Johnson, B.W. 1901. "Hardships at Johnson's Island: Record of Privation in Prison." *Confederate Veteran* 9.4 (April): 164–65.

Johnson, Guy B. 1927a. Letter. "'John Henry—Pile Driving Man!'" *The Chicago Defender (National Edition).* February 12: A2. Available through http://pqasb.pqarchiver.com/chicagodefender/advancedsearch.html.

_____. 1927b. To C.C. Spencer. Guy B. Johnson Papers (#3826), Southern Historical Collection, Manuscripts Department, Wilson Library, University of North Carolina at Chapel Hill, Chapel Hill, North Carolina. Letter to Mr. C.C. Spencer, 1400 East 21 Street South, Salt Lake City, Utah. March 1.

_____. 1927c. To C.C. Spencer. Guy B. Johnson Papers (#3826), Southern Historical Collection, Manuscripts Department, Wilson Library, University of North Carolina at Chapel Hill, Chapel Hill, North Carolina. Letter to Mr. C.C. Spencer, 1400 East 21st South, Salt Lake City, Utah. March 17.

_____. 1927d. "John Henry." *The Southern Workman* LVI.4 (April): 158–60. Published by the Hampton Normal and Agricultural Institute, Hampton, Virginia, from 1872. Hampton was founded in 1868 to educate ex-slaves. It is now Hampton University.

_____. 1927e. To Leon R. Harris. Guy B. Johnson Papers (#3826), Southern Historical Collection, Manuscripts Department, Wilson Library, University of North Carolina at Chapel Hill, Chapel Hill, North Carolina. Letter to Mr. Leon R. Harris, P.O. Box 209, Moline, Illinois. April 5.

_____. 1927f. To Mrs. C.L. Lynn. Guy B. Johnson Papers (#3826), Southern Historical Collection, Manuscripts Department, Wilson Library, University of North Carolina at Chapel Hill, Chapel Hill, North Carolina. Letter to Mrs. C.L. Lynn, Rome, Georgia. September 6.

_____. 1927g. "John Henry: A Negro Legend." *Ebony and Topaz.* Ed. Charles S. Johnson. New York: Opportunity, National Urban League.

_____. 1928. To L.W. Chappell. Guy B. Johnson Papers (#3826), Southern Historical Collection, Manuscripts Department, Wilson Library, University of North Carolina at Chapel Hill, Chapel Hill, North Carolina. Folder No. 1056. Personal letter to Mr. L.W. Chappell, Chicago, dated June 23, responding to a letter from Chappell dated June 2. Evidently Chappell had learned of Johnson's continuing work on John Henry, including Johnson's visit to the Big Bend Tunnel area in June 1927, where Chappell had been in September 1925.

_____. 1929. *John Henry: Tracking Down a Negro Legend.* Chapel Hill: University of North Carolina Press.

_____ 1990. Guy Benton Johnson Papers (#3826). Southern Historical Collection, Manuscripts Department, Wilson Library, University of North Carolina at Chapel Hill, Chapel Hill, NC. Donated to Wilson Library.

Jones, Dewey R. 1927. "Lights and Shadows." *The Chicago Defender (National Edition).* February 12: A2. Chicago, Illinois. http://pqasb.pqarchiver.com/chicagodefender/advancedsearch.html.

Keefer, Jane. 1996. "Folk Music Index." February 19, 2009. http://www.ibiblio.org/folkindex/.

Kennedy, Peter. 1971. "Harry Cox 1886–1971." *Folk Music Journal* 2.2: 160–62.

_____. 1975. *The Bald-Headed End of the Broom: Songs of Uneasy Wedlock.* Cassell/Shirmer. Oak, 1985. http://folktrax-archive.org/menus/cassprogs/019wedlock.htm. The FolkTrax WWW site is maintained by the Loomis House Press, Northfield, Minnesota.

Kennedy, Peter, Harry Cox, and Francis Collinson. 1958. "Harry Cox: English Folk Singer." *Journal of the English Folk Dance and Song Society* 8.3: 142–55.

Kentucky Thoroughbreds. 1928. "Only a Miner." Recorded in Chicago, September 19–21, 1927. Doc Roberts, mandolin; Ted Chestnut, banjo-mandolin and vocal; Dick Parman, guitar and vocal. Issued as a 78-rpm audio record, Paramount 3071.

Kerlin, Robert T. 1921. *Contemporary Poetry of the Negro.* Hampton, Virginia: Press of the Hampton Normal and Agricultural Institute.

_____. 1923. *Negro Poets and Their Poems.* Washington, D.C.: Associated Publishers.

Kilham, Elizabeth. 1870. "Sketches in Color." *Putnam's Magazine. Original Papers on Literature, Science, Art, and National Interests. New Series.* Vol. 5 (January–June: 31–38). New York: G.P. Putnam and Sons.

Kiser, Rob. 2012. "Chatauqua Park, Crystal Springs, Ms." *Peenie Wallie.* November 18. January 9, 2013. http://www.peeniewallie.com/2012/08/chautauqua-park.html.

Klann, Fred. 1952a. "Off the Beaten Path: A Poet and a Crusader, for Steel and Railroad Workers, and, Though He's 75 Percent White, for the Negro; Story of a Nationally Known Moline Man." *The Moline Dispatch,* January 23. Moline, Illinois.

_____. 1952b. "Off the Beaten Path: Have Courage, Work Hard, Fight for Your Rights, Is

Message to Negro Youth from Veteran Crusader for Colored; a Mellowing Poet Grows More Hopeful." *The Moline Dispatch*, January 25. Moline, Illinois.

_____. 1959. "Off the Beaten Path: A Racial Problem Novel by Ex-Moliner—Poet-Crusader Harris Writes Fascinating Book." *The Moline Dispatch*, July 8. Moline, Illinois.

Kundahl, George G., and United States Civil War Center. 2000. *Confederate Engineer: Training and Campaigning with John Morris Wampler.* Knoxville: University of Tennessee Press.

Kurtz, Kenneth S., Editor-in-Chief. 1925. *The Monticola 1926: The Annual of West Virginia University and Class Book of the Junior Class.* Morgantown: West Virginia University. Online at www.archive.org.

Lane, Ron. 2010. "Great Bend Tunnel." Charleston, West Virginia. *e-WV: The West Virginia Encyclopedia.* Ed. Becky Calwell. Ken Sullivan and the West Virginia Humanities Council. February 1, 2011. http://www.wvencyclopedia.org/articles/2154.

Laplace, Pierre Simon. 1902. *A Philosophical Essay on Probabilities.* Trans. Frederick Wilson Truscott and Frederick Lincoln Emory. 1st ed. New York: John Wiley & Sons, 17. Translated from the sixth French edition.

Laws, G. Malcolm. 1964. *Native American Balladry, a Descriptive Study and a Bibliographical Syllabus.* Publications of the American Folklore Society. Bibliographical and Special Series. Rev. ed. Philadelphia: American Folklore Society. Original edition 1950.

Leach, MacEdward. 1966. "John Henry." *Folklore and Society: Essays in Honor of Benj. A. Botkin.* Ed. Bruce Jackson. Hatboro: Folklore Associates. 93–106.

Ledbetter, Huddie. 1934. "Ella Speed." Collected by John A. and Alan Lomax, Angola Prison, Louisiana. Issued on Document CD xxxx.

Ledbetter, Huddie (Lead Belly). 1944. "Take This Hammer." Recorded October 4, 1944, in Hollywood, California, for Capitol Records. Reissue: Audio CD, *Leadbelly,* BGO Records, BGOCD403, 1998, Track 7.

Letwin, Daniel. 1998. *The Challenge of Interracial Unionism: Alabama Coal Miners, 1878–1921.* Chapel Hill: University of North Carolina Press.

Levee Board. 2011. Clarksdale, Mississippi. Yazoo-Mississippi Delta Levee District. http://www.leveeboard.org/about_the_levee/history/father_levee.html.

Lewis, Robert S. 1914. "The Book Cliffs Coal Field, Utah." *Bulletin of the American Institute of Mining Engineers* 91: 1729–49. Google Books.

Lewis, Ronald L. 1987. *Black Coal Miners in America: Race, Class, and Community Conflict, 1780–1980.* Lexington: University Press of Kentucky.

Lewis, Walter "Furry." 1929. "John Henry." Vocalion 1474. Recorded September 22, 1929, Peabody Hotel, Memphis, Tennessee. Available on CD reissues such as Document Records DOCD-5004.

_____. 1959. "John Henry." *Furry Lewis.* New York: Folkways Records FS 3823. Recorded October 3, Memphis, Tennessee, by Sam Charters.

_____. 1961. "John Henry." *Shake 'Em On Down.* Berkeley, California: Fantasy Records FCD-24703-2. Recorded April 3 and 4. Originally issued on Prestige/Bluesville 1037 (LP).

_____. 1968a. "John Henry." *Party! At Home. Furry Lewis, Bukka White, & Friends*: Arcola Records A CD 1001. Recorded July 5, Memphis, Tennessee, at Furry's apartment on Fourth Street, between Beale and Vance, by Bob West. CD published 2001. Originally released 1972 by Asp Records, Asp #1.

_____. 1968b. "John Henry." *Furry Lewis.* Blues Masters Vol. 5. New York, New York: Blue Horizon Records. Distributed by Polydor. Recorded July 21, 1968, at Ardent Studios, Memphis, Tennessee.

_____. 1969. "John Henry." *Fourth & Beale.* Cambridge, Massachusetts: Lucky Seven Records CD 9202 AAD, distributed by Rounder Records Corp. Recorded March 5, near Fourth and Beale streets, Memphis, Tennessee, at the home of Furry Lewis.

Library of Congress. 2011. *American Memory.* http://memory.loc.gov/ammem/index.html. To find "John Henry," by Arthur Bell, search "john henry arthur bell cummins" at this site.

Lomax, Alan. 1960. *The Folk Songs of North America, in the English Language*. Garden City, New York: Doubleday & Company.

Lomax, John Avery. 1915. "Some Types of American Folk-Song." *The Journal of American Folklore* 28.107: 1–17.

_____. 1947. *Adventures of a Ballad Hunter*. First ed. New York: Macmillan.

Lomax, John Avery, and Alan Lomax. 1934. *American Ballads and Folk Songs*. New York: Macmillan.

Lomax, John Avery, et al. 1941. *Our Singing Country*. New York: Macmillan. 2000. Mineola, NY: Dover.

Long, Priscilla. 1989. *Where the Sun Never Shines: A History of America's Bloody Coal Industry*. 1st ed. New York: Paragon House.

Lucas, Paul. 2011. "The Etta Baker Project." http://www.ettabakerproject.com/.

Lynn, Mrs. C.L. 1927. Guy B. Johnson Papers (#3826), Southern Historical Collection, Manuscripts Department, Wilson Library, University of North Carolina at Chapel Hill, Chapel Hill, North Carolina. Letter to Guy B. Johnson, September 29.

Macon, Uncle Dave. 1926. "Death of John Henry." Audio recording, 78 rpm. Vocalion 15320.

Magowan, Alma. 2002. Personal communication. Telephone conversation with John Garst. Pulaski, Tennessee, October 25.

Mamet, David. 1999. *Jafsie and John Henry: Essays*. New York: Free Press.

Mancini, Matthew J. 1996. *One Dies, Get Another: Convict Leasing in the American South, 1866–1928*. Columbia: University of South Carolina Press.

Marbury, Carl. 2002. "John." Comments at a meeting of the Leeds (Alabama) Historical Society, February 6.

Mason, Polly Cary. 1947. "The Story of Elmington, Gloucester County, Virginia." *The Virginia Magazine of History and Biography* 55.3: 247–58.

Mather, Frank Lincoln. 1915. *Who's Who of the Colored Race: A General Biographical Dictionary of Men and Women of African Descent*. Chicago: Memento Edition; Half-Century Anniversary of Negro Freedom in U.S. Biography of Leon R. Harris, p. 130. Google Books.

Matteson, Richard L., Jr. 2005. "Uncle Dave Macon." Louisville, Kentucky. Bluegrass Messengers. http://www.bluegrassmessengers.com/uncle-dave-macon-.aspx.

Mayhew, Tim. 2008. "Empire Mine SHP." Camino, CA. February 12, 2008. http://www.pashnit.com/roads/cal/Empire.htm.

McCormick, Kyle. 1957. Press release, West Virginia Industrial & Publicity Commission. *West Virginia Division of Culture and History, West Virginia Archives & History*. Charleston, West Virginia, November 4.

McDonald, Elbert. 1934. *Middlesboro Daily News*. "The Saga of John Henry." June 1: 2.

McElhaney, James. 2005. *Mcelhaney's Trial Notebook*. 4th ed. Chicago: Section of Litigation American Bar Association.

McGrayne, Sharon Bertsch. 2011. *The Theory That Would Not Die: How Bayes' Rule Cracked the Enigma Code, Hunted Down Russian Submarines, & Emerged Triumphant from Two Centuries of Controversy*. New Haven: Yale University Press.

Meade, Guthrie T., Richard K. Spottswood, and Douglas S. Meade. 2002. *Country Music Sources: A Biblio-Discography of Commercially Recorded Traditional Music*. Chapel Hill: Southern Folklife Collection, University of North Carolina at Chapel Hill Libraries in Association with the John Edwards Memorial Forum.

Meier, John. 1906. *Kunstlieder Im Volksmunde: Materialien Und Untersuchungen*. Halle a.S.: Max Niemeyer.

Miller, C.S. (Neil). 1930. "Certificate of Death." Hinton: West Virginia State Department of Health. March 16. http://www.wvculture.org/vrr/va_view.aspx?Id=1933503&Type=Death. Accessed January 28, 2011.

Miller, James H., and Maude Vest Clark. 1908. *History of Summers County from the Earliest Settlement to the Present Time*. Hinton, West Virginia: James H. Miller. Accessed at Google Books on January 26, 2011.

Miller, Leitia Dabney. 1926. "Recollections of Letitia Dabney Miller." *Miller Album*. Eds.

Kay Amick et al. July 16, 2008. October 7, 2008. http://milleralbum.com/tmm/docs/ LDM-Recollections.html.

Millner, Beverly R. 2006. *Something to Build On: Genealogy of African American Families of Henry County, Virginia and Surrounding Area with Surnames "A–Z."* Axton, Virginia: B.R. Millner.

Mississippi Department of Archives and History. n.d. "Confederate Graves Registration."

M'Neilly, J.H., D.D. (the Reverend James Hugh McNeilly). 1919. "Under Fire at Port Hudson." *Confederate Veteran* 27.9: 336–39.

Moore, Gregory. 2008. "John Henry." Personal communication. Personal interview, Leeds, AL. September 20.

Moore, Robert. 2008. "John Henry." Telephone interview, Athens, GA (Garst), and Birmingham, Alabama, October 14.

Moorehead, Singleton P., A. Lawrence Kocher, and Howard B. Dearstyne. 1951. "John Coke House Architectural Report, Block 9, Building 27." Williamsburg, NC. 1990. Colonial Williamsburg Digital Library. Accessed November 30, 2008. http://research. history.org/DigitalLibrary/View/index.cfm?doc=ResearchReports\RR1145.xml.

Morrow, J.D.A. 1918. "The Coal Operators' Case." *The American Review of Reviews* 57, January–June: 290. Google Books. A search for "coal shortage" within this volume yields several other reports.

Musgrove, Warren. 1955. "Alabama's John Henry Country." *Birmingham News Magazine.* Birmingham: Birmingham News. Sunday, September 11: 10–11.

Myers Sisters and Leasie. 2007. *Music from Apple Pie Ridge.* New York: Global Village Music.

Nason, Henry B. 1887. *Biographical Record of the Officers and Graduates of the Rensselaer Polytechnic Institute, 1824–1886.* Troy, NY: William H. Young, 307. http://openlibrary. org/details/biographicalrec00nasogoog.

Nelson, Scott Reynolds. 2005. "Who Was John Henry? Railroad Construction, Southern Folklore and the Birth of Rock and Roll." *Labor: Studies of Working Class History of the Americas* 2 (Summer): 53–80.

_____. 2006. *Steel Drivin' Man: John Henry, the Untold Story of an American Legend.* Oxford: Oxford University Press.

Nelson-Easley, LaTricia M. 2007. *Copiah County.* Images of America. Charleston, South Carolina: Arcadia, 30.

Nevada State Museum. 2008. "20,000 Spectators at the Drilling Contest, Goldfield." Nevada Department of Cultural Affairs. July 2, 2009. http://nevadaculture.org/ museums/new_exhibits/cc-goldfield/exhibit6/e60004b.htm.

Nickerson, Raymond S. 1998. "Confirmation Bias: A Ubiquitous Phenomenon in Many Guises." *Review of General Psychology* 2.2: 175–220.

Niles, John Jacob. 1936. *More Songs of the Hill-Folk.* "John Henry." Schirmer's American Folk-Song Series, Set 17. New York: G. Schirmer.

Ninnis, Lillian. 1961. "Brawny Men and True Steel. The Story of Hard-Rock Drilling: The Desertland's Forgotten Sport." *Desert: Magazine of the Outdoor Southwest.* Palm Desert, California: 14–17.

NMD Inc. 2010. "Slidell History." Slidell, Louisiana. City of Slidell. December 1, 2011. http://www.slidell.la.us/about_history.php.

Ocheltree, Cliff. 2008. "C.C. Spencer." Personal communications. E-mail messages and attached documents, October 29–30.

Odum, Howard W. 1927a. Howard Washington Odum Papers, 1908–1982 (#3167), Southern Historical Collection, Manuscripts Department, Wilson Library, University of North Carolina at Chapel Hill, Chapel Hill, NC. Letter to Louis Chappell dated March 7.

_____. 1927b. Howard Washington Odum Papers, 1908–1982 (#3167), Southern Historical Collection, Manuscripts Department, Wilson Library, University of North Carolina at Chapel Hill, Chapel Hill, North Carolina. Letter to Louis Chappell dated April 15.

_____. 1927c. Howard Washington Odum Papers, 1908–1982 (#3167), Southern Historical

Collection, Manuscripts Department, Wilson Library, University of North Carolina at Chapel Hill, Chapel Hill, North Carolina. Letter to Louis Chappell dated May 6.

Odum, Howard Washington, and Guy Benton Johnson. 1926. *Negro Workaday Songs.* Chapel Hill: University of North Carolina Press.

Oliver, Paul. 1984. *Songsters and Saints: Vocal Traditions on Race Records.* Cambridge: Cambridge University Press.

Oursler, Bill. 2008. "Ringing." Personal communications, e-mail, February 8.

Palmer, Larry. 2007. "Palmer/Mennega Heirlines > Fly into History." Frisco Lakes, Texas. February 1, 2011. ttp://trees.ancestry.com/tree/4731320/person/-1556645284. This link is for the Brice Miller page.

Pattman, Neal. 2002. "John Henry." Performance. Athens, Georgia. August 13. State Botanical Garden of Georgia.

_____. 2003. "Maggadee." Interview. Athens, Georgia. September. State Botanical Garden of Georgia.

Perrow, E.C. 1913. "Songs and Rhymes from the South." *Journal of American Folklore* 26. Apr-June: 123–73. "John Henry": 163–65. This is part two of a three-part series, 1912–15.

Pettit, J.E. 1911. "Report of the Coal Mine Inspector for the State of Utah." Ed. Utah Department of Mines and Mining. Salt Lake City: Tribune-Reporter Ptg. Co. A volume that is online at Google Books contains reports for the years 1907 (pp. 4–46), 1908 (pp. 51–103), 1909 (pp. 1–64), and 1910 (pp. 68–153).

_____. 1913. "Biennial Report of the State Mine Inspector of the State of Utah: 1911–1912." Ed. Utah Department of Mines and Mining. Salt Lake City: The Arrow Press, of *Public Documents: State of Utah. Part 2* Google Books.

Pezzoni, J. Daniel, and Harrison S. Toms. 2001. "Grassdale Farm." NPS Form 10–900 (Rev 10–90), United States Department of the Interior, National Park Service, National Register of Historic Places, Registration Form. A link to a PDF file of this document is at http://www.dhr.virginia.gov/registers/Counties/register_Henry.htm. The historic context of Grassdale Farm is given in Section 8, pp. 10–15. The quoted sections are from pp. 10–13.

Poor, Henry V. 1889. *Manual of the Railroads of the United States for 1889* 22. New York: H.V. & H.W. Poor, 662.

Potter, Albert F. 1902. "Diary of Albert F. Potter." Available as a PDF file at http://extension.usu.edu/forestry/UtahForests/ForestHist_PotterDiariesIntro.htm.

Pound, Louise. 1933. "John Henry, a Folk-Lore Study. By Louis W. Chappell." *The Journal of American Folklore* 46. No. 182 (October–December): 421–22.

Powell, Charles D. 1993. *Moncure Holdings.* Dallas, Texas. Information provided by Rebecca Drake.,Ella Tardy, and Patricia Moncure Thomas.

Racer, James M., ed. 1903.. "College Items." *The Citizen* 4, no. 36 (February 26), 4.

The Railroad and Engineering Journal. 1887. 61.5 (May): 235. January 9, 2012 .http://www.archive.org/stream/5088829_61#page/n257/mode/2up.

Railway World. 1888. "Railway Projects: Columbus and Western." Quarto Volume 14.16 (April 21): 375. Google Books.

Ramella, Richard. 1992. "John Hardy: The Man and the Song." *Goldenseal* 18.1 (Spring): 47–50. Green was state historian. G.A. Bolden was state archivist. This article incorrectly assigns Bolden's position to Green.

Rees, Nigel. 2002. *Cassell's Dictionary of Word and Phrase Origins.* Third ed. London: Cassell. For a compilation of mondegreens from popular songs, see Gavin Edwards, *'Scuse Me While I Kiss This Guy and Other Misheard Lyrics.* 1995. New York: Fireside. The title is from a line in "Purple Haze," The Jemi Hendrix Experience: 'Scuse me while I kiss the sky." Here the mondegreen makes more sense than the original.

Reid, Debra A. 2010. "The National Federation of Colored Farmers: Constructing Separatist Networks During the 1920s-1930s." *Rural History 2010.* Brighton, England, September 13–16. Conference paper. PDF file available at http://www.ruralhistory2010.org/abstWed1C.html. I am grateful to Debra Reid for providing me with copies of several documents concerning Leon R. Harris.

Riddlebarger, Kim. 2010. "Riddlebarger Family History." Anaheim, California. http://kimriddlebarger.squarespace.com/.

Robinson, William Henry. 1969. *Early Black American Poets; Selections with Biographical and Critical Introductions.* Dubuque: W.C. Brown Co.

Rocha, Mona, and James Rocha. 2011. "A Feminist Scandal in Holmes's Generalizations." *Sherlock Holmes and Philosophy: The Footprints of a Gigantic Mind.* Ed. Josef Steiff. Chicago: Open Court. 147ff.

Rock Drilling. 1907. International Library of Technology, Section 35. Scranton: International Textbook Company. Google Books.

Romalis, Shelly. 1999. *Pistol Packin' Mama: Aunt Molly Jackson and the Politics of Folksong.* Music in American Life. Urbana: University of Illinois Press.

RootsWeb. 1997. "Blankenship-L Archives." Provo, Utah. Ancestry.com. September 19, 2010. http://archiver.rootsweb.ancestry.com/th/index/BLANKENSHIP.

_____. 2010. "Blankenship: Surname and Family Lists." Provo, Utah. Ancestry.com. September 19, 2010. http://lists.rootsweb.ancestry.com/index/surname/b/blankenship.html?cj=1&o_xid=0001546952&o_lid=0001546952#BLANKENSHIP.

Rosner, David, and Gerald E. Markowitz. 1991. *Deadly Dust: Silicosis and the Politics of Occupational Disease in Twentieth-Century America.* Princeton: Princeton University Press.

Roud, Steve. 1985. "Roud Folksong Index." February 21, 2009. http://library.efdss.org/cgi-bin/query.cgi?cross=off&index_roud=on&access=off.

Royster, James F. 1927a. Personal letter to Louis W. Chappell, February 27. Chappell, Louis Watson (1890–1981), English Professor and Folklorist. Research Papers, Sound Recordings, and Other Material, 1815–1980, West Virginia & Regional History Collection, Charles C. Wise Library, West Virginia University. A&M No. 2480. Morgantown, West Virginia.

_____. 1927b. Personal letter to Louis W. Chappell, March 12. Chappell, Louis Watson (1890–1981), English Professor and Folklorist. Research Papers, Sound Recordings, and Other Material, 1815–1980, West Virginia & Regional History Collection, Charles C. Wise Library, West Virginia University. A&M No. 2480. Morgantown, West Virginia.

Russell, Tony. 2004. *Country Music Records: A Discography, 1921–1942.* Oxford: Oxford University Press. Editorial Research by Bob Pinson, assisted by the staff of the Country Music Hall of Fame and Museum.

Salt Lake Telegram. 1922a. "Posses Conduct Hunt for Slayer in Two Counties." December 27.

_____. 1922b. "Slayer of Carbon County Man in Card Game Jailed." December 30.

The Salt Lake Tribune. 1926. "Life Term Commuted." November 21: 24.

_____. 1929. "Sunday School at 9:45." October 12: 24.

_____. 1931. "Pilgrim." August 22: 20.

_____. 1932. "Colored Organization to Hold Yearly Meet." November 12: 5.

_____. 1940. "Lula L.D. Spencer." December 20: 29. Lula L.D. Spencer obituary.

_____. 1944. "Death Claims Negro Pastor." April 22: 24. Rev. Charles C. Spencer obituary.

Sandburg, Carl. 1927. *The American Songbag.* New York: Harcourt.

Sanders, Charles W. 2005. *While in the Hands of the Enemy: Military Prisons of the Civil War.* Conflicting Worlds. Baton Rouge: Louisiana State University Press.

Saunders, W.L. 1910. "The History of the Rock Drill." *Cassier's Magazine: An Engineering Monthly* 38 (May–October): 43–44. New York: Cassier Magazine Company. http://books.google.com/books?id=borOAAAAMAAJ&pg=RA2-PA43&dq=ingersoll+%22rock+drill%22. Several pages here are numbered 43.

Saunders, William L. 1889. "Rock Drills." *Souvenir and Official Programme of the Centennial Celebration of George Washington's Inauguration as First President of the United States.* New York: Garnett & Gow, 376–79. http://books.google.com/books?id=1DMFAAAAYAAJ&dq=%22centennial+celebration%22+%22george+washington%22&printsec=frontcover&source=bl&ots=PQWjNsUVGA&sig=6zxnqqe0X

CenqFG8TZoDktrTWjs&hl=en&ei=DMFLSvXSJpSm8AS3gN3yBw&sa=X&oi=b
ook_result&ct=result&resnum=6.

Savage, Charles R. 1895. "Coal Mine in Cedar Creek Canyon." Photograph. The date is estimated. http://www.ilovehistory.utah.gov/place/counties/emery.html.

Saxton, Edward H., and Phil C. Bowman. 1979. "Men of Steel: The Hard Rock Drilling Contestants." *Desert: Magazine of the Southwest* (January): 28–29. Palm Desert, California: William and Joy Knyvett.

Scarborough, Dorothy, and Ola Lee Gulledge. 1925. *On the Trail of Negro Folk-Songs.* Cambridge: Harvard University Press.

Schaefer, Edward F. 1919. "Rock Drills and Rock Drilling." *Encyclopedia Americana.* Encyclopedia Americana Corporation. July 3, 2009. http://books.google.com/books?id=a7 5PAAAAMAAJ&pg=PA594&lpg=PA594&dq=%22inches+per+minute%22+rock+dri lling&source=bl&ots=iHekKr7XhS&sig=DYdW64PSSs1juhJC_AgGL8YtoXs&hl=en& ei=SnBOStrIGJSVtgeBoaWiBA&sa=X&oi=book_result&ct=result&resnum=2.

Scheife, Richard T., and Wendy R. Cramer. 2007. "'How to Be a 5-Star Scientific Journal Reviewer.'" Lenexa, Kansas, and Boston, Massachusetts. American College of Clinical Pharmacy. June 29, 2010. www.pharmacotherapy.org/pdf/5-star_Reviewers.pdf.

Schulze, Bruce, and Steve Robinson. 2010. "Port Hudson." Kingston, Oklahoma. *Civil War Album.* Ed. Bruce Schulze. CivilWarAlbum.com. December 1, 2011. http://www. civilwaralbum.com/porthudson/southern2.htm. Photo of the Gibbons, or Gibbens, house near Port Hudson, Louisiana. At the time of the Civil War, it was the home of James H. Gibbens. Officers of the Confederate Engineering Corps were housed here in the fall of 1862.

Schwartz, Barry. 2004. *The Paradox of Choice: Why More Is Less.* 1st ed. New York: Ecco. Vivid interviews and the availability heuristic are discussed on pp 58–59.

Sharp, Cecil James, Olive Dame Campbell, and Maud Karpeles. 1932. *English Folk Songs from the Southern Appalachians.* 2nd ed. London: Oxford University Press. Reprints 1952, 1960.

Shea, William L., and Terrence J. Winschel. 2003. *Vicksburg Is the Key: The Struggle for the Mississippi River.* Great Campaigns of the Civil War. Lincoln: University of Nebraska Press.

Shearin, Hubert G., and Josiah H. Combs. 1911. *A Syllabus of Kentucky Folk-Songs.* Transylvania University Studies in English 2. Lexington, Kentucky: Transylvania Printing Company. Available at Google Books.

Sheer, Steven. 2011. "A Rider's Journal." September 5. November 17, 2011. http://ssscheer. us/aridersjournal/. Includes a photograph of the Thomas G. Dabney memorial.

Shepherd, Henry E. 1917. *Narrative of Prison Life at Baltimore and Johnson's Island, Ohio.* Baltimore: Commercial Ptg. & Sta. Co.

ShopSugarHouse.org. 2011. "Sugar House History." Salt Lake City. *The Official Website for Sugar House in Salt Lake City.* Sugar House Merchant's Association. http:// shopsugarhouse.org/?page_id=191.

Shorter, Henry R., et al. 1887. *Seventh Annual Report of the Railroad Commissioners of Alabama.* June 30. Nashville: Marshall & Bruce, Stationers and Printers, 52–53. Google Books.

Simpson, Jacqueline, and Stephen Roud. 2000. *A Dictionary of English Folklore.* Oxford: Oxford University Press.

Smedes, Susan Dabney. 1887. *Memorials of a Southern Planter.* Baltimore: Cushings & Bailey. http://docsouth.unc.edu/fpn/smedes/smedes.html as part of "Documenting the American South," University Library, University of North Carolina, Chapel Hill, North Carolina.

———. [1887] 1965. *Memorials of a Southern Planter.* Ed. Fletcher M. Green. New York: Knopf.

Smith, Harry Everett. 1997. *Anthology of American Folk Music.* Sound recording. Smithsonian Folkways/Sony Music Special Products, Washington, D.C. Originally released by Folkways Records, 1952, as LP records (FP 251--FP 253).

Smith, Tyrie J. 2008. "'A Voice That Was Thin and Pure': Folklore as Literature and

Literature as Folklore in the Works of Byron Herbert Reece." University of Louisiana at Lafayette. Ph.D. Dissertation. Advisor: Marcia Gaudet.

Smitty22031. 2010. "Maine Family Tree: Tenney Maten." Provo, Utah. Ancestry.com. October 21, 2010. http://trees.ancestry.com/tree/2160406/person/-1730996684?pg=32810.

Speer, Lonnie R. 1997. *Portals to Hell: Military Prisons of the Civil War.* Mechanicsburg, Pennsylvania: Stackpole Books.

Spencer, C.C. 1927a. Guy B. Johnson Papers (#3826), Southern Historical Collection, Manuscripts Department, Wilson Library, University of North Carolina at Chapel Hill, Chapel Hill, NC. Letter to Guy B. Johnson, February 24.

_____. 1927b. Guy B. Johnson Papers (#3826), Southern Historical Collection, Manuscripts Department, Wilson Library, University of North Carolina at Chapel Hill, Chapel Hill, NC. Letter to Guy B. Johnson, March 10.

Spencer, Charles C. 1927. "Application of C.C. Spencer #4201." April 22. February 16, 2011. To find a download link for a PDF file, search "Charles C. Spencer" at http://images.archives.utah.gov/cdm4/search.php.

_____. 1944. "State of Utah Certificate of Death." Salt Lake City. March 4, 2011. http://images.archives.utah.gov/data/81448/2260782/2260782_0001324.jpg.

Spencer, Lula V. Stevens. 1940. "State of Utah Certificate of Death." Salt Lake City. March 4, 2011. http://images.archives.utah.gov/data/81448/2260354/2260354_0001676.jpg.

Spencer, Onah L. 1927 (?) "John Henry." Cincinnati, Ohio. Version sent to Guy B. Johnson.

Spencer, Terries. 1879. "Mathews, Hairston." http://lva1.hosted.exlibrisgroup.com/F. At this URL, search "Mathews Hairston" and select the 1879 link. The document is a death record for which Terries Spencer was the informant.

Stamper, Georgia Green. 2011. "Re: Leon Harris, Ward of Silas Hudson." Personal communication: e-mail. August 24. Lexington, Kentucky.

Stamper, Georgia Green, and Ernie Stamper. 2011. Personal communications: e-mail correspondence. August 24–September 12. Lexington, Kentucky.

State of Utah. 1923. *7th District Court, Emery County, Series 4126, Criminal Case Files, Case #190, State of Utah vs. Charles C. Spencer.* Utah State Archives & Records Service, Salt Lake City. CD-ROM from microfilm in the collection of the Utah State Archives, 300 S. Rio Grande, Salt Lake City, Utah 84101.

Steedman, I.G.W., M.D. 1870. "A Medical History of the United States Military Prison on Johnson's Island, Lake Erie." *Camp, Field and Prison Life; Containing Sketches of Service in the South, and the Experience, Incidents and Observations Connected with Almost Two Year's Imprisonment at Johnson's Island, Ohio.* By W.A. Wash. Saint Louis: Southwestern Book and Publishing Company. 351–82. January 10, 2012. http://www.archive.org/details/campfieldprisonl01wash.

Stern, Alexander. 2009. "Old Shoes and Leggins'—Uncle Eck Dunford." Altamont, New York. *Where Dead Voices Gather: The Anthology of American Folk Music Project.* Ed. Alexander Stern. April 20, 2011. http://theanthologyofamericanfolkmusic.blogspot.com/2009/11/old-shoes-and-leggins-uncle-eck-dunford.html.

Strack, Don. 2000. "Utah Territorial Prison, Sugar House, 1855–1951." Centerville, Utah. November 6, 2012. http://utahrails.net/utahrails/utah-territorial-prison.php.

Swem, E.G. 1941. *Provisional List of Alumni, Grammar School Students, Members of the Faculty, and Members of the Board of Visitors of the College of William and Mary in Virginia, from 1693 to 1888.* Vol. 2008. Richmond, Virginia: Division of Purchase and Printing. Page 14. A PDF file can be downloaded at http://hdl.handle.net/10288/13856.

Taff, Joseph A. 1906. "Book Cliffs Coal Field, Utah, West of Green River." *Contributions to Economic Geology 1905.* Eds. S.F. Emmons and E.C. Eckel. Washington, District of Columbia: United States Geological Survery. 289–302. Bulletin No. 285. February 16, 2011. Google Books.

Talbott, E.H., and H.R. Hobart, eds. 1885. *The Biographical Directory of the Railway Officials of America.* Chicago: The Railway Age Publishing Company. Google Books.

Taniguchi, Nancy J. 2004. *Castle Valley, America: Hard Land, Hard-Won Home.* Logan: Utah State University Press.

Terry, D.M. 1999. "Passing Along a Tale About John Henry." Letter to the Editor. *The Leeds News.* January 14.

Thomas, Arthur L., Secretary of the Territory of Utah. 1880. "Laws of the Territory of Utah Passed at the Twenty-Fourth Session of the Legislative Assembly, Held at the City of Salt Lake, the Capitol of Said Territory, Commencing January 12, A.D. 1880, and Ending February 20, A.D. 1880." Salt Lake City: Deseret News Printing and Publishing Establishment. 4–5. Google Books.

Thomas, Cecil. 2002. Personal communication: telephone conversation with John Garst. October 24. Huntsville, Alabama.

_____. 2010. Personal communication: digitally recorded interview with John Garst. About 51 minutes in two segments. November 23. Huntsville, Alabama.

Thomas, Gomer. 1899. *Report of the State Coal Mine Inspector for 1899.* Salt Lake City. February 16, 2011. Google Books.

Thompson, Katherine Beidleman. 2010. Interview with the author. July 19. Richmond, Virginia.

Thwaites, Reuben Gold. 1910. *The Colonies, 1492–1750.* New York: Longmans, Green, and Company. Twenty-second printing. Fourth revision. Google Books.

T.M.C. 1909. Letter to H.F.S., Jr. December 3. Includes the quoted sentence, taken from the General Manager's Report of 1888 for the Central Railroad and Banking Company of Georgia.

Travis, Merle. 1947. "Dark as a Dungeon." Written and performed by Travis. Recorded August 8, 1946, in Hollywood, CA. Released on audio album *Folk Songs of the Hills,* Capitol AD 50.

Tredwell, J.H. 1868. "The Pathway of a Great Enterprise." *Putnam's Magazine of Literature, Science, Art, and National Interests* (September): 360–64. http://digital.library. cornell.edu/cgi/t/text/pageviewer-idx?c=putn;cc=putn;idno=putn0012-3; node=putn0012-3%3A1;size=l;frm=frameset;seq=376;view=image;page=root.

Tribe, Ivan M. 1993. *The Stonemans: An Appalachian Family and the Music That Shaped Their Lives.* Music in American Life. Urbana: University of Illinois Press.

Turner, Peter. 1998. "Origins: John Henry." The Mudcat Cafe. January 13, 2013. http:// mudcat.org/thread.cfm?threadid=4018#21244. Posted February 12.

Twain, Mark. 1959. *The Autobiography of Mark Twain [Pseud.] Including Chapters Now Published for the First Time, as Arr. And Edited, with an Introd. And Notes.* New York: Harper.

U.S. War Department. 1891. *List of Staff Officers of the Confederate States Army. 1861–1865.* Washington, D.C.: Government Printing Office. Internet Archive.

_____. n.d. "Roll of Prisoners of War at Depot: Prisoners of War, Near Sandusky, Ohio." *Selected Records of the War Department Relating to Confederate Prisoners of War, 1861–1865.* Ancestry.com.

University of Alabama. 2012. "Historical Map Archive." Tuscaloosa, Alabama. *Alabama Maps.* November 7. December 10, 2012. http://alabamamaps.ua.edu/historicalmaps/.

Utah State History. 2010. "Staff Directory." http://history.utah.gov/about_us/index.html. Greg Walz, Librarian.

Utah State Prison. 1923. "List of Prisoners in the Utah State Prison." Prison Registry. Salt Lake City. Entry for Chas. C. Spencer, confined on February 20, 1923. Mug shots are included.

van der Merwe, Peter. 1989. *Origins of the Popular Style: The Antecedents of Twentieth-Century Popular Music.* Oxford: Oxford University Press (Clarendon Press). A paperback edition, with minor changes and additions, was published in 1992 by Oxford University Press, USA.

_____. 2004. *Roots of the Classical: The Popular Origins of Western Music.* Oxford: Oxford University Press. A paperback edition, with minor changes and additions, was published in 2007 by Oxford University Press, USA.

Virginia State Penitentiary. 1866. "Prison Register." Library of Virginia, Richmond.

Walshaw, Chris. 1995. "Earl Brand." London, England. *abc notation.* Ed. Chris Walshaw. March 16, 2011. http://abcnotation.com/searchTunes?q=earl+brand&f=c&o=a&s=0.

Waltz, Robert B., and David G. Engle. 1996. "The Traditional Ballad Index." February 19, 2009. www.csufresno.edu/folklore/BalladIndexTOC.html.
Ware, Mary Dabney. 1923. "Reminiscences from My Life." New York. Putnam. Accessed December 11, 2008. From the book *A New World Through Old Eyes.* http://milleralbum.com//tmm/docs/MaryWare.html.
The Weekly Iron Age. 1887a. "In the Dark." September 8: 3. Birmingham, Alabama.
_____. 1887b. September 29: 8. Birmingham, Alabama.
_____. 1888. "The Road Complete." June 21. Birmingham, Alabama. Reprinted in *Leeds, Her Story,* Leeds, Alabama: Leeds Bicentennial Commission, 1979, pp 127–28.
Weiser, Kathy R. 2010. "Utah Legends: Castle Gate Lost Treasure." Warsaw, Missouri. *Legends of America: A Travel Site for the Nostalgic & Historic Minded.* March 2, 2011. http://www.legendsofamerica.com/ut-castlegate.html.
White, Newman Ivey. 1928. *American Negro Folk-Songs.* Cambridge: Harvard University Press.
Wilgus, D.K. 1959. *Anglo-American Folksong Scholarship since 1898.* New Brunswick: Rutgers University Press.
_____. 1961. *Obray Ramsey Sings Folksongs from the Three Laurels.* Prestige/International LP 1320, Liner Notes.
_____. 1966. "The Oldest (?) Text of 'Edward.'" *Western Folklore* XXV: 77 ff.
_____. 1967. "Foreword." *Folk-Songs of the Southern United States.* Ed. John Harrington Cox and D.K. Wilgus. Austin: University of Texas Press for the American Folklore Society.
Wilgus, D K., and Eleanor R. Long. 1985. "The *Blues Ballad* and the Genesis of Style in Traditional Song." *Narrative Folksong, New Directions: Essays in Appreciation of W. Edson Richmond.* Eds. Carol L. Edwards and Kathleen B. Manley. Boulder: Westview Press (printer), 434–82.
Wilgus, D.K., and Lynwood Montell. 1968. "Clure and Joe Williams: Legend and Blues Ballad." *The Journal of American Folklore* 81, no. 322 (October–December): 295–315.
Willard, Eugene B., et al. 1916. *A Standard History of the Hanging Rock Iron Region of Ohio.* Vol. 1, pp. 219–20. [Chicago?]: The Lewis Publishing Company, 219–20. 1983. Marceline, Missouri: Walsworth. Google Books.
Williams, Brett. 1983. *John Henry, a Bio-Bibliography.* Popular Culture Bio-Bibliographies. Westport, CT: Greenwood Press.
Williamson, Stanley. 1999. *Gresford: The Anatomy of a Disaster.* Liverpool: Liverpool University Press.
Wilson, Joseph T. 1890. *The Black Phalanx.* Hartford, Connecticut: American Publishing Company. Google Books.
Woodside, James L. 1862. "A Plan of Port Hudson and Its Defenses." Chapel Hill, North Carolina. *Jeremy Francis Gilmer Papers #276.* Gilmer Map Number 409. Southern Historical Collection, Wilson Library, University of North Carolina at Chapel Hill. December 1, 2011. http://dc.lib.unc.edu/cdm4/item_viewer.php?CISOROOT=/gilmer&CISOPTR=97&CISOBOX=1&REC=2.
Woulfe, Rev. Patrick. 1923. *Irish Names and Surnames.* Dublin, Ireland. 2007. Baltimore: Genealogical Publishing Company.
Wright, Howard C. 1863. "Port Hudson: Its History from an Interior Point of View. The Mule Diet at Port Hudson." Washington, D.C. *Teaching with Historic Places.* Ed. National Park Service. National Park Service. December 14, 2011. http://www.nps.gov/nr/twhp/wwwlps/lessons/71hudson/71facts2.htm. Teaching with Historic Places Lesson Plans: "The Siege of Port Hudson: Forty Days and Nights in the Wilderness of Death."
Wright, John. 1993. *Traveling the Highway Home: Ralph Stanley and the World of Traditional Bluegrass Music.* Music in American Life. Urbana: University of Illinois Press.
Writers' Program, Montana. 1943. *Copper Camp; Stories of the World's Greatest Mining Town, Butte, Montana.* New York: Hastings House.
WVA&H. 2011. "John Henry." Charleston, West Virginia. *West Virginia Division of*

Culture and History, West Virginia Archives & History. May 24, 2012. http://www.wvculture.org/history/notewv/henry.html.

Wyman, Mark. 1979. *Hard Rock Epic.* Berkeley: University of California Press.

You Tube. 2009. June 2. <http://youtube.com/>. A "John Henry" search gave "about 1,980" hits.

Yronwode, Catherine. 2007. E-mail. Yronwode brought the significance of the wife to my attention.

Index

Numbers in *bold italics* indicate pages with illustrations